THE
AVATAR

JONATHAN CAHN

THE AVATAR by Jonathan Cahn
Published by FrontLine, an imprint of Charisma Media
1150 Greenwood Blvd., Lake Mary, Florida 32746

Copyright © 2025 by Jonathan Cahn. All rights reserved.

Unless otherwise noted, all Scripture quotations are taken from the New King James Version®. Copyright © 1982 by Thomas Nelson. Used by permission. All rights reserved.

Scripture quotations marked ESV are from The ESV® Bible (The Holy Bible, English Standard Version®), copyright © 2001 by Crossway, a publishing ministry of Good News Publishers. Used by permission. All rights reserved.

Scripture quotations marked KJV are from the King James Version of the Bible.

Scripture quotations marked LEB are from the Lexham English Bible. Copyright 2012 Logos Bible Software. Lexham is a registered trademark of Logos Bible Software.

Scripture quotations marked NASB are taken from the (NASB®) New American Standard Bible®, Copyright © 1960, 1971, 1977, 1995, 2020 by The Lockman Foundation. Used by permission. All rights reserved. www.lockman.org.

Scripture quotations marked NET are from the NET Bible® copyright ©1996-2016 by Biblical Studies Press, L.L.C. http://netbible.com. All rights reserved.

Scripture quotations marked NIV are taken from the Holy Bible, New International Version®, NIV®. Copyright © 1973, 1978, 1984, 2011 by Biblica, Inc.® Used by permission of Zondervan. All rights reserved worldwide. www.zondervan.com. The "NIV" and "New International Version" are trademarks registered in the United States Patent and Trademark Office by Biblica, Inc.®

Scripture quotations marked THE VOICE are taken from The Voice™. Copyright © 2008 by Ecclesia Bible Society. Used by permission. All rights reserved.

Noted Scripture quotations are the author's own translation.

All italics in quoted material is the author's emphasis.

While the author has made every effort to provide accurate, up-to-date source information at the time of publication, statistics and other data are constantly updated. Neither the publisher nor the author assumes any responsibility for errors or for changes that occur after publication. Further, the publisher and author do not have any control over and do not assume any responsibility for third-party websites or their content.

For more resources like this, visit MyCharismaShop.com and the author's websites at jonathancahn.com and booksbyjonathancahn.com.

Cataloging-in-Publication Data is on file with the Library of Congress.

International Standard Book Number: 978-1-63641-523-9

E-book ISBN: 978-1-63641-521-5

1 2025

Printed in the United States of America

Most Charisma Media products are available at special quantity discounts for bulk purchase for sales promotions, premiums, fundraising, and educational needs. For details, call us at (407) 333-0600 or visit our website at charismamedia.com.

CONTENTS

PART I
THE MYSTERY

1 The Avatar 1
2 The Return of the Ancients 3
3 The Journey 6

PART II
KINGDOM OF THE GODS

4 Footsteps of the Apostle 11
5 The Man on the Mountain 15
6 The Trickster 21
7 The Sound of Entities 25

PART III
HAUNTED ISLAND

8 The Mask of the Gods 31
9 Gods and Guerrillas 37
10 Chango 40
11 Crown of the Goddess 47

PART IV
ORISHA LAND

12 Gods on the Lake 57
13 The Yoruba King 60
14 Lady of the Forest 66
15 Gods and Kingdoms 71

PART V
THE OLYMPIAN MYSTERY

16   Festival of the Gods.................79

17   The Return of the God..............86

18   The God of Madness................90

PART VI
AMERICAN GODS AND KINGS

19   The American Gods.................99

20   The Eve of Repossession 104

21   The Prototype 110

22   House of the Gods.................117

PART VII
THE RETURN OF JEHU

23   The Man on the Stairs..............123

24   Return of the Warrior..............130

25   Return of the Witches 134

26   Return of the King Slayer 140

27   Return of the Queen 143

28   The Mystery of Risings 148

29   The Sign of Jehu 152

PART VIII
THE MYSTERY OF JEHORAM

30   The Other Kingdom................159

31   Jehoram the Apostate.............161

32   The Retreat.....................164

Contents vii

33 The Breachable Kingdom 171
34 The Arabian–Philistine Invasion 173
35 Jehoram and the Gods 176
36 The Twentieth Day of Kislev 180
37 The Mystery of Ahaziah 183
38 Jehoram the Feeble 186

PART IX
THE MYSTERY OF ATHALIAH

39 Jezebel's Daughter 193
40 City on the Sea 196
41 Athaliah and Jehoram 199
42 Daughter of the Gods 202
43 King Athaliah 205
44 Jehosheba 209
45 The House of David 214
46 Athaliah's End 217
47 The Yard and the Valley 223

PART X
THE STORM KING

48 King Jehu 229
49 The Deconstructor 233
50 The Purger 236
51 Sword of Jehu 240
52 The Meaning of Jehu 243
53 The Twenty-Eighth Year 247

PART XI
AVATAR

54	Agents of the Gods	253
55	The God-Kings	255
56	The Avatar	258
57	The House of Brahmin	261
58	Lotus	264
59	Goddess	268
60	The Gopalan	271
61	Lady of the Waters	274
62	Cosmic Queen and Sleeping God	277
63	The Mahavidya	280
64	A Necklace of Skulls	284
65	The Laughing One	287
66	Day of the Goddess	291
67	Night of the Visitation	294
68	Birth	297
69	Image of the Avatar	300
70	The Eastern and Western Goddess	305
71	The Altar of Ishtar	310
72	Sign of the Avatar	316

PART XII
MYSTERY OF THE VESSEL

73	The Trumpet	323
74	The Appointed Scripture	327
75	The Appointed Time	330
76	The Trumpet and the Gods	333

Contents ix

PART XIII
REDEMPTION

77 The Return of God................ 341

78 The Window.................... 344

79 The Anointing of the Priest......... 348

80 The Investiture 354

81 The Obelisk.................... 360

82 Judgment, Redemption,

and Eternity 363

About Jonathan Cahn................ 369

Notes........................ 370

PART I

THE MYSTERY

Chapter 1

THE AVATAR

THE AVATARS HAVE returned.

Avatar—the manifestation of a god or goddess on earth, the embodiment of a released soul or spirit, that which embodies or personifies something or someone else.

The word originates in Hinduism, where it speaks of a deity manifesting, assuming, or embodying itself in another form or being. Typically the deity assumes the form of an avatar to accomplish a specific purpose, mission, or end, or to move or operate in a specific setting or way in which it could not otherwise move or operate. The avatar could manifest in the form of another god, goddess, or supernatural being. The avatar could be born into the world as a child and grow up to become a man or woman. The avatar could even manifest as an animal.

Avatars existed in the realm of mythology. But could there be another side to the story?

Is there another context in which the avatars could, in some way, assume a reality?

Could the avatars, in some way or form, actually exist in the modern world?

Could they, even now, be moving within our culture,

affecting our lives, operating in the political and governmental realms that rule our lives?

As the avatar is the manifestation of something other than itself, in order to open the mystery, we must first open the mystery of that which lies behind it, beneath it, and within it—the spirits and the gods.

The mystery we are about to uncover begins in ancient times and yet is fully at work in the modern world and in our day. It affects virtually every facet of modern life and every person in the Western world.

The mystery operates in the realms of modern society, culture, politics, and government. It involves ancient gods and modern spirits, ancient rulers and modern leaders, ancient embodiments and modern vessels. It underlies a war that manifests in the political and cultural realms but is ultimately spiritual—with spirits, gods, and avatars on one side; vessels, instruments, types, and antitypes on the other. And though it involves institutions, organizations, and people, it is not ultimately about them but that which lies beyond them. It is, by nature, an explosive mystery.

We now enter the realm that lies behind the mystery of gods and goddesses, kings and queens, vessels and avatars.

Chapter 2

THE RETURN OF THE ANCIENTS

Is it possible that behind the central movements and issues of our time are entities of ancient origin, with consciousness and volition? Could they be the unseen agents behind the transformation of our culture, indwelling movements, institutions, agendas, and even the people of our times?

In *The Return of the Gods* I wrote of the deities of the ancient world. Behind the gods and goddesses of the nations lies another realm—a realm of entities. In the Hebrew Scriptures they are identified as the *shedim*. In the Greek New Testament they are identified as the *daemonia*—from which we get the word *demon*. Both shedim and daemonia refer to entities with volition and consciousness—spirits.

There is an ancient warning concerning what happens when the door is opened for the entering of the spirits and the return of the gods. We have ignored that warning. We have opened that door. In *The Return of the Gods* I wrote how we did so and chronicled how the spirits, entities, and gods have returned to American and Western civilization. But since I wrote of it, the mystery has not stopped unfolding and the transformation has not stopped progressing. This now raises other questions.

Is it possible that the spirits, the entities, the gods have

3

entered the political realm, impelled campaigns, chosen candidates, and altered elections?

Is it possible that their aim is to crystallize their hold on modern culture by taking possession of the political and governmental realms?

Can their agenda be withstood?

And could the answers to these questions determine the future of America, the West, and much of the modern world? The gods have returned. For what purpose? They have not returned for the sake of returning—but for the purpose of dominion. In this they have increasingly assumed control of the central institutions of American and Western culture and, as in ancient times, now vie for the highest platforms and seats of power.

They are, by nature, possessing spirits, and so they seek to possess all things, people, movements, cultures, and civilizations. And by nature, they wage war against the ways, the nature, and the works of God and seek to vilify His people.

They gained their entrance in the name of tolerance and freedom. But such things were never their goal, only the means by which their goal, dominion, could be achieved. And so it is no accident that American and Western civilizations have witnessed the emergence of a cultural totalitarianism, a repressive consensus that seeks the cancellation of all opposition and the elimination of the Judeo-Christian foundation upon which those civilizations have, for ages, stood.

The Return of the Ancients

The metamorphosis was inaugurated by the gods and culminates in the takeover of the civilization that hosts them. It is then that they decisively penetrate the realm of politics, law, and government. Government, by which civilizations, nations, and peoples are ruled, is the final prize, the end goal. We will now see how the realms of ancient gods and modern government have increasingly intersected and how that intersection has triggered a cultural and civilizational crisis and conflict that has altered the course of America and the world.

We will also uncover the template of an ancient nation that underwent the same metamorphosis, the same crisis, and the same conflict, a template of gods and goddesses, kings and queens, altars and temples, uprisings and revolutions. That template, which has continued to unfold since I first wrote of it, will eerily describe and reveal what is now transpiring in America, what it is leading to, and what we do in light of it.

Chapter 3

THE JOURNEY

WE NOW EMBARK on a journey across the globe.

It will take us first to the East, to a land the gods never left, to a cursed mountain, to a trickster god, to an ancient showdown, and to the sounds of mass deliverance.

We will then go to a haunted island in the Caribbean where a ruler walked in the footsteps of an ancient god, where the gods disguised themselves as saints, and to a mountain on which a hallowed goddess was uncrowned.

We will pass through a South American lake of gods and goddesses on the way to an African land, to the birth-place of spirits, to a man venerated as Lord of the Earth, and to the lady of the forest.

Then we will return to the West, where we will see the gods who lurk just beneath its surface and one that appeared before the eyes of the entire world.

We will then come back to America, where we will see how the gods have now ascended to the point where they vie for the nation's future and the dominion of its government.

We will open up the ancient mystery that lies behind one of the most controversial and consequential of world leaders, a mystery that foreshadowed his rise to the world stage thousands of years before it happened.

Then the template of an ill-fated ancient king whose life constitutes the mystery at work behind a recent American president.

The Journey 7

Then that of a little-known ancient queen whose reign was characterized by blood and who bears a warning concerning America's future.

We will then open the mystery of a goddess from a faraway land and the avatar that has become a prominent leader in the American political realm—the instrument of the gods, the avatar, who rose to the heights of power and vied to determine the future of America.

We will see how close America and the West came to the possession of the gods, what almost was and might be again.

We will then witness how behind one of the most dramatic events in recent political history lies the consecration of an ancient priesthood.

We will uncover an ancient obelisk and the message it holds for America.

Finally, we will bring together all the pieces of the mysteries to see what they reveal concerning the future. What is it all leading to? What do we need to know and do?

In *The Return of the Gods* I wrote of the *dark trinity*, the three ancient gods, spirits and principalities, at work in our culture. We will return to them. But in order to understand what is now taking place in America and the West, we begin our journey to lands and cultures in which the gods and principalities manifest themselves more overtly and exercise their dominion with thinner masks.

I have thus far written of the gods, but now I will write on how I encountered them.

Our first journey will take us to a land saturated by deities, gods and goddesses whose reign and dominion have continued through the ages unbroken.

PART II

KINGDOM OF THE GODS

Chapter 4

FOOTSTEPS OF THE APOSTLE

IT IS, IN many ways, the last great repository of the gods: India. Unlike the gods of Western civilization, the gods of India were never rejected. There was no mass repudiation, no civilizational exorcism, no spiritual or cultural transformation regarding them. Unlike the gods of the West that departed in the wake of the gospel, they were never cast out.

LAND OF SPIRITS

Because of its unbroken worship of the gods, Eastern religion serves as a type of time capsule of what once was in the West, before the impact of monotheism and the gospel. Filled with gods and goddesses, human gods, animal gods, and combinations of each, temples, altars, and sacrifices, Indian religion gives us a glimpse of what once permeated Western civilization and what would come to be known as *paganism*.

If behind the gods are what the Bible calls the shedim and the daemonia, words denoting spirits, the latter more specifically denoting demonic spirits, then a land of countless gods would be a land of countless spirits. And a land of numberless gods would also be a land of countless spirits. It is that which will unlock and make sense of the events that took place on my journey through India.

THE FOOTSTEPS OF THOMAS

It was a Friday night worship service at Beth Israel, the congregation I lead in northern New Jersey. That night, we had a guest speaker, an Indian evangelist named Dr. Job. He spoke of the connection between his land and the apostle Thomas. According to church tradition, Thomas took the gospel from Israel to India.[1] The land, the churches, and the believers of India are thus marked by the name of the apostle to this day.[2]

In the middle of Dr. Job's address he turned to me and said, "Jonathan, I am inviting you to go to the land of India to walk in the footsteps of the apostle Thomas." It was for that reason he had come to Beth Israel. It was his burden that since Thomas was a Jewish believer in Jesus, another Jewish believer should go to India, walk in the former's footsteps, and likewise proclaim the gospel.

A DANGEROUS JOURNEY

I was to give him an answer before he left. Complicating the decision was the fact that not long before he came to Beth Israel, a new party and government had come to power in India, a radical agent of Hindu nationalism.[3] It was known for championing the worship of Hindu gods and the persecution of non-Hindu religious minorities, prominent among whom were Christians.[4] It was an example of the convergence of the spiritual and physical realms, in this case of the gods and government of India.

Under the new government, churches were burned down, Christian schools and cemeteries were destroyed, and Christians were assaulted, raped, and murdered.[5] I

Footsteps of the Apostle 13

was now being asked to walk through the land of India, proclaiming the gospel in the footsteps of the man who the people of India believed had brought the gospel to their land. Under such circumstances, it promised to be a dramatic and potentially dangerous journey. I prayed and was led to say yes.

ANOTHER KIND OF WARFARE

The other part of the story was of a much stranger nature but in line with the mystery of the shedim, the spirits behind the gods. As soon as I said *yes* to going to India, an array of strange events began taking place at the congregation, most of which I cannot put in these pages. But some of them affected my travel plans. It was as if every step taken toward the journey was being countered, obstructed—but not by human agency. With every advance, a new obstacle would appear. Hardly a day went by when those in charge of arranging for the journey weren't dealing with confusion, erroneous information, false reports, and strange impediments.

As the time of departure drew near, we discovered that our plane tickets had disappeared. The travel agent in charge of obtaining them, we learned, had left the country, leaving behind no contacts. On the day I was to leave for India, I headed to the airport with no tickets and no assurance I would be able to board the plane. That was the first flight; the second would be more dramatic.

I had just taken off from Amsterdam on a flight to New Delhi. As I gazed out my airplane window, I noticed something strange: dark objects flying past my view, what appeared to be pieces of the airplane's machinery. The plane quickly turned around and headed back to the airport.

The dramatic events did not stop upon my reaching India. Two days after our arrival my team and I were almost killed. And it was just the beginning.

None of these events was connected by any outworking of natural causation. But in the realm of the spirits it all made sense. We were entering the realm of the gods, the shedim. It was inevitable that there would be warfare. And the closer we came to our final destination, the greater that warfare would become.

Chapter 5

THE MAN ON THE MOUNTAIN

I T WAS LIKE something out of a movie. I was being led across India in the footsteps of Thomas with multitudes of Indian Christians, often thousands, waiting at each site. They welcomed me as if they were welcoming the apostle after a two-thousand-year absence. At one site I was greeted by an elephant adorned with festive decorations. In its trunk was a garland, which it placed around my neck.

THE MARTYR

The journey would culminate in the land of Tamil Nadu and the city of Chennai. It was there, according to church tradition, that Thomas ministered. And it was there, by the same tradition, that he was assassinated by a Hindu priest.[1] When I was asked to follow in Thomas's footsteps, that part of the story was left out of the invitation. Nor was I told that our final destination would be the same mountaintop that marked the apostle's death. Thus I was to minister on the mountaintop of the apostle's martyrdom and hopefully not get martyred in the process.

A MULTITUDE OF FACES

It was not long into our journey that we began noticing strange occurrences of another kind—we were being followed. We would travel over a thousand miles to our destination, and yet the same faces, a multitude of faces, all of them male, would reappear over and over again in the

15

crowds, by our vehicles, on city streets, in restaurants, in alleyways, in our hotels, everywhere we went. It was as if they knew where we were going before we got there, even when our plans had not been made public. It appeared as well that they were intensely interested not merely in observing but in trying to gain proximity to me. They appeared most often to be on edge, tense, and deadly serious. We took as many precautions as possible. But there were other things, stranger things, against which no precautions were possible. I will mention just one of them here.

SEIZURE

It happened at night in a hotel in Tamil Nadu as we were getting ready to sit down to eat. I was about to lead the team in prayer over the dinner. But I never prayed that prayer. It was just as I was about to open my mouth that the leader of my security team, the man who had served as my principal bodyguard, a former New York City policeman, was suddenly and violently thrown backward. He came crashing down on the dinner table, then onto the floor, where he began convulsing in seizures, out of control and foaming at the mouth. Those witnessing it feared for his life. Emergency medics were called in.

LAND OF THE SHEDIM

He had never experienced anything remotely like what happened to him that night. Nor, after leaving India and returning home, did anything like it ever happen to him again. Back in America he underwent several medical tests

The Man on the Mountain 17

to find the cause. No cause was ever found. It made no sense in the natural. But we had come to a land of many gods and thus a land of many shedim, principalities and spirits. We were there on a mission that would put us in conflict with such things. In the New Testament Greek it meant we were in a land of many daemonia—demonic spirits. And so it was no accident that what took place that night manifested the signs of the demonic.

COMMANDOS ON THE MOUNTAIN

As we neared Chennai, our final destination, the persecution of Indian Christians by radical Hindus had reached a fever pitch.[2] News of what was happening across the land filtered back to our families and friends at home, who sent us messages pleading that we stop the journey and avoid going up that mountain.

Upon arriving in Chennai, we were visited by one of the city's police chiefs. He informed us that because of the increased danger of violence to Christians, he sent commandos to the mountain to accompany us on our ascent. It turned out he was a Christian. Before leaving our hotel room, he was led to recite the words of Psalm 91:

> I will say of the LORD, "*He is* my refuge and my fortress; my God, in Him I will trust.
>
> "Surely He shall deliver you from the snare of the fowler and from the perilous pestilence....You shall not be afraid of the terror by night, nor of the arrow that flies by day."[3]

THE MARTYRS OF ORISSA

The day arrived for us to ascend the mountain of Thomas's martyrdom, the site that epitomized the war of the gods against the gospel. As we prepared to do so, the war exploded into world headlines. That same day, another martyrdom took place in India, and another missionary had been killed in the land, as an Australian minister and his two sons were brutally murdered by a mob of radical Hindus in the Indian state of Orissa.[4] The authorities now feared that a similar event would take place as we went up the mountain.

AS IF THE LAST

On the mountaintop was a centuries-old church bearing the name of Thomas and commemorating his martyrdom. Outside the church was a platform on which I was to speak. Between the church and the platform were thousands of Indian men, women, and children. According to the program, after giving my address, I was to walk into the crowd to the church of Thomas. There I would light a torch from the flame that burned in the sanctuary and that stood for the apostle's testimony. I was then to carry the lit torch back through the crowd and onto the stage.

As I approached the podium to deliver my message, in front of the multitude was a crowd of men standing as close to the stage as possible. We had seen their faces before, as they followed us throughout our journey across India. They were pressing in toward the gate in the security fence separating the stage from the people, the same

The Man on the Mountain 19

gate through which I was to pass upon entering the crowd. Again the men appeared tense, focused, and deadly serious.

It is said that ministers should preach every message as if it were their last. It is hard to do that. But on that day, it was easy. I delivered that message on the mountain of Thomas as if it would be my last.

THE RETURN OF THE TORCH

At the last moment, Dr. Job informed me he had made a change in the program. He had decided that he would go out to get the flame of Thomas instead and hand it to me upon his return. So he did. And there, on top of the mountain of Thomas, he placed the torch alit with the flame of Thomas into my hands. It was a symbolic moment. Two thousand years earlier, Jewish disciples of Messiah passed the torch of the gospel to the Gentiles, the light of God to the nations. That mountain represented its passing. Now, two thousand years later, a minister from the nations, from India, returned the torch back into the hands of a Jewish follower of Messiah on that same mountain.

PROPHECY ON THE MOUNTAIN

While on the mountain of Thomas, I encountered an Indian Christian who was waiting there with a message to give me. A year before the event, he was led to ascend the same mountain to pray. While praying, the Spirit spoke to him of a curse on the land of India, birthed in its rejection of the gospel. The mountain of Thomas embodied that rejection and the blood of the martyrs shed in the land. The Spirit, he said, then told him that a Jewish man had to

come to India, had to ascend the mountain of Thomas—
and not get killed. It would be part of the breaking of the
curse.

After receiving that word, he traveled through Chennai
and Tamil Nadu proclaiming to the churches and whom-
ever would listen that a Jewish man had to come to
Chennai and ascend the mountain of Thomas. He had
no idea that a Jewish man was, in fact, coming to India
and would ascend that mountain. Nor did any of those
who invited me or planned that event have any idea of the
word he had given. But I had ascended the mountain. I
had given the message. I had received back the torch. And
I had not been killed.

But there was one more puzzle piece to the mystery of
India and the gods. It happened at the beginning of the
journey and almost brought it to a sudden end.

Chapter 6

THE TRICKSTER

IT WAS SOON after arriving in India that our host informed us he had arranged for us to see one of the most famous tourist sites in the country. It was the seventeenth-century white marble monument built by the Mughal emperor Shah Jahan as a mausoleum for his deceased wife Mumtaz Mahal—the Taj Mahal.[1]

THE FOG

Our host had hired a driver for the day to take us there and back. It took us over three hours from New Delhi, where we were staying, to Agra, the city of the Taj Mahal. By the time we had walked through the site and were ready to go home, it was getting dark. We had been warned to head back before dark, before the fog had settled on the roads. But it was too late. It was now dark, and the fog had descended.

The fog was so thick that at times we could barely see twenty or thirty feet ahead. But because our driver was nervous about getting home late, he drove much faster than was wise or safe. At times he seemed to be racing. Objects would suddenly materialize out of the fog, many of them vehicles stranded on the road as a result of accidents. We had never seen so many accidents on a single road in a single night as we saw on that road that night.

But even more striking was the nature of those accidents: a four-wheeled cart turned over with produce scattered all

21

over the road, another cart overturned with hay scattered across the road, and then another with more spilled produce. Then we drove past an overturned truck and then an overturned car. All along the road that night were carts, trucks, and cars motionless on the road, several of them on their sides or overturned.

THE CRASH

And then it happened. At a speed far above what was safe, our car crashed into the vehicle ahead of us. The vehicle was hidden by the fog until it was too late. It was a truck. The car rammed into the truck in such a way that it became latched onto it. The truck, also going much faster than it should have been, was now dragging the car through the fog. The driver of the truck did not, at first, realize what was happening. The car began swerving dangerously back and forth, each swerve putting us in danger of flipping over.

Finally, we came to a stop. The front of the car was badly damaged, the driver and his passengers, shaken, but the car hadn't flipped over, and we hadn't been killed. It was only our second day in the land, and our journey had almost been brought to a sudden end.

THE AVATAR-GOD

After returning home from India, I came across an article on Hindu mythology. It spoke of Krishna. Krishna was an avatar, an avatar-god, the bodily manifestation of the Hindu god Vishnu. According to his myth of origin, Krishna was born or incarnated in a place called Mathura.

The Trickster 23

Mathura is located in the Indian state of Uttar Pradesh. Uttar Pradesh is the state that contains Agra, the city of the Taj Mahal. We had come to the land of Krishna. Beyond that, Krishna's birthplace, Mathura, was located between two major Indian cities—*on the road connecting Agra and New Delhi*—in other words, on the very route we were driving. Krishna is known as the "trickster god." He was famed for performing pranks on the villagers of his land.[2]

THE OVERTURNER OF VEHICLES

According to his myth, the power of Krishna was first displayed when he was a child. It was his first act of warfare. According to the story, a spirit named Sakatasura took on the form of *a cart*. As a cart, Sakatasura attempted to crush the baby Krishna, who was lying underneath it. But Krishna kicked *the cart and overturned it*. By this, Krishna broke the cart and killed his enemy, Sakatasura. Thus the power of the god Krishna was first manifested in the *overturning of a cart*.[3] And the overturning of the cart was the act by which Krishna first destroyed his enemy.

Now we were traveling the route and land in which Krishna was said to have been born, whose power was manifested in the overturning of the cart. And it was the night of the overturning of the carts and four-wheeled vehicles, one after the other. And then it was our vehicle that just barely escaped becoming one of the overturned, and we inside it, becoming victims of the overturning.

MYTH AND SPIRITS

Mythology is an expression of fantasy. And yet what we experienced in real time and space as we traveled through the land of a god, on the particular route associated with his birth, matched the mythology of that particular god and the very same strategy he employed to destroy his enemy. It was a myth. And yet it almost killed us.

We were not battling mythology. Mythology is inert. But the principalities are present, active, and moving. What we witnessed that night aligned with what the Bible says of the gods. Behind the gods are spirits, the shedim, the daemonia—and they were present, active, and dangerous.

How did the mythological account of the overturned cart translate into reality? How did the shedim relate to the gods? Did the mythologies follow the existence of spiritual entities? Did they contain elements of the spirits they represented? Or did the spirits follow, utilize, and play upon the mythologies and beliefs of men regarding the gods? Or could it be both?

It was our last event in the land that would prove the most dramatic—and the scene of a mass phenomenon.

Chapter 7

THE SOUND OF ENTITIES

AFTER OUR ASCENT of the mountain of Thomas, we prepared for the last major event of our journey, a series of gatherings in which we would share the gospel with a massive sea of Indian people. The meetings took place at night outdoors.

THE SEVENTY THOUSAND

As darkness began to fall, the grounds began filling with people, an enormous sea of Indians, men in white shirts and women in robes of every color. At the end of the last night, I spoke to the multitude of God's love, the gospel of Messiah, then led those who were willing in a prayer of salvation. It was estimated that the number of Indian men and women who prayed that night to receive salvation was over seventy thousand. Everything that had taken place from the moment I said yes to that journey, all the obstacles, setbacks, and dangers, was more than worth it for that one night and that one moment.

THE SOUNDING

But something else happened at that gathering that would leave those standing with me on the stage in stunned awe. It happened on the first night. I held up a shofar, the ancient biblical trumpet, the ram's horn, before the multitude. It is unlikely that anyone at that gathering had ever seen one before. I explained that the sound of the trumpet was the sound of freedom and a representation of the power of God. And we would pray for God's power to break any bondage in their lives, to bring release and freedom. We would then sound the trumpet that the ancient sound of freedom would go out to them. I set the trumpet to my mouth and blew. We couldn't, at first, make sense of what happened next.

MASS EXORCISM

Waves of sound came back to the stage from the multitudes as if in response. I sounded the trumpet a second time. Again came the waves of sound. They were waves of bloodcurdling screams. The only thing we could liken it to was what one would imagine one might hear in the exorcism of a demon-possessed man. But the screams weren't coming from any one person or direction but from the many. It was as if the trumpet blast had triggered a mass deliverance, as if we were witnessing some kind of colossal exorcism.

WHEN YOU GO TO WAR

Upon returning home from India, I opened a Jewish encyclopedia to an article on the meaning of the trumpet, or shofar, in Jewish history. The article spoke of the trumpet as an instrument of freedom but also as a vessel of war and the power of God. It went back to a scripture in the Book of Numbers:

> When you go to war in your land
> against the enemy who oppresses
> you, then you shall sound an alarm

> with the trumpets, and you will be
> remembered before the LORD your
> God, and you will be saved from your
> enemies.[1]

At the sound of the trumpet, the people of Israel would defeat their enemies. In Jewish belief this extended into the spiritual realm. The trumpet was deemed a vessel of war against the satanic and demonic realms. Its sounding would cause the enemy to be defeated and the spirits of darkness to flee.

TRUMPETS AND ENTITIES

But the tens of thousands of Indians who stood before us that night had never seen, much less read, a Jewish encyclopedia. And yet the sounding of the trumpet triggered massive waves of bloodcurdling screams, as if legions of spirits were fleeing the blast and departing from the multitudes.

We had entered a land of many gods, spirits, principalities, and powers, into the midst of spiritual warfare. We had sounded the ancient biblical instrument of Israel's warfare by which its enemies fled or were defeated. The result was the sound of a mass fleeing of another kind.

THE AVESA AND THE POSSESSION OF THE GODS

The question must now be asked: If behind the gods are spirits, and if spirits seek to possess, then could spirit possession play a part in Hinduism? It could and it does. It is called *avesa*—the possession of human bodies by spiritual entities. And in accordance with the scriptural connection

28 THE AVATAR

of the gods to the possessing shedim and daemonia are the Hindu gods themselves that often possess their devotees. It is known as *divine possession* and is considered to be a form of *yoga*, becoming one with the god.

Though the textbook definition may vary, the one possessed by the inhabiting spirit becomes a type of avatar, the embodiment of the Hindu deity, the vessel by which it moves and acts. Whether it is a god or goddess seeking embodiment in the avatar, or a spirit seeking to possess a flesh-and-blood host, it is, in the end, and in its essence, the same. The spirits seek embodiment. The result is possession, or an avatar.

Beyond the phenomenon of *divine possession*, it is part of Hinduism to recognize certain human beings as living avatars. These include hallowed religious leaders, teachers, masters, and gurus. Each is seen as a living incarnation of a particular Hindu god or goddess.

Soon after coming home from India, I received word that a man had come to America to request a meeting with me. He would invite me to another land, very different from that of India. It was an island haunted by the gods.

PART III

HAUNTED ISLAND

Chapter 8

THE MASK OF THE GODS

A VISITOR TO CUBA in the late twentieth century would see the signs of Marxist-Leninist ideology and totalitarianism in nearly every realm of life. Plastered on its walls and billboards were images of the island's dictator, Fidel Castro, and its hallowed revolutionary, Che Guevara, along with those of communism's older icons, Marx, Engels, and Lenin. But beneath its Marxist and secular veneer was another realm—a kingdom of gods.

RULE OF THE GODS

Beginning in the sixteenth century and continuing up to the nineteenth century, masses of Africans were brought as slaves to the island of Cuba. There they were introduced to the Roman Catholicism of the Spanish settlers. But the slaves did not come alone; they brought their gods.[1]

To continue worshipping and serving their gods and idols, they gave them masks. Their masks were taken from the Catholic veneration of saints. While appearing to give honor to the saints, they were, instead, worshipping their native gods. The practice or religion of worshipping gods disguised as saints came to be known as Santeria. The word *Santeria* can be translated as the way or worship of the saints. But it is known at the same time as *Regla de Ocha*, or *Regla de Orishas*. The words *ocha* and *orisha* refer to an African deity. Thus the religion known as the

31

"worship of the saints" can also be rendered the "rule of the gods."[2]

GODS DISGUISED AS SAINTS

So in Santeria the gods are served and worshipped in the guise of saints. Behind the mask of Saint Peter is Ogun, the African god of war.[3] Behind the mask of Saint Anthony is Eleguá, the trickster god of the gates.[4] Behind the mask of Saint Barbara is the god Chango,[5] king of the orishas. Behind Saint Joseph is Osain,[6] god of plants, woods, and jungles. And behind Mary are several Santerian gods, including Oshun, goddess of rivers, fertility, and sensuality;[7] and Yemayá, goddess of the sea.[8]

SANTEROS, SANTERAS, AND SACRIFICES

The priests of the Santerian gods are known as *santeros*, if male, and *santeras*, if female.[9] They officiate over Santerian ceremonies, feasts, and sacrifices. It is written in the Scriptures that the shedim required sacrifices, even human sacrifices.[10] So too the gods of Santeria, the orishas, require their followers to offer up sacrifices at their altars. In past times and in their native land, the orishas required human sacrifices.[11] But in the late nineteenth century the practice was outlawed.[12] Now the Santerian sacrifices consist largely of common objects such as food, flowers, and money, along with birds and four-legged animals. But rumors persist of Santerian sacrifices of children.

The Mask of the Gods

TOQUE DE SANTO AND THE POSSESSION OF THE GODS

Does the biblical connection between the gods and the shedim and daemonia hold true for the world of the Santerian gods? It does. It is in one of the most central of Santerian rites, the *Toque de Santo*. In it the worshippers sing and dance to the beat of drums to summon the manifestation of a god. The god is then invited to take possession of one of the worshippers.[13]

The possessed worshipper is then taken into another room and arrayed in the ritual garments of the particular deity indwelling them. The worshipper then becomes an *avatar*, the embodiment of the Santerian deity. It is now the orisha, the god or goddess, who moves, acts, and speaks through its indwelled vessel.[14] The worshippers see it as a sacred event; others would call it demonic possession.

MARXISM AND SANTERIA

The gods seek to possess more than individuals. They seek as well to indwell kingdoms and governments. What then in the case of Cuba? Could there be any connection between the government of Fidel Castro and the gods of Santeria?

With Castro's embrace of Marxism, Cuba became an officially atheistic state.[15] Christians and clergy were persecuted. Churches were cut off from access to media and from influencing the larger culture.[16] Church schools were shut down.[17] And Marxism replaced Christianity as the nation's official creed and dogma.[18] Priests and pastors were arrested and sent to prison.[19]

As for Santeria, since it was likewise deemed a religion, the government at first discouraged and suppressed its practice.[20] One could not openly engage in Santeria and be a member of the Cuban communist party.[21] To hold a Santerian ceremony, practitioners had to receive government permits, at least officially.[22] But Santeria continued to be practiced.[23] In fact, the Cuban government increasingly saw Santeria as beneficial in promoting a unified Cuban identity.[24] To that end the government began sponsoring performances of Santerian dances and rites.[25] Though one could view such things as folklore, the Santerian dances and rituals were designed to invoke the gods and summon the spirits.

INTO THE EMPTY HOUSE

Instead of weakening the practice of Santeria, Castro's regime ended up empowering it. In the spiritual realm the power of Jesus was the antidote to the Santerian spirits and gods. But the government's relentless war against the gospel would largely remove that antidote, along with its restraining force, from Cuban culture. At the same time, the absence of the gospel would create a spiritual void that Marxism was unable to fill.

The result was that Cubans increasingly turned to Santeria to fill the God-shaped void their government had created. Furthering the transformation, Santerian practices were increasingly allowed, if not promoted by the Cuban government, which could have led to the undermining of the Christian faith.[26] And so under Cuba's Marxist-Leninist government, Santerian practices

The Mask of the Gods   35

proliferated throughout the island. The government even began broadcasting Santerian ceremonies on national television.[27] The result was that over time the majority of those on the island would take part in Santerian practices in one form or another.

That was the irony. Castro had removed God from Cuban culture. But he could not remove the need for God's presence. And so instead of eliminating spiritual hunger, it increased it. And in closing the door to God's presence, it had opened the door to the gods and spirits. And in Cuba they were already there, waiting and well prepared to fill the void.

AN ISLAND POSSESSED

When a demonic spirit rules or possesses an individual, the unique and unmistakable signs of demonic possession will inevitably manifest. When such spirits rule or possess a society or nation, those same signs will manifest but on a much larger scale. So as the Cuban government waged war to remove God from the island while encouraging the entrance of the gods, the daemonia, the signs of possession would manifest on a national level.

An individual possessed by a spirit will become darkened and will live a life characterized by oppression, bent toward death, destruction, even self-destruction, and war against God's presence. So life on the island became darkened and characterized by oppression. It became bent toward self-destruction, even to the point that it almost brought the entire world to the edge of nuclear destruction. So too it warred against God and His people.

Beyond this, as the gods demanded sacrifices of blood, even human sacrifice, the Castro regime would oblige them. It was not long after coming to power that Cuba's revolutionary government proved itself adept at shedding blood as it inaugurated an era of executions. Anyone deemed an enemy of the state could be imprisoned and killed.[28] The orishas now had their blood sacrifices brought to their altars by their new Marxist priests. In that sense the atheistic Marxist government of Cuba became, itself, an avatar of the gods.

If Castro's regime would in the end empower the practice of Santeria, could its relationship to the Santerian gods go even deeper? Could it be that the spirits were involved in its reign, even from the very beginning?

Chapter 9

GODS AND GUERRILLAS

THE CITY OF Santiago lies near Cuba's southeastern coast. It is the island's second-largest city. But it is the city's spiritual nature and function that makes it especially significant to the mystery of the gods.

CITY OF SPIRITS

Santiago is a central hub of Santerian worship, filled with Santerian priests and priestesses, rites and rituals, sacrifices, the invocations of spirits, the casting of spells, and the manifestations of possession, a wellspring of the Santerian gods and goddesses, spirits, and orishas. On July 26, 1953, Fidel Castro led a small band of revolutionaries in an attack on the Moncada Barracks.[1] Though the attack was unsuccessful, it marked the birth of the revolution that would end the reign of Fulgencia Batista.[2] The Moncada Barracks are located in the city of Santiago.[3] Thus the Cuban Revolution and all that it would bring to the island and to the world, the movement that would wage war against the gospel, was born in the city of spells and possessions, spirits and gods.

OUR LADY THE GODDESS

In the shadow of Santiago is the nearby town of El Cobre. El Cobre houses the shrine of Cuba's patron saint, Nuestra Senora de la Caridad, Our Lady of Charity.[4] But the title is a mask. It is common practice to approach the shrine of El Cobre not in veneration of Mary but in the worship of a Santerian deity. Behind the mask of Our Lady is Oshun, the Santerian goddess of love and fertility.[5] Thus Oshun occupies a most venerated and powerful position in the Santerian pantheon, having been merged with Cuba's patron saint.

THE IDOL AND THE FIGURINE

It was there that a mother, seeking intervention on her son's behalf, brought a golden figurine to present at the side of the idol at the shrine linked not only to Nuestra Senora de la Caridad but to the goddess Oshun. It was the figurine of a guerrilla fighter. The woman was Fidel Castro's mother.[6] So the figure representing Fidel Castro stood at the side of the figure venerated as Oshun.

Beyond the figurine, it was reported that Castro, while leading his guerrilla fighters in the mountains of the Sierra Maestra, commissioned local Santerian priestesses to make magic amulets and talismans to bring protection to himself and those around him.[7] And when his men came down from the mountains, they were observed wearing metal amulets dedicated to the lady of El Cobre, Oshun. He reached the capital city on January 8, 1959. That night, he would address the nation.[8]

THE DOVES OF OBATALA

One of the most revered gods of Santeria is Obatala. Obatala is worshipped as creator of the earth[9] and the Great White God. In Santeria, Obatala was joined to or worshipped in place of Jesus. Obatala is connected to kingship, thrones, authority, and the coronation of rulers.[10]

Gods and Guerrillas 39

Among the foremost of his symbols is the dove. Doves are often depicted as hovering over Obatala, resting on his body, or perched atop his altar.[11]

At an outdoor gathering on the night of his victorious entrance into Havana, Castro addressed the nation. In the midst of his speech a white dove landed on his shoulder and another on his podium.[12] Castro continued preaching, adorned with doves just like Obatala and his altar. In the Santerian world the event was taken as a clear sign that Obatala had placed his mark of approval on Castro to lead the island, having sent to Castro the sign of his throne at the moment of the future dictator's coronation. The priests of Santeria declared that Castro had been chosen by the gods, and they would stand behind him.[13]

Throughout Castro's reign it was considered something of an open secret among Cubans that those in his inner circle were worshippers of the Santerian gods.[14] It was also rumored that he himself had dabbled in it.[15]

But could the relationship of Castro to the gods and spirits of Santeria be of a still deeper mystery?

Chapter 10

CHANGO

THE GODS SEEK avatars; the spirits seek physical embodiment. In the case of possession, the spirits indwell their human hosts. But there are other ways. And to use a king as one's vessel is to gain dominion over a kingdom. Could the gods be connected to Fidel Castro? And is it possible that behind Castro's rise to power was a Santerian god?

THE WARRIOR GOD

Chango is one of the most powerful and popular gods in the Santerian pantheon and, at the same time, among the most controversial. He is adored by some, feared by others.[1] For nearly five decades Fidel Castro was unquestionably the most powerful figure on the island of Cuba. He was also among the most controversial of world leaders—loved and adored by some, hated, feared, and reviled by others.

In Santerian mythology Chango was a warrior god, known for his many battles and military campaigns. He was celebrated as a symbol of masculinity and virility, a risk-taker, strong and courageous, and at the same time volatile, temperamental, violent,[2] and murderous. Starting with his first uprising against Batista, Castro took on the role of warrior and became known throughout Cuba for his military campaigns and battles, a symbol of masculinity and virility, a risk-taker—strong and courageous on

Chango   41

one hand, volatile, temperamental, and murderous[3] on the other.

THE SEDUCER

Chango was a flirtatious god, a charmer, and a seducer, a womanizer with lovers and affairs too numerous to recount. A handful of these took on the functions or attributes of a wife.[4] So too it was well known that Castro was a womanizer, a seducer, with lovers too numerous to recount except that one of his aides put the number at thirty-five thousand. His inner circle reportedly scoured the beaches of Cuba daily, searching for women to serve as new conquests for their leader.[5] And as with Chango, a handful of these took on the functions or attributes of a wife.[6]

THE USURPER

While Chango engaged in battle, his brother Ajaka reigned as king. But Ajaka lost the support of the people. He would be removed from power. Some accounts relay that it was Chango who overthrew him. Chango then took the throne and reigned in his place.[7] While Castro was likewise engaging in battle as a guerrilla fighter, Batista was ruling the nation. But Batista also lost the support of the people and would fall from power. It was Castro who overthrew him. He would then rule the island in Batista's place.

THE RED TYRANT

Chango is associated with the color red. He is typically depicted as arrayed in red garments just as his worshippers typically dress in red to honor him.[8] So too Fidel Castro was associated with the color red. He saturated the island in red, with red flags and red banners hanging from flagpoles and buildings. So too the posters and paintings that bore his image across the nation were typically highlighted or awash in red.

Chango was said to have ruled his kingdom with an iron fist. He was a powerful and violent leader, a tyrant, feared for his tyrannical ways. He was given to vengeance and showed no reluctance in putting his enemies to death. He was a despot.[9] So too Castro ruled Cuba with an iron fist. He too was a powerful and violent leader, feared for his tyrannical ways. He too was vengeful and showed no hesitation in imprisoning and executing his enemies.[10] He ruled as a dictator.[11]

THE GOD WITH THE CIGAR

Among the objects associated with Chango is the cigar. His worshippers would place cigars on his altars as offerings in the hope of procuring his favor.[12] We might then expect the cigar to be uniquely associated with Fidel Castro. And so it was. In fact, no major world leader in the late twentieth century had become so uniquely associated with the cigar as Fidel Castro. So strong was the association that the American CIA came up with more than one plot to assassinate him by means of a deadly cigar.[13] And as far as assassination attempts went, in the mythology of Chango, the god was famous for escaping the prospect of death.[14] So too was Castro.

THE AMULET

Chango was especially associated with the goddess Oshun.[15] So too Castro, as we have seen, was associated with the goddess Oshun, his figurine placed on the goddess's altar next to her idol. Chango was said to have worn an amulet around his neck. So too as he entered Havana to take power, Castro was said to have been wearing a metal amulet around his neck—and the amulet bore the image of the lady of El Cobre, behind which was the goddess Oshun.

THE POWER OF DESTRUCTION

Chango was believed to possess terrifying powers of destruction. He mastered the secret of fire and employed it against his adversaries.[16] Indeed, he was the god of lightning and thunder. He utilized them as weapons.[17] He sent down lightning from the skies to strike down his enemies. He learned the magical use of thunderstones to bring destruction on the earth.[18] According to the mystery of Chango, we might expect Castro to likewise acquire terrifying powers of destruction. And so he would. It happened as he worked with the Soviet Union to place nuclear missiles in Cuba aimed at the United States. The act would trigger the Cuban Missile Crisis[19] and perhaps the most dangerous moment in world history up to that point. Chango's avatar, Fidel Castro, had brought the world to the brink of destruction.

THE FIRE OF THE SHEDIM

As with Chango, Castro had now acquired the power to send objects through the sky to bring fire and destruction upon the earth. As Chango sent fire down from the skies to bring destruction to his enemies, so Castro sought to compel the Soviet Union to launch a preemptive nuclear strike,[20] to send fire down on his enemy, America. So the mystery of the god operating through the Cuban ruler, the embodiment of a Santerian god, now brought the world to the brink of nuclear destruction. It was all there in the Hebrew word used in the Bible to describe the gods—the *shedim*, derived from a word meaning *to destroy*.

THE FESTIVAL OF CHANGO

Once a year Cuba pauses to give homage to the god Chango. The people of the land dress up in red, Chango's color, gather in temples and shrines, light candles, present red roses on his altars, and hold festive processions.[21] It is the Day or Festival of Chango. On Chango's day, gatherings for the orishas, known as *bembes*, are held throughout the island. It is in these gatherings that they beat drums to ancient rhythms to summon the spirits of the gods.[22] The gods are then invited to possess one of the worshippers. The Festival of Chango is one of the most important celebrations of the Cuban year, a day appointed to give homage to its king of the gods.[23]

NINE DAYS TO THE GODS

After dominating Cuban life for half a century, Fidel Castro died on November 25, 2016. The Cuban government

Chango

announced there would be nine days of mourning until the funeral.[24] The nine-day rite of mourning can be found in varied Catholic cultures, but in Cuba it is known to be a Santerian rite with roots in Africa, where it is given to facilitate the journey of the deceased's spirit to the gods.[25] Castro was now following the journey ordained for souls to enter the realm of the gods.

BACK TO THE CITY OF SPIRITS

Castro came to power by journeying from Santiago to Revolution Plaza in Havana. Now his remains were taken from Revolution Plaza in Havana and carried back to Santiago along the same route. His journey to power was being replayed in reverse.[26] And so Castro returned to the place where his rise began, the city of Santerian priests and gods, and by which sat the shrine of Oshun, the island's ruling deity. The ninth and final day of mourning was the day of his funeral, the burial of his remains, and his final departure.

His coffin, carried by a military caravan, made its way through the multitudes that lined the streets of Santiago to his final resting place. Some saluted as it passed by; others shouted his name. All over the island, life came to a standstill.[27] The commandant's final journey was televised so every Cuban could take part in it. The nation paused to pay its final respects, to honor his memory, and to say farewell.

DAY OF THE AVATAR

But while all this was happening, an ancient mystery was at work that went back to the rulers of Egypt and Mesopotamia, to the days of the god-kings. Castro had come to his final resting place on December 4. It was no accident. *December 4 was the Day of Chango.*

All the parallels between the Cuban ruler and the Cuban god had been leading up to that last day and that one final convergence. The day appointed to pay homage to Fidel Castro fell on the day appointed to pay homage to Chango. So now the day on which Cubans set up candles and red roses in memorials in honor of Castro fell on the same day that Cubans were to set up candles and red roses in honor of Chango. It was only because Castro died on the day he died that it all converged on the Day of Chango.

In the ancient pagan world, it was believed that the king who had served as the avatar of the god would, upon his death, become one with the god he embodied, having fully attained godhood. So in Castro's departure from the world, the avatar was joined to the god he embodied. The Day of Chango became the Day of Castro and the Day of Castro, the Day of Chango. As in the world of ancient paganism, the god and his avatar became as one.

As Chango was the king of Santerian gods, Oshun was their queen, the island's patron deity. It would be Oshun that I would encounter before I had any idea who she was.

Chapter 11

CROWN OF THE GODDESS

BEFORE I ARRIVED in Cuba, I had never heard of the gods of Santeria, much less a goddess named *Oshun*. That would change when I ascended another mountain. On the top of that mountain I would come into a biblical mystery that hearkened back to an event recorded in the Hebrew Scriptures.

VESSEL OF FREEDOM

I traveled through the island of Cuba from east to west over the span of one month as part of the first public and nationwide expression of the gospel since Castro declared the island to be officially atheist.[1] The celebration was to culminate in a mass event in Revolution Plaza, Havana, which Castro would attend. Throughout the journey, I shared of God's love, power, and freedom and sounded the shofar, the biblical trumpet embodying freedom and the power of God. It was the same trumpet I had sounded before the multitudes in India.

THE MAN FROM THE MOUNTAIN

It was in the province of Orientes, while I was at dinner, that a man came off the streets with a word he said he had to give me. He told me his story. A few weeks before I came to Cuba, he and other Christians were led to ascend one of the island's mountains to pray. It was while they were in prayer that the Spirit of God spoke to them. The

47

48

THE AVATAR

island was under a curse. A Jewish man would come to the island on a visit having to do with that curse. When they gathered on that mountain, they had no idea I was coming.

The story and its elements were eerily similar to that which I had been told as I ascended the mountain in India. Cuba and India share little in common. But each is home to a multitude of gods. The man in India had told me of a cursed mountain. The man in Cuba told me the same.

CURSED MOUNTAIN

It was a nearby mountain, looming over the city in which I was staying. "The mountain is cursed," he said. "On the mountaintop, they cast spells and incantations. They offer up sacrifices to the gods, sacrifices of blood." It appeared God was giving me a new calling—going up cursed mountains. I gathered my team together and relayed what I had been told. The next day, we went up the mountain. In my hand was the shofar. I would sound it on the mountaintop.

THE CERAMIC PLATE

Resting on the mountain's pinnacle was a structure that looked like a kind of pavilion. It was a house given to the gods and idols. A man was standing in front of it, staring at me from a distance. "Hola, Jonathan," he said. I didn't speak Spanish, but I assumed he was greeting me *by name*. I nodded in return but didn't approach him. About a minute later he approached me and my translator.

"I've been waiting for you," he said. "I knew you would come." In the man's hand was an object—a ceramic plate.

Crown of the Goddess 49

On the plate was a painting. It was an image *of me*. In the image, I was holding a shofar, the same shofar I had brought up the mountain and was now holding.

IN THE HOUSE OF THE GODS

The man was a Christian. He told us that the Lord had led him to make a ceramic plate and paint on it a picture of me. He had seen my image on posters plastered in the city, announcing the monthlong celebration. He said the Lord then told him to go up to the mountaintop and place the picture inside the pavilion. Inside the pavilion were idols of the Santerian gods and goddesses. He went inside and hung the plate on one of its walls and went home.

THE SIGN OF DAGON

That night, something happened in the house of the gods. The new leather strap holding the ceramic plate against the wall somehow broke apart. The plate came down. Before reaching the ground, it struck the head of an idol. The idol was a representation in clay of the island's chief orisha and ruling spirit. It was Oshun.

The Bible records the story of the god Dagon and the ark of the covenant. The Philistines, Israel's ancient enemies, had captured the nation's most sacred possession, the ark of the covenant, the vessel of God's presence. They brought the ark into the temple of their god Dagon. They set it down as a spoil of war in front of the idol of their god Dagon. The Bible records what happened next:

> And when the people of Ashdod rose
> early the next day, behold, Dagon had

> fallen face downward on the ground before the ark of the LORD. So they took Dagon and put him back in his place. But when they rose early on the next morning, behold, Dagon had fallen face downward on the ground before the ark of the LORD, and the head of Dagon and both his hands were lying cut off on the threshold. Only the trunk of Dagon was left to him.[2]

Modern critics of Scripture dismiss such accounts as fanciful inventions of ancient storytellers. But on top of that mountain in Cuba we saw its reality. The same elements, the same dynamics, the same act had again manifested in real time. The same power of the same God broke the idol of Oshun.

UNCROWNING THE GODDESS

On top of the idol, on the head of Oshun, was a crown. The crown represented her power, authority, and rule over the island. When the plate came down, it was not only the goddess's head that was struck but her crown.

As in the story of Dagon and the ark, the next morning, the worshippers of the gods returned. When they opened the doors of the pavilion, they found their chief deity, the goddess, struck down, lying on the ground. The crown of her glory and authority that had adorned her head was removed. It was now lying on the ground next to the fallen idol. Oshun had been uncrowned.

Crown of the Goddess 51

TRUMPETS, GODS, AND SPIRITS

Lying next to the fallen idol they saw a ceramic plate with the image of a bearded Jewish man. In his hands was the trumpet of God. The plate was chipped. The chip revealed that the plate had struck the idol at the opening of the trumpet's end, where the sound of its blast would go forth. The crown of the goddess was removed by the trumpet of God.

I could not help but think of Numbers 10:9, in which God tells His people that at the sounding of the trumpet in war, the enemy would be defeated. It was the sounding of the trumpet in India that had produced the sound of mass exorcism, of spirits fleeing the multitudes. Now it was the image of that same trumpet that had struck the image of the goddess and removed its crown.

THE KING UNCROWNED

From the figurine that stood next to the goddess of Santiago to the amulets worn by his men as they entered the capital city were the connections between Fidel Castro's rise to power and the gods of Santeria. Most prominent and central in those connections was the goddess Oshun. So then could the removal of Oshun's crown on top of that mountain be linked to the removal of Castro's power, the end of his reign?

When I journeyed across Cuba, I was led to share of the Jubilee, the biblical year of restoration, return, release, and freedom. It was in connection to the Jubilee that I sounded the trumpet, the instrument by which the Jubilee was inaugurated. At the end of the journey, after the mass gathering in Revolution Plaza, Havana, I gave Fidel Castro three objects: a Bible, a piece of paper with a prophetic word concerning the Jubilee, and a shofar, the vessel of Jubilee and sign of God's power.

The Jubilee was the fiftieth year. Nine years after the giving of those three objects, Castro entered the fiftieth year of his reign, the Jubilee. It was in that fiftieth year that the reign of Fidel Castro was brought to an end, on the fiftieth day of the fiftieth year. As the vessel of Jubilee had removed the crown of Oshun, so the Jubilee removed the crown of Fidel Castro, his power, his authority, and his rule.

SMASHING THE GODS

But there was more to what happened on the mountain that day. In the case of ancient Israel, the breaking of idols was linked to spiritual revival and return to God. So it was in our journey throughout the island that we witnessed the beginning signs of a mass revival. People were flooding into the churches, lives were being changed, multitudes were coming to God, and a new confidence was taking hold of the Cuban believers. Many would cite that month of gatherings across the island as the beginning of revival in Cuba.

The man who had told me of the mountain's curse had also told me that its curse would be turned to blessing and the blessing would come down the mountain to the people below. Months after the encounter on the mountain, a pastor from Cuba came to America to give me a message. He told me that in the city and region surrounding the

Crown of the Goddess 53

mountain, something major was happening. People were coming out to the churches with objects, the idols of their gods. "Smash them," they told the ministers, "for we heard what happened on the mountain."

The curse was breaking. Blessing was coming down from the mountaintop. And revival had begun.

On the island of Cuba, we saw again the connection between gods and kingdoms, spirits and governments. In this case they lay behind a revolution, a dictator, a tyrant-god, an avatar, the removal of an idol's crown, and a darkened kingdom. But there was more to the mystery and more to the gods. In fact, what happened on the mountaintop would not be my last encounter with the goddess. There would be another journey. This one would begin at a lake of floating gods and would take me to their homeland.

PART IV

ORISHA LAND

Chapter 12

GODS ON THE LAKE

A FTER COMING BACK from Cuba, I was invited to minister in Brazil's most populous city, São Paulo. I would speak there in an indoor arena over a series of nights. In the daytime I was free. One afternoon my hosts took me to a lake. It was that which was *on the lake* that they wanted me to see.

THE GODS REAPPEAR

In the middle of the water were strange, colossal figures, each one appearing to be at least twenty feet high. Each was holding an object: a knife, a lance, a staff, a sickle, a bowl, an axe, a bow and arrow. Each floated on the water, adorned in robes and headdresses of different colors: yellow, white, green, blue, and red. It was a lake of gods.

I had seen them before but in different guises. Behind the slight variations in their names and appearances were the same gods that haunted Cuba, the orishas of Santeria. And there, arrayed in yellow garments and holding a mirror and a dagger, was Oshun, the goddess I had seen on the mountaintop. Though I had never heard of her before those journeys, now, in a short span of time, I had encountered her twice, thousands of miles apart.

THE TRANSMUTATIONS

As with the gods of Mesopotamia, the Mediterranean, the Nordic and Slavic lands, and many others, it was their nature to spread and transmute their names and appearances in accordance with the new surroundings and cultures in which they found themselves.

In Cuba they manifested as the gods of Santeria. In Haiti they became the possessing iwa of voodoo.[1] In Brazil, they manifested as the orixas of candomblé.[2] But in every manifestation, they followed the biblical truth of the shedim and daemonia. Behind the gods were spirits. The word *voodoo* means both god and spirit.[3] The word *candomblé* speaks of a "dance in honour of the gods."[4] In each of these religious streams, the gods, orishas, or spirits possessed their worshippers, and their worshippers served as their avatars.

MATRIX OF THE GODS

The gods on the lake were a sign of things to come. Before arriving in São Paulo, I had received an invitation from an African pastor to come to his land. After praying about it, I said yes. One month after standing at the edge of the lake of gods, I was in Africa. Though I had no idea when I arrived there, it was all part of the same journey that began when I set off for India, a journey that took me through the fog of Agra, to a goddess on a Cuban mountaintop, to a lake of gods in Brazil, and now to Africa, a journey of gods and mysteries.

LAND OF THE YORUBA

When I set out for Africa, I didn't realize the connection between where I was going and where I had been. Santeria, voodoo, and candomblé all had their roots in Africa, more

Gods on the Lake 59

specifically, in West Africa, and still more specifically, in Nigeria, in the land of the Yoruba. I had been invited to minister in West Africa, more specifically, in Nigeria, in the land of the Yoruba.[5] In every case, I had simply gone to where I was invited to go. But it was as if an unseen hand was arranging each journey and guiding every footstep.

TEMPLE OF CHANGO

The journey and its mystery would be still more specific. The mystery of the gods centered on the Nigerian state called *Oyo*.[6] The pastor who invited me to come happened to live in the city of Ibadan—in the Nigerian state of Oyo.

According to Yoruban mythology, the god Chango, or Shango, ruled as king from Oyo.[7] And the temple of Chango was housed in the city of Ibadan.[8] Without having any idea, I had been brought to the city of Chango and to the matrix from which the gods of Santeria, voodoo, and candomblé had sprung.

It would be there in that city that we would receive a visit from one believed to be the Lord of the Earth.

Chapter 13

THE YORUBA KING

THOUGH I DIDN'T yet realize the connections between where I was and what I had encountered in my other journeys, I knew I was in a land where gods and idols were worshipped. So I had planned to tell the people of Ibadan the story of the idol on the mountaintop.

THE IMAGE ON THE WALL

When my hosts showed me the platform from which I would be speaking, I was stunned. It was a large outdoor stage with a massive back wall. The wall was covered with a colossal painting...*of me*. I was wearing a tallit, the Jewish prayer shawl, and I was sounding the shofar. It was the same painting, the same image that was on the ceramic plate in Cuba. So as I shared the story of what had happened on the mountaintop in Cuba, the people of Ibadan could see for themselves the same image, magnified many times over, that adorned the plate that struck the crown of the goddess.

"LORD OF THE EARTH"

Oshun, Chango, Obatala, Ogun, Yemayá, and the other gods of Santeria had come from the pantheon of the Yoruban gods. The pantheon had a guardian, the supreme leader of Yoruban worship, the keeper of the gods. He was called the *Ooni of Ife*. It was a royal title. The Ooni was

The Yoruba King 61

king and priest over the Yoruba religion, the latest to sit on a hallowed throne that went back ages.[1]

According to the mythology of that throne, its first occupants were some of the most prominent of the Yoruban pantheon. The Ooni reigned on the throne of gods. He was their representative on earth.[2] He was their avatar, an avatar of avatars. Indeed, he was reckoned as an orisha himself, a spirit deity, a god in flesh and blood.[3] He was so highly esteemed that Nigerian leaders, chiefs, princes, tribal kings, and other government officials would bow down in his presence. He bore the title Oluaye, which can be translated as "Lord of the Earth" or "Master of the World."

THE GATHERING

The day after I spoke of what happened on the mountaintop, an event would take place that would reverberate throughout the Yoruban world and make headlines throughout Nigeria. It would take place in a sacred gathering of prayer and repentance on behalf of the nation on that same stage. Nigerian leaders, governors, senators, civil leaders, administrative leaders, spiritual leaders, tribal leaders, and even the president's representative converged on Ibadan. One by one they ascended the stage and led the people in prayer, in the confession of sin, and in declarations of repentance.

ENTRANCE

It was while one of Nigeria's political leaders was speaking from the podium that a commotion broke out to the side of the audience. It was the Ooni of Ife. He had decided to come to the event. He entered the grounds in an ornate royal robe of purple with a purple ornate head covering, representing his crown. He was accompanied by a company of royal attendants and servants, a royal procession.

The event came to a standstill. Political and civil leaders bowed down in reverence before him as he approached and passed them by. He ascended the stage and stood before the podium to speak. The representative of the Yoruban gods, the keeper of the goddess Oshun, the Yoruban king revered as a living representation of the gods, was now standing in front of the towering backdrop of the image that had removed the crown of Oshun. A hush came over the audience. The Ooni began to speak.

THE UNCROWNING OF THE OONI

"I will first purge myself," he said. "I want to make myself pure." The Ooni then told the gathering and the nation that from that moment on he would be known by a new title, *Alayeluwa Oba Okunade Sijuade, Olubuse II.* For the Nigerians hearing those words as he uttered them and those who would later hear or read of them, the announcement was stunning. The Ooni of Ife was removing his title of *Oluaye.*[4] He was no longer to be called or seen as a god who presided over all. He was no longer to be spoken of as "Master of the World."

The Ooni went further. "There is no other god," he told the people, "but the divine God, the King of all kings." After ages of presiding over the gods as "Lord of the Earth," the Ooni of Ife had renounced his title and his godhood.

The Yoruba King   63

Before the nation, he had borne witness that only God was God.[5] The act sent shock waves through the Yoruban world. The avatar had renounced his godhood.

THE SAME IMAGE

After issuing the proclamation, the Ooni performed another unprecedented act. In the Yoruban world, he was to be bowed down to, not to bow down himself. But before the other leaders, the people, and the nation, the Ooni dropped to his knees and bowed down before God.[6] Crowning the moment, he removed his purple head covering.

The Ooni of Ife had uncrowned himself. It was not only what took place that day but where it happened. The Ooni had removed his title of Oluaye, his crown of godhood, in front of the colossal image that had removed the crown of Oshun. He had uncrowned himself in front of the image of the uncrowning. The Ooni was Oshun's keeper. Her uncrowning was connected to his, and his uncrowning to hers. Those who had painted that image on the back wall of that stage had no idea of its significance, nor did they or anyone but the Ooni have any idea what he was planning to do before it.

THE SHOFAR'S EDGE

From the vantage point of the photographers recording the event in front of the stage, the Ooni was in the same place in relation to the image of the trumpet as had been the idol on the mountain relative to the ceramic plate that struck its head. The end of the trumpet that had removed the crown of the goddess was now touching the head of the Ooni as he uncrowned himself.

Again there was the trumpet, and again it had touched the gods. When it had sounded in the land of the gods of India, it unleashed the cries of deliverance. It was there as well in the form of the image that struck the head of the idol on the mountain in Cuba. And now it was in Africa, where its image formed the colossal backdrop of an epic moment on the Yoruban throne, the uncrowning of another god.

THE AARONIC BLESSING

Before the close of that event, I was asked to sound the shofar and then seal it with the giving of God's ancient blessing, the Aaronic Benediction, first in the original Hebrew, then in English.

As I stood at the podium, about to give the blessing, I felt led to ask the Ooni of Ife to join me on the stage in its giving. He came up beside me. I lifted my right hand to give the blessing—the Ooni did the same. As I began chanting the ancient Hebrew words of God's blessing, the Ooni closed his eyes and bowed his head. The moment was captured by the newspaper photographers who had come to cover the event.

"THERE IS NO OTHER GOD"

The next day the photograph of the Ooni with his head bowed, his eyes closed, and his arm outstretched as I gave the Aaronic Blessing made front-page headlines in the newspapers of Nigeria. Under the photograph were the words of the Ooni's proclamation, "There is no other god but the

The Yoruba King 65

divine God, the King of all kings." And in large letters the headline read "Ooni Drops Oluaye Title." Under the headline was a photograph showing the Ooni bowed down on his knees, with his head covering removed. And under that was the caption describing the Ooni as "kneeling down in submission to the Almighty."

What happened that day was, in the Yoruban world and the spiritual realm, earthshaking. The former "Lord of the Earth" had bowed down in submission to the Almighty.

And yet the mystery was not finished. Our time in the land would not be complete until we encountered the lady of the forest.

Chapter 14

LADY OF THE FOREST

WHEN I SHARED the story of the goddess's uncrowning in Cuba before the people of Ibadan, the response was striking. The moment I spoke the name *Oshun*, there was something of a collective gasp and more than that. At the end of the night I asked my host, "Why did they react like that when I said, 'Oshun'?" "Because they all know her," he said. "She's from this land. You've come to her home."

THE LAND OF OSHUN

I was now in the birthplace of the gods I had encountered in the nations. And yet it was more specific than that. Bordering on Oyo was another Nigerian state—the state of *Osun. Osun* is another version of the name *Oshun. The entire state was named after the goddess.* The same mystery that had brought me to Oshun on the Cuban mountaintop had now brought me to her homeland. Of all the places on earth I could have come to, I had been brought to her home.

The goddess had many shrines, groves, and temples in Africa, South America, and even North America and Europe, but we were now standing in the epicenter of her kingdom. Oshun is the goddess of rivers. So in the land of Osun runs a sacred river dedicated to her worship, the Osun River.[1] Along the river is the goddess's Sacred Grove. It was the global center of her cult and veneration. People

Lady of the Forest 67

would come there from all over the world to partake in her worship.[2]

Beyond that, it was the last prominent sacred grove of the Yoruban religion. And so though dedicated to Oshun, it had become the home of the Yoruban gods. Over forty idols and shrines could be found on that site. The mystery that had led me to her grove concerned the goddess and more than the goddess, all the gods of the Yoruba.

THE SACRED GROVE

Upon hearing of the Osun state, I knew we could not return home without making one more journey. We had to visit the Sacred Grove. So on the day after the Ooni of Ife renounced his godhood, we set out for the shrine of the goddess. It was set in something of a forest. Along the forest, one could see the waters of the Osun River. We gathered there by one of her altars and prayed for all those involved in her worship, rites, and rituals.

After we finished praying, we noticed a figure in the distance, watching us. It was a woman clothed in a light blue garment, something of a cross between a robe and a summer dress. When we moved, she moved. When we stopped, she stopped. She was the keeper of the grove. She was the priestess of Oshun, the consecrated vessel of the goddess.

PRIESTS OF THE YORUBA

Spirit possession is not only present in Yoruban worship but occupies a central place. Ceremonies are performed to invoke gods and goddesses and trances entered into to allow them to enter the body of the medium. The medium is, more often than not, the deity's priest or priestess, especially trained to invite and be possessed by the summoned spirit. As in the ceremonies of Santeria, the Yoruban minister then acts, moves, and speaks as the god. They become, in effect, its avatar. The priestess of Oshun was thus trained to be taken over, indwelled, and used by the possessing spirit of the orisha. She had undoubtedly served many times as avatar of the goddess.

PRAYER OF THE AVATAR

I was led to approach her. There were two male attendants at her side. I came with a translator, as she spoke no English. I spoke to her of God, His love, and His salvation in the Messiah, Jesus. It was a long conversation. She had been dedicated to the gods since childhood. It was all she had known. But there she had an openness of heart and a longing for something more. At the end of the conversation, I asked her if she wanted to receive Jesus and salvation into her heart and to begin following Him. She answered yes.

I led her in a prayer of salvation, of turning away from all darkness, all bondages, all gods, all sins, of receiving God's love, His forgiveness, His cleansing, and the new birth. She prayed with me, repeating my words in her native tongue. She who had served as the vessel of the possessing spirit, the avatar of the goddess, now prayed to receive the Spirit of God.

At the end of her prayer, she opened her eyes and looked up. I don't know that I have ever seen a face so glowing

Lady of the Forest 69

with the joy and peace of God as I saw that day in the face of the priestess of Oshun.

THE PEOPLE WHO WALKED IN DARKNESS

I asked one of those assisting me to give her a Bible that she could read in her native tongue. "In this," I said, "are the oracles of God. He will speak to you through it." I took out my own pocket Bible and opened it up at random. It opened to the beginning of Isaiah 9. I read her the passage:

> The people who walked in darkness have seen a great light; those who dwelt in the land of the shadow of death, upon them a light has shined.[3]

The rule of Oshun had been broken, this time in the heart of her priestess. The one who dwelt in the land of the shadow of death, the light had shined upon her.

REVIVAL IN THE OONI'S PALACE

Shortly after returning home from Nigeria, I received an invitation to come back, this time from a Nigerian minister in the city of Lagos. He was holding a mass gathering and wanted me to speak there. I agreed.

While in Lagos, I felt led to pay a visit to the Ooni of Ife. A meeting was arranged. I entered his royal residence and into his royal chamber, where we sat down together and spoke at length. After the meeting I walked through the outlying courtyards. All over the palace walls were fliers. On the fliers was the picture of the Ooni and me giving the blessing of God. Next to the photograph were the words "Revival! Revival! Revival!" Under that was a scripture and a series of dates. So now, on the throne of the Yoruban gods, there would be praise, prayer, and the worship of God—revival.

THE NIGHT OF MILLIONS

Later that night, I stood on an outdoor stage in the midst of a sea of Nigerians numbering into the millions. I shared of God's love and power, then led them in a prayer to receive His salvation and to dedicate their lives to following Him. Then I took out the biblical trumpet, the shofar—the same that I had blown in India, Cuba, and Ibadan—and sounded it. Millions of Nigerians heard the sound of the trumpet that night, and millions prayed with me to dedicate their lives to God. There was revival in the land.

In the land of idols and spirits, matrix of the gods, the priestess of Oshun had found salvation, the Yoruban king had removed his crown and bowed down before the King of all kings, and a people who dwelt in darkness had seen a great light.

Chapter 15

GODS AND KINGDOMS

THE JOURNEY HAD taken me to three continents and an island, from Asia to the Caribbean, South America, and Africa. And yet all were connected to the others in a mystery of gods and spirits. What did those connections reveal?

TIMELESS

First, the gods are not bound by time. They are older than recorded history and yet are worshipped to this day. They may disappear from view. They may reappear and rise again. But they are never entirely gone.

BORDERLESS

Second, the gods are not bound by geography or culture. They can be found throughout the world and in cultures holding virtually nothing else in common with each other but the gods. In ancient times the worship of gods was a near-universal phenomenon. It was, by and large, the spread of the gospel, of monotheism, and that which was birthed from monotheism, that restrained it or brought it to an end.

BEHIND THE GODS

Third, the gods are joined to spirits. It was there in every journey and land. And it was there thousands of years earlier and revealed in the Bible. Behind the gods are the shedim and the daemonia. Where there are gods, there are spirits.

THE MORPHERS

Fourth, it is the nature of the gods to morph and transmute themselves, to alter their appearances and names. So Inanna became Ishtar, Ishtar became Ashtarte, and Ashtarte became Ashtoreth, Aphrodite, and Venus. It happened in the ancient world. It has happened ever since.

THE MASKED

Fifth, it is the nature of the gods to mask and disguise themselves. This can most overtly be seen in Santeria and candomblé, where the Yoruban gods come in the guise of saints. The gods will mask themselves according to the dictates of their surroundings. And yet the masking of the gods is universal, as the gods themselves are the masks of the spirits behind them.

THE POSSESSORS

Sixth, the gods, being in reality shedim and daemonia, possessing spirits, will seek to possess their worshippers. The connection was there in ancient paganism and was likewise there in the worship of the gods that had survived into modern times. In every land I visited, India, Cuba, Brazil, and Nigeria, the worship of the gods was accompanied by the phenomenon of spirit possession.

THE AVATARS

Seventh, where the gods are present and dominant, so too will be their avatars. In India belief in avatars was a central tenet of faith. They were worshipped as gods and revered in flesh-and-blood incarnations. And the gods could take over vessels of flesh and blood in the form of divine possession. In Cuba the Santerian orishas could likewise possess their worshippers and, through them, move, speak, and act upon the world. And a revolutionary guerrilla could serve as an avatar of a tyrant-king. And in Nigeria the Yoruban gods and spirits could likewise indwell and possess their priests and worshippers, and the people would bow before an avatar-king who ruled as a living representative of the gods and "Lord of the Earth."

THE RULERS

Lastly, the gods seek to possess more than people—societies, cultures, nations, thrones, governments, and kingdoms. And so in each of the visited lands, the interplay of gods and government was present. In India, the ruling government venerated the gods, championed their worship, and supported the building and dedication of their shrines and temples and, at the same time, facilitated the persecution of Christians and those who opposed the worship of the gods.[1]

In Cuba the officially godless government launched a relentless persecution against Christians and the church. The resulting absence of the gospel's influence on Cuban society opened the door to empowering and increasing the worship of Santerian gods. The island's communist

74 THE AVATAR

government would later openly celebrate and encourage the worship of the gods as an expression of a unified Cuban identity.[2]

In West Africa the gods were, from the start, connected to government. Its first kings were believed to have been gods themselves, and the thrones of their rulers, the seat of the gods. And so governmental and national leaders would still bow down before those believed to walk the earth as the embodiments of the gods.

THE WARNING

The deep interplay of gods and kingdoms, spirits and rulers, was characteristic of ancient pagan civilization. The people were ruled by the gods. Kings and queens functioned as priests and priestesses, representatives, agents, or avatars of the gods themselves. Gods were hallowed and avatars reigned.

In this is a warning to any culture or nation that opens its door to the gods or, in any way, removes its safeguards against them. If the gods, or shedim, are not bound by time, then they are still present and a present danger to the modern world. If they are not bound by geography, then they can touch any land, any people, and any nation. And if they can change their appearance, if they come in disguise, then we might not recognize them when they come or discern their manifesting.

THE INDWELLERS

As they come to indwell, to inhabit, and to possess, the gods will never be content to merely be tolerated or, in any

Gods and Kingdoms   75

way, contained. They will seek to indwell every habitation and possess every realm of society, culture, and civilization. To that end they will vie to gain control of kings and governments. The nature of the particular government is irrelevant. The gods can possess a modern government as easily as an ancient one, a secular government as much as a pagan one, a democracy as well as a dictatorship. And if they attain possession, they will use the machinery of state to war against all that stands in their way and, most specifically, God. And so the ascendancy of the gods will inevitably involve the realm of government, oppression, and subjugation, if resisted, and, if necessary, the shedding of blood.

Could this lie behind what is now taking place in our own day and midst? Could it underlie the changes that are transforming our culture? Could it reveal the real battle being waged behind what appears as a war of culture? And could it determine the future of America and the world?

We will now see how the mystery has manifested in a civilization that most would think is immune to the gods—the West. In fact, we will now see how an ancient god manifested itself in the West, openly, brazenly, and before the eyes of the modern world.

PART V

THE OLYMPIAN MYSTERY

Chapter 16

FESTIVAL OF THE GODS

IT IS LARGELY assumed that the phenomenon of the gods is confined to the ancient past, to the non-Western world, or to anomalous pockets of modern culture. But the assumption is wrong. The mystery of the gods most critically applies to the West. It is, in fact, with regard to the West that the mystery takes on its greatest powers and dangers.

THE GODS OF THE WEST

The modern West is not immune to the gods. That fact is critical to understand if we are to comprehend the forces that are now at work transforming our world. The gods of the modern West are, for the most part, veiled and move, by and large, in secret. But with regard to the world's future, it is these gods, rather than those openly worshipped in temples, shrines, and groves, that are by far the most potent, critical, and dangerous. The fact that they are largely masked makes them more, not less, dangerous. And yet at times their masks may be removed. The unmasking of one such Western god took place in the middle of a strange spectacle displayed before millions of witnesses around the world.

FESTIVAL OF ZEUS

Every four years the eyes of the world turn to a nation chosen to host the Olympics. The Olympics are, of course, the world's preeminent athletic event and that to which the nations send their best athletes and athletic teams to compete. For the associations and individuals who partake in the Olympics, that is all it is. But that is not all there is. The world's preeminent athletic competition has, and always has had, another side.

The Olympics came into the world as pagan convocations. The very name *Olympics* comes from *Olympia*, which was, in turn, named after *Mount Olympus*, the dwelling place of the Greek gods. The Olympics were never just athletic competitions but, in essence, religious celebrations of pagan deities. In the midst of the athletic competitions were rites and rituals, prayers, feasts, and sacrifices to the gods of the Greek pantheon.[1] The Olympian athletes would typically compete in the nude. Married women were not allowed to attend, only the unmarried and a multitude of prostitutes.[2] The Olympics were overtly pagan festivals convened specifically for the glory and honor of Zeus,[3] king of Olympus, king of the gods.

THE OLYMPIAN SACRIFICES

Central to the ancient Olympics were blood sacrifices. Priests were present throughout the games to oversee them. The Olympian athletes partook in the hecatomb ceremony, which involved the sacrifice of one hundred oxen before a colossal statue of Zeus. The ancient Olympics were thus not only pagan religious festivals convened for the glory and worship of the gods but were anointed and soaked with blood.[4]

Festival of the Gods

THE OLYMPIC HYMN

That was then, but it is also now. The paganism of the ancient Olympics survives in its modern reincarnation. Each Olympics of the modern era is inaugurated with the singing of the "Olympic Anthem," also known as the "Olympic Hymn." A *hymn* is defined as a song or poem in praise of a god. So too the Olympic hymn praises its god:

> O Ancient immortal Spirit, pure father...
> Descend, reveal yourself and flash like lightning
>   here...
> And hurries at the temple here, your pilgrim...[5]

What temple? And what god is being invoked to descend? Zeus was, indeed, the god of lightning.

FLAME OF THE GODS

But there was more. A sacred element of the ancient Olympics was the eternal flame, which burned in veneration of the goddess Hestia. The fire from the flame was used to ignite the other sacrificial flames used in the Olympian ceremonies. So too the element of the "sacred fire" plays a central role in the modern Olympics. The world watches as the Olympic torch is brought into the Olympic stadium of the hosting nation. But its flame is first lit by the temple of Hera in a ceremony performed by a company of women representing the high priestess and priestesses of the goddess.[6] Every modern Olympics is inaugurated by a pagan ceremony involving the gods.

THE ANCIENT PARABLE

For those who have not read *The Return of the Gods*, the key to understanding the mystery is found in a parable given by Jesus of a possessed man. The man is delivered of the possessing spirit but remains empty of God's presence. The disembodied spirit then returns to the man, finds him empty, an empty house, and brings in seven other spirits to repossess him. The man who was possessed by the one spirit is now repossessed by the eight. His end is thus worse than his beginning.

RETURN OF THE DISEMBODIED

But the parable applies to more than individuals. Jesus Himself sealed the story by saying, "So also will it be with this evil generation."[7] The issue of spirits, possession, deliverance, and repossession applies not only to individuals but to generations, cultures, nations, and civilizations. When taken to its largest application, the parable contains a warning unbound by time. It is this: If any civilization that has been set free of the gods, cleansed of paganism, and delivered of the spirits by the power of God should empty itself of God, then that which was cast out of it will return and come back into it, and more so. It will undergo a repaganization—a repossession.

THE REPOSSESSION

No civilization has ever been so transformed by God as Western civilization. Unlike the East, where the gods never left, the West was exorcised of its gods and spirits. The entrance of the gospel drove out the gods and thus the

Festival of the Gods 83

shedim and daemonia that had inhabited the pagan West. It was the greatest mass exorcism in human history.

But the modern West began emptying itself of God's presence, His Word, and the gospel. As in the parable, its house could not stay empty. Therefore, according to the ancient warning, the gods and spirits that were cast out of it would return into it. The West would be re-indwelled, repaganized, repossessed. It is that transformation, the return of the gods, the repossession of the spirits, and the repaganization of culture, that is now transforming Western civilization.

THE GOSPEL AND THE END OF THE OLYMPICS

What does this have to do with the Olympics? Everything. The ancient exorcism of Western civilization that came with the advent of Christianity involved the Olympics. When the gods were cast out of Greco-Roman civilization, the Olympics, as a religious convocation to Zeus and the gods, were cast out with them. Though there may have been some competitions that survived for a short time afterward, the last recorded Olympics of ancient times took place in AD 393.

The timing was no accident. The Olympics came to an end in the days of the house of Emperor Theodosius. It was Theodosius who sealed the ascendancy of Christianity as the official faith of the Roman Empire. It was just one year after the last recorded Olympic Games that the fate of paganism was likewise sealed in the emperor's victory in the Battle of the Frigidus.[8] And so the disappearance of the Olympics coincided with the disappearance of the gods and the ascendancy of the Christian faith.

RETURN OF THE FESTIVAL

But what if the West was to turn away from God and empty itself of His Word, His ways, and His Spirit? We would then expect, in accordance with the parable, that the gods would return. We might likewise expect the Olympics to return. That is exactly what happened. One and a half thousand years after the official end of paganism and the Olympian games, the Olympics were resurrected. The resurrection took place at the end of the nineteenth century, in the same era that was critical in laying the groundwork for a post-Christian Europe. And it is no accident that the post-Christian Europe to be ushered in would be devastated by the post-Christian, demonic, and deadly movements of modern times—communism, fascism, Nazism—to the destruction of millions.

THE INVOKING OF SPIRITS

If, then, the disappearance of the Olympics coincided with and marked the Christianization of the West, we might expect that the reappearance of the Olympics would coincide with and mark the *de-Christianization* of the West. And if the disappearance of the Olympics accompanied the casting out of the gods, we might expect that its reappearance would coincide with their return. And as the apostasy of the West from God progressed and intensified, we might expect that the Olympics would assume an increasingly and overtly pagan nature, especially in its

Festival of the Gods 85

opening and closing ceremonies. And as the Olympics served as platforms for the gods and as convocations for their invoking, we might expect that they would again invoke a long-departed god.

What we might expect to happen actually did. The modern Olympics would invoke an ancient god. It would manifest before the world. And it would embody the metamorphosis and the exchange overtaking Western civilization and much of the modern world.

We now open up what was likely the most widely viewed act of blasphemy since the dawn of Christianity—and the return to the West of a long-exorcised god.

Chapter 17

THE RETURN OF THE GOD

Among the most iconic of Christian images in Western civilization is Leonardo da Vinci's *Last Supper*, in which Jesus sits with His disciples to partake of His last meal before the crucifixion. It was that image that the 2024 Olympics in Paris evoked and broadcast to the world.[1]

THE OLYMPIAN BLASPHEMY

It was a spectacle performed in the opening ceremony. Some claimed the spectacle was based on a seventeenth-century painting titled *The Feast of the Gods* or the sixteenth-century engraving titled *Preparations for the Wedding Banquet of Cupid and Psyche*, both paintings focusing on ancient pagan gods. But for most of those who witnessed the spectacle, there was no doubt as to what was being portrayed. Regardless of intention, the presentation was a clear evocation of the Last Supper. The gods war against God, and the spirits against the Spirit. The ancient deities had been exorcised from the West in the name of Jesus. So it would be in perfect accord with their nature and the mystery that they would seek to make a mockery of Jesus and ridicule, subvert, and desecrate the most sacred of acts before the world.

The Return of the God

RETURN OF THE DESECRATION

The desecration had an ancient precedent. At the beginning of the age, when Christianity began its spread into the Roman Empire, it was the sacrament of Communion, the Lord's Supper, the same as depicted in DaVinci's *Last Supper*, that was especially attacked, slandered, and vilified by the defenders of the pagan world. Christians who partook in the Lord's Supper were vilified as partaking in cannibalism.[2]

Those planning the Olympic spectacle were undoubtedly not thinking back to the ancient war of the gods and the gospel. But in the realm of the spirits, it was the replaying of an ancient war. Again the sacred act of the Christian faith, that which represented Jesus' sacrificial death, was being mocked, attacked, and desecrated, but now via television, satellites, and the internet.

THE GOD ON A PLATTER

It was a blasphemous act and, more than that, a manifestation. The *Last Supper* centers on the elements of bread and wine, the food of the sacred meal. So did the Olympic spectacle. Only there was a switch. Instead of the bread and wine, the representation of Jesus, a covered platter was set out on the festive table, as if keeping warm the festival meal. But something very different was waiting inside.

When the covering was lifted, there lying on the plate was an ancient god, a god that had been cast out of the Greco-Roman world at the coming of the gospel. Embodying the god was a nearly naked man covered in blue paint, reclining on the plate with a yellow beard and a garland around his head. It was the ancient god Dionysus.[3] He appeared before the world as a living representation of the deity. In the realm of the gods he appeared as an avatar.

THE RETURN OF DIONYSUS

In the beginning of the age the gods were replaced by Jesus. Now Jesus was being replaced by the gods. And as the Lord's Supper had, in ancient times, replaced the sacrifices and celebrations of the gods, now the celebration of the gods was replacing the Lord's Supper, with the body of Dionysus taking the place of the elements representing the body of Jesus.

The god at the center of the Olympian spectacle, Dionysus, was significant. Many observers believe that the worship of Dionysus constituted a direct competition to the worship of Jesus in the first centuries. Both Jesus and Dionysus were associated with wine.[4] Both died violent deaths. And both were brought back to life. But the similarities were superficial. In actuality the two could not have been more different. The death and resurrection of Jesus was an act of redemption. Dionysus was torn apart and brought back to life in a redemptionless mythological tale of violence and gore.[5] And while the wine of Jesus was connected to His sacrifice, the wine of Dionysus was connected, rather, to drunkenness, lasciviousness, and debauchery, as was the god himself.[6]

THE RETURN OF THE GODS TELEVISED

What happened in the opening ceremony of the Olympics of 2024 was the inverse of what had happened at the

The Return of the God 89

beginning of the age. At the beginning of the age, the West turned away from the gods to God. Now it was turning away from God and back to the gods. At the beginning of the age, it had exchanged Dionysus for Jesus, now Jesus for Dionysus. At the beginning of the age, it abandoned the wine of Dionysus, of debauchery and sexual immorality, for the wine of Jesus, of holiness and redemption. Now it was turning from the wine of Jesus to that of Dionysus, from holiness and redemption to the carnality, the sexual immorality, and the debauchery of a feast to a pagan god.

It was a manifestation of Jesus' parable and warning. The house had emptied itself of God and would not stay empty. Others would come in, the same others that had, in ancient times, been cast out. The reappearing of Dionysus before the eyes of the world was a sign that others—the shedim and the daemonia—were likewise coming back, the return of the gods.

The appearance of Dionysus before the world and the return of the ancient gods is a far more ominous sign than the Olympic spectacle might suggest. Just how ominous, we will now see.

Chapter 18

THE GOD OF MADNESS

IN THE PARABLE of spirits, the span of time between the casting out of the demon and the time of its return was presumably, at the least, a matter of days, and, at most, of years. But the span of time between the casting out of Dionysus and his return to the world stage encompassed centuries and separated the ancient world from the modern. And yet at the same time, it was as if no time had elapsed between the two events.

THE LURKERS

As the West turned away from Jesus, the same god that had been replaced by the worship of Jesus in ancient times now reappeared in the Olympic ceremony as the replacement of Jesus. All it took was that turning, and he again manifested. Those who planned the Olympian spectacle undoubtedly had no idea of the parable's implications or warning or, likely, of the parable itself. And yet they manifested it. It was as if the spirit of Dionysus was there all along lurking, with the others, just below the surface of Western civilization. In the case of the West, it was either the One or the others. There was no middle ground or era of neutrality. If not the One, it would be the others. But the Olympic ceremony was not the first time that the switch had been made or that Dionysus had returned.

The God of Madness

THE SUBVERTER

Dionysus was among the most subversive of gods, even in the context of ancient paganism. He broke norms and transgressed the accepted bounds of convention and morality, even of pagan conventions and morality. He was known not only as the god of wine and licentiousness but as the god of possession. Those who worshipped him, those who partook in his mystic rites, were especially given to be possessed by the god of their worship. He drove them into frenzies of insanity. For Dionysus was the god of madness, and his worshippers, the avatars of insanity.[1]

THE GOD OF MADNESS RETURNED

In ancient times the god of madness thus warred against the Jewish people, the Word of God, the Christian faith, and the name of Jesus. What then would his reappearance before the world signify? The civilization into which he returned not only was in the midst of turning away from Christianity but was beginning to wage war against it. Beyond that it was as well increasingly at war against the nation of Israel and Jewish existence.

What then would the return of Dionysus portend for the world? We have already been given an answer.

THE WAR OF FRIEDRICH NIETZSCHE

The replacement of Jesus for Dionysus in the Olympian spectacle had a precursor. It did not involve a global audience but a single person. The ramifications of that replacement and that single person would shake the world.

His name was Friedrich Nietzsche. Nietzsche was born in Prussia, of the German Confederation, in 1844. He was the son of a Lutheran pastor. In college he came under the influence of anti-Christian literature and thought. He would turn against God, against the Bible, against Christianity, and against Jesus. He would become known for waging a rabid, all-consuming war against God and Christianity through his many writings. To Nietzsche, God was the ultimate enemy, and Christianity was a curse. He would war to wipe it off the face of the earth.

APOSTLE OF THE GODS

At the same time of his raging against God and Christianity, Nietzsche became increasingly obsessed with an ancient god. It was Dionysus. Nietzsche devoted his first book to showing how important Dionysus was. He would continue to write of the ancient deity throughout his career. If, in Nietzsche's thought, Jesus was the problem for Western civilization, Dionysus was the answer. It was either Dionysus or the "Crucified One."

Through his writings, Nietzsche would actively and openly advocate for the replacement of Jesus for Dionysus, the Crucified One for the god of frenzies, and Christianity for a revived paganism. It was in perfect accordance with the warning of the ancient parable. Nietzsche would argue that Western civilization should empty itself of God and Christianity and open itself up to the ancient spirits. It was the same exchange that would later manifest in the Olympic spectacle: Jesus for Dionysus, God for the gods. The exchange took place first in Nietzsche's own mind

The God of Madness 93

and heart. He had emptied himself of God and opened the door to a god.

DESCENT INTO MADNESS

And then something strange happened. As Dionysus is the god of madness, the god who drove his worshippers to insanity, Nietzsche began descending into madness. Just as strange, Nietzsche connected his insanity to Dionysus, the god of madness. And as Dionysus was also and especially the god of possession, who would indwell, control, and use his worshippers as agents of destruction, so Nietzsche wrote as if possessed by Dionysus and would, in turn, become an agent of destruction.

In his adoration of Dionysus, Nietzsche would pen books advocating a new ethos and spirit to be taken up in the rejection and destruction of Christianity, a new morality of amorality in which the weak are vanquished by the strong, in which man becomes a superman, and which is summed with Nietzsche's most famous words, "God is dead."[2]

THE FRUIT OF THE POSSESSED

Nietzsche's rejection of the Crucified One for Dionysus would have far-reaching, even world-shaking, repercussions. In the years ahead he would be hailed as the philosopher and prophet of a new movement—Nazism.[3] The Nazis saw themselves as translators of Nietzsche's philosophical concepts into political, cultural, and geopolitical reality. That translation would lead to the Third Reich, the Second World

War, the destruction of Europe, the Holocaust, and the blood of millions.

THE AVATAR OF MADNESS

The shedim, as we have seen, are destroyers. Nietzsche had cast God and the "Crucified One" out of his life and opened the door to a god, one of the shedim, the daemonia. He, in turn, would become their agent to bring forth an evil of a magnitude that the world had never witnessed.

Before Nietzsche, in his madness, grew silent, he began signing his letters with a new name—*Dionysus*.[4] It was as if the god, the spirit of the god, had taken him over entirely. He had become the avatar of Dionysus, an avatar of madness. And yet at the same time, the sign of the conflict and the replacement would also manifest, as Nietzsche would also now sign his name as the *Crucified One*.

A MORE DANGEROUS POSSESSION

The case of Nietzsche and the Third Reich bears witness, most dramatically, to the warning of Jesus' parable. Greater than the danger of being possessed by a spirit is the danger of being repossessed by a returning spirit. And far more dangerous than a pagan god is a post-Christian god. The warning now most specifically applies to the modern West and the danger posed by its returning gods. For as Nietzsche and Hitler have demonstrated, for a Christian civilization to turn away from God, to empty itself of Jesus, is a most dangerous thing.

Nietzsche's exchange of Jesus for Dionysus was manifested a century and a half later in the Olympian spectacle.

The God of Madness 95

His turning away from God is now reflective not of a peculiar national movement such as Nazism but of a mass civilizational metamorphosis. In Nietzsche's case the possession of a god drove him to madness and then, through him, a nation to an even darker, more demonic, and more deadly madness.

So then what will that exchange now mean for the West and the world? We have seen the effect of the gods in varied cultures and lands. But their effect with regard to the West, though veiled, is, as we have seen, in the end far more dangerous. The mystery now turns to one of the West's most central battlegrounds in the war of the gods—America.

PART VI

AMERICAN GODS AND KINGS

Chapter 19

THE AMERICAN GODS

As America emptied itself of God, it was inevitable that other gods would come in to fill the void of His absence. Which gods?

THE UNHOLY THREE

American civilization was founded after the pattern of ancient Israel. From the vision of John Winthrop to the moral foundations laid by its early colonists to the admonitions of its first leaders and ministers, the template of ancient Israel was embedded in America's spiritual DNA. But ancient Israel turned away from God. So did America. In Israel's apostasy it became indwelled by the gods and spirits, three in particular. In *The Return of the Gods* I identified them as the *dark trinity*. Could, therefore, America in emptying itself of God become indwelled by the same? It could. Though here I can give only the briefest of overviews, it is crucial that we identify the gods that now dominate American culture, the dark trinity of American gods.

THE POSSESSOR

His name meant the *Master*, the *Lord*, and the *Possessor*. He was called *Baal*. He was the god who turned a nation away from the God it had once known. Baal caused Israel to forget God, to overturn His ways and precepts, and to drive Him out of its public life. Baal blurred the lines

99

between the world and God, truth and illusion. He turned the nation of Israel from God to the gods, from monotheism to polytheism and pantheism, and from biblical faith to paganism.

RETURN OF THE POSSESSOR

Though there is no single date to mark the definitive turning of America away from God, the early 1960s marked a critical milestone. The spirit of Baal began penetrating American culture, causing it to drive God out of its national life, out of its schools, out of its public squares, out of its culture, out of its life. As the spirit of Baal had done to ancient Israel, so it likewise caused America to forget its God, to overturn His ways and precepts, and to blur the lines between truth and subjectivity. He moved America from God to the gods and from biblical faith to post-Christian neo-paganism.

THE ENCHANTRESS

She was a goddess, a seductress, and an enchantress. In Babylon she was called *Ishtar*, in the Bible, *Ashtoreth*, the goddess of unbridled sexuality, lust, and prostitution. Indeed, she was worshipped as the great prostitute. The goddess paganized ancient Israel through the realm of sexuality, overturning biblical values and replacing them with pagan ones. She took sexuality out of the marital covenant and into the marketplace and public square. Thus she weakened marriage and sexualized the culture. Her images in clay and stone and the erotic writings composed

The American Gods

101

in her name constitute the world's first official examples of pornography.

RETURN OF THE ENCHANTRESS

In the biblical account, Baal is listed first, then the goddess. So first comes the turning away from God, and then the turning of sexuality. So it was no accident that America's apostasy from God in the early 1960s was followed by what would come to be called a *sexual revolution*. The biblical values and ethics that had, for thousands of years, undergirded marriage and sexuality were overturned and replaced with pagan or neo-pagan ethics and values. The goddess wrested sexuality out of the marriage covenant and placed it in the public square and in the marketplace. Marriage was undermined, and American culture was sexualized, flooded with pornographic images and writings. The Enchantress had cast her spell to draw American and Western civilization away from God by means of seduction.

THE DESTROYER

The last of the dark trinity was Molech, the god of destruction, the killer of children. The Scriptures had declared that life was sacred and children, a gift from God. But Molech required his worshippers to present him with human sacrifices, their sons and daughters. And so as Israel turned away from God, the altars of Molech covered its valleys and high places, and the Holy Land was defiled by the cries and blood of the most innocent. The prophets cried out to warn them that the blood of their children would be answered with judgment, even the nation's destruction. And so it would be.

RETURN OF THE DESTROYER

As Baal leads to Ishtar and Ishtar to Molech, so the sexual revolution that overtook American and Western culture would lead to the sacrificing of the most innocent. And so it was no accident that in the wake of the sexual revolution, mothers and fathers began offering up their children as sacrifices. Molech now came in the guise of self-interest, liberation, convenience, and the pursuit of happiness, gain, and success. His shrines now took the form of abortion clinics, and his stone altars became operating tables. But it was nonetheless Molech. The act was again enshrined in the trappings of a sacred rite, if not a sacrament. But there was a difference; Israel had offered up thousands of its children—America had offered up millions. The ancient warning of the prophets against Molech now echoed to another nation that had given itself to his altars.

THE TRANSFORMER

One more must be noted, not another deity but another side to one of them, a side so potent that it warrants another title. In her ancient inscriptions, the goddess announces, "*I am a woman; I am a man.*" The hymns of the goddess praise her for *turning a man into a woman and a woman into a man.* She was the *Transformer.* She blurred the lines between male and female, altered sexuality and gender, emasculated men, and defeminized women.

Her priesthood included men who dressed as women

The American Gods 103

and those who had been surgically altered to appear as the opposite sex. Her parades flowed through the streets with color and spectacle to celebrate the confusing and merging of genders. Among the signs with which she was associated was that of the rainbow. And in one month of the year, she especially possessed the culture. In Latin that month was known as *Iunium* or *Junium*. Today it corresponds with the month of June.

RETURN OF THE TRANSFORMER

The bending and twisting of sexuality and gender was the goddess's deeper work. And so it was only a matter of time, as her possession of American and Western culture deepened, that this side of her workings would manifest. And so it did. Men were increasingly emasculated, women, increasingly defeminized. The priests of the goddess, the men who dressed as women, now performed in libraries, on television, and throughout popular culture. Boys were transitioned to appear as girls, and girls as boys. The parades of the goddess again coursed through city streets with color, spectacle, and music in celebration of the confusing and merging of genders. The sign of the goddess, the rainbow, now appeared in schools, public squares, and government buildings. And the goddess again especially possessed the culture in the month of June.

But if the gods have returned, then for what purpose? What is their agenda and their end goal?

Chapter 20

THE EVE OF REPOSSESSION

IN THE YEARS after I first wrote of it in *The Return of the Gods*, the mystery of the gods has continued to manifest. In fact, it accelerated and deepened, penetrating virtually every sphere and front of American culture. This now is to give a short glimpse into that acceleration and deepening.

CHILDREN OF BAAL

The work of Baal, to cause a nation that had known of God to apostatize and turn against His ways, became increasingly manifest and brazen, penetrating virtually every realm and segment of American culture. The young were especially targeted. Polls of American youth and young adults revealed that, barring a massive change in the nation's course, for the first time since the Christianization of Western civilization, Christians would become a minority and non-Christians, a majority. The Western apostasy was now producing a generation completely alienated from God. The United Kingdom offered a glimpse of America's future as polls revealed that the moment of a non-Christian majority had already arrived.[1]

IN PRAISE OF MOLECH

As for Molech, though *Roe v. Wade* was overturned, the war against innocent life only intensified. Those advocating for the killing of the unborn now did so all the

The Eve of Repossession 105

more openly and brazenly. They now sought to remove all hedges and restraints that might hinder the practice or its expansion. And in their zeal they now began crossing the line into the realm of infanticide, advocating that babies born alive in a failed abortion attempt should not be saved but left to die.[2]

Molech's work was not limited to the unborn. There were other ways to kill. And so the number of those contemplating suicide, attempting it, or committing it now reached epidemic proportions. The young were especially prone to contemplate self-destruction. And it wasn't only the young who were in danger—but the old. The same culture that devalued human life at its beginning would do so at its end. Once condemned in Western culture as murder, euthanasia was increasingly legitimized, legalized, and spreading. In this, Canada now offered a dramatic glimpse into America's future. In one year's time the number of its citizens legally put to death had exceeded ten thousand.[3] Where the gods reign, death also reigns.

THE DEEPENING SPELL

As for Ishtar, her possession of American and Western culture only deepened. Through the internet, pornography was everywhere and accessible to nearly everyone, including children. Her war against family and the marital bond was so effective that by the mid-2020s, the US marriage rate had plummeted by more than 60 percent from where it had been half a century earlier.[4]

And as for the goddess's war against the natural order, the strange doctrine that one's gender was whatever one believed it to be became the culture's official ruling dogma. The largest medical association in America now advocated for the removal of the words *male* and *female* on birth certificates.[5] Children were now being openly sexualized from kindergarten and even earlier. The school system that had once led American children in the Lord's Prayer now recruited them, step by step, into gender confusion while hiding what they were doing from the children's parents. The entire culture was complicit, using children's programming, cartoons, video games, social media, and the entertainment industry to indoctrinate them. The agenda of the goddess was so effective that for the first time in human history, almost one out of every three young adults now claimed to be something other than heterosexual.

THE NEW WHITE HOUSE FLAG

The radical metamorphosis of American culture came into focus in the summer of 2023 when its president hosted the largest and most brazen celebration of *Pride*, the alteration of sexuality and gender, ever held on White House grounds[6]—an event unimaginable in earlier days. But in the midst of the celebration it was a single piece of cloth that most clearly manifested what had happened to America.

Three flags draped the White House between the stone pillars that lined its facade. Two were the American flag. The third was the flag of Pride with the colors of the rainbow representing groups including the transgendered. It was not the American flag that was hung in the center, the place of greatest importance; it was the flag of Pride.

The Eve of Repossession 107

The American flags were merely flanking it.[7] The sign of Ishtar on the nation's highest house had now superseded the flag of America.

TAKEOVER

It was not an accident. In a statement released that same day, the president said, "Today, the People's House—your house—sends a clear message to the country and to the world, 'America is a nation of *pride*.'"[8] The word *pride*, in this case, was a euphemism for the alteration of sexuality. The president was proclaiming America as a nation of altered sexuality—a nation no longer under God. It was now one nation under the goddess. When a nation is taken over by a revolutionary faction, among the first signs of its victory is the flying of the flag of that faction over the highest of government buildings and all over the land. So the flying of the rainbow flag, the sign of Ishtar, on the White House was the sign of a revolution, ascendant and on the verge of gaining total control and dominion over a civilization.[9]

REVOLUTION OF THE GODS

Another sign of an ascendant revolution is the war waged against any dissent or "counterrevolutionary" opinions and individuals—persecution. This also became an increasingly prominent part of the new cultural regime. Those who did not support the new worldview and values were increasingly marginalized, censored, deplatformed, banned, fired, and demonized. The suppression or persecution typically set as its target conservatives and

Christians. No dissent was tolerated. And in accordance with classic revolutionary and totalitarian practice, many of those who dissented were compelled to issue apologies, confessing their sins and denouncing their lack of loyalty to the dogmas of the new regime, the new gods. And even the uncensored would now censor themselves, watching every word that passed through their lips.

THE TOTALITARIAN

As in a totalitarian dictatorship the dogmas of the regime were propagated and enforced in nearly every realm of culture. Even the business world fell in line, with corporation after corporation seeking to prove its loyalty to the new gods by requiring its employees to attend special indoctrination sessions and punishing those who dissented. And as a revolution is not complete without the takeover of the nation's military and enforcement agencies, so the gods invaded the Departments of Justice and Defense with indoctrination classes, celebrations of "Pride," and retribution against those who resisted.

THE TIPPING POINT

The gods had done it. The nation that once proudly declared itself to be "under God" and the upholder of Christian values was now turning pagan, increasingly and more brazenly so. The gods had ascended its high places. In 2024 America was standing at a critical juncture, in danger of passing the point of no return. A pivotal election was looming. On one side of that election was a presidential candidate fully aligned with the agenda of the

The Eve of Repossession 109

gods. Had that candidacy prevailed, it would have proved a tipping point, and, likely, the sealing event of the repossession, the takeover of the American government and American civilization.

In order to open up the mystery of our times, it is necessary to add one more puzzle piece. We have looked at the American gods; we must now open the template of kings.

Chapter 21

THE PROTOTYPE

THERE WAS ANOTHER critical juncture and another tipping point in another nation's history, one that likewise threatened to seal its future to the gods. What happened then will give us an uncanny revelation into what is now transpiring in America.

THE ANCIENT TEMPLATE

Ancient Israel was heading for judgment. An apostate king and a pagan queen had initiated a war against God and His ways while leading the nation into the worship of Baal and his fellow gods. The war would continue for decades into the reigns of their sons. By then, the apostasy had become so ingrained in the nation's cultural and governmental fabric that it was rapidly approaching the point of no return.

What we are now about to open is not a prophecy but a shadow, a pattern, a template, a revealing of our times, and a warning concerning the future. I first wrote of it in the book called *The Paradigm*. Since the book's release, the template has continued to play out and manifest on America's national stage—to this very day. The template is crucial to understanding what is now taking place on the world stage. For those unaware of it, I can here only give a brief glimpse into its mystery. Before doing so, it is important to note that the modern-day leaders who have become players and agents in the template's fulfillment

The Prototype   111

have done so unknowingly. We are not to presume their motives nor make enemies of any leader but rather to pray for them and even seek their salvation.

AHAB

The departure of Israel from God had already been long underway when a man ascended its throne to take that departure to an entirely new level. He was a divided and compromised man, having known of God's ways but now warring against them.[1] He would be the first king in Israel's history to openly champion the worship of Baal. And so he would become an emissary for child sacrifice, sexual immorality, and the uprooting and overturning of biblical or traditional values. He thus triggered a culture war. His name was *Akhav*. We know him as *Ahab*.

THE AMERICAN AHAB

The template of King Ahab would find its modern fulfillment in President Clinton. As with Ahab, Clinton was a divided and compromised man, having known of God's ways but warring against them.[2] He would become the first president in America's history to openly champion the sacrifice of children in the form of abortion and the first to advocate for elements of the LGBT agenda. And as the reign of Ahab triggered a culture war in Israel, so Clinton's rise to the presidency would trigger a culture war in America. In fact, the phrase *culture war* would enter America's national debate at the time of Clinton's rising.[3]

THE TWENTY-TWO YEARS OF AHAB

Could the mystery be even more exact? Bill Clinton entered the national stage when he was sworn in as governor of Arkansas in 1979. He left the national stage at the close of his presidency in 2001. And so his time on the national stage was *twenty-two years*. As for King Ahab, it is recorded in 1 Kings 16:29,

> Ahab the son of Omri reigned over
> Israel in Samaria *twenty-two years*.

Thus both the ancient and the modern Ahab inhabited the national stage of their lands for twenty-two years.

JEZEBEL

Ahab was not alone in his war against God. He ruled in a coregency with his wife. The queen saw biblical faith and traditional values as something to be warred against, even stamped out. She incited her husband to promulgate and enforce the worship of her god Baal and the gods of Phoenicia. She was the driving force and chief agent in the promulgation of child sacrifice in the land of Israel. Her name was *Izevel*. We know her as *Jezebel*.

THE AMERICAN JEZEBEL

Though there would be another modern leader who would step into the role at a later time, the prototype of Jezebel belongs most centrally to Hillary Clinton. As Ahab reigned in a coregency with his wife, so Bill Clinton governed in what observers saw as a copresidency with his wife, Hillary. As did Jezebel, so Hillary Clinton saw biblical

The Prototype

and traditional values as obstacles to be warred against and eliminated. During her campaign for the presidency she was publicly quoted as saying that "deep-seated... religious beliefs" needed to be overcome so that abortion could expand.[4] And as Jezebel was the chief advocate of child sacrifice in the land, so Hillary Clinton would be named as Planned Parenthood's abortion champion of the *century*.[5]

THE SCANDAL

The reign of Ahab was plagued with scandal; so too the presidency of Bill Clinton. The greatest scandal of Ahab's reign was exposed in *the nineteenth year* of his time on the national stage. The greatest scandal of Clinton's presidency, the Clinton–Lewinsky scandal, was exposed in 1998. 1998 was *the nineteenth year* of his time on the national stage. Clinton was sworn in as governor in *January* of 1979, so the scandal was exposed nineteen years later, in the same month, *January* of 1998.

Three years after the exposure of the scandal, the reign of King Ahab came to an end. Three years after the exposure of the Lewinsky scandal, the years of the Clinton presidency came to an end. The exact day of that end was January 20, 2001. Counting back three years from that date pinpoints the date January 20, 1998. The scandal broke on *January 20, 1998, the same day—three years to the exact date*.[6]

THE THREE-YEAR CALAMITY

Three years after King Ahab confessed the sin of his scandal, misfortune struck his nation. After much denial Clinton would come to confess the sin of his scandal in September of 1998. Thus three years later misfortune would strike America in *September of 2001*. Clinton's confession came on the morning of September 11, 1998.[7] The calamity struck three years later *to the exact day—on the morning of September 11, 2001.*

THE QUEEN ON HER OWN

When the reign of Ahab came to an end, Jezebel continued on the national stage, walking the halls of power in the capital city.[8] When the presidency of Bill Clinton came to its end, Hillary Clinton likewise continued on the national stage, first as senator and then as secretary of state, in the halls of power in the capital city. She would attempt to become the foremost leader of her nation but would fail. It was all according to the ancient template. Jezebel would never become the primary leader in Israel. The office would go to a man, her junior.

SON OF AHAB

The most significant of Ahab's sons, Joram would reign on his father's throne and follow, by and large, in his father's footsteps. So Barack Obama would follow, by and large, in the ways and policies of the Clinton presidency. When Joram reigned as king, his mother, Jezebel, dwelt in the royal palace, undoubtedly influencing him and giving counsel.[9] When Obama walked the halls of the White House, so too

The Prototype   115

did the nation's former first lady, Hillary Clinton, bearing influence and giving him counsel.[10] Joram's reign would be marked by hostility against the ways of God and His people. The Obama administration would likewise be marked by hostility against the ways and people of God. As Joram further led his nation away from God and in the way of apostasy, Obama would further lead America away from God and in the way of apostasy.

THE TWELVE YEARS OF JORAM

Obama entered the national stage when he addressed the Democratic National Convention of 2004. By that single event, he became a celebrity in the Democratic Party and ultimately its candidate for the presidency.[11] His final year on the national stage as president was 2016. Thus Barack Obama was on the national stage for *twelve years*. Of King Joram it is written in 2 Kings 3:

> Now Joram the son of Ahab...*reigned twelve years.*[12]

THE YEARS OF THE QUEEN

The end came for Joram and Jezebel at the same time, in the same political struggle.[13] The end of Barack Obama's political career and that of Hillary Clinton came in the same year, at the same time, and in the same political struggle. Clinton had been on the national political stage without her husband, twelve years in public office and two years running for the presidency. Altogether, she had been on the national stage with her husband for twenty-two years, and on her own, fourteen years. Jezebel had been on the national stage with her husband, Ahab, for *twenty-two years* and on her own, *fourteen years.*[14]

We have opened the realm of American gods and kings or rulers. We will now see in America, as we have seen in other lands, the coming together of gods and kings.

Chapter 22

HOUSE OF THE GODS

THE GOVERNMENT THAT led Israel into the worship of Baal and the gods and persecuted the people of God is identified in Scripture as the *house of Ahab*. What was it? And what *is* it?

HOUSE OF AHAB

The house of Ahab was first a dynasty beginning with Ahab and his family and continuing through his heirs. It was the central catalyst of Israel's radical departure from God, leading the nation and dominating its culture for nearly four decades. The house of Ahab was a house of gods. It became their chief ally and sponsor. Under its reign the worship and cult of the gods would become the kingdom's state-sponsored, state-compelled, and state-enforced religion.

Which gods did the house of Ahab promulgate? They included Baal, Ishtar, and, in the cult of child sacrifice, Molech. In other words, the house of Ahab championed the same gods that now dominate American culture. So if the gods of the house have returned to American culture, could the house of the gods have returned as well? In other words, could there now exist an American house of Ahab?

THE AMERICAN HOUSE OF AHAB

The American house of Ahab would have to be an institution, a government, party, faction, or segment of society that holds to the same overall views, ideologies, causes, and practices once championed by the ancient house of Ahab. It would be that segment of American culture that most strongly promulgates turning away from God and the overturning of biblical or traditional values, as in Baal; the alteration of sexuality and the bending of gender, as in Ishtar; and the sacrifice of children, or abortion, as in Molech.

Thus, in its broadest application the American house of Ahab would include that which would become known as the *woke*.

PARTY OF AHAB

But there is also a more specific answer. The house of Ahab was a political faction, heirs to the throne and their attendants, relatives, and allies. The ancient template, with its modern-day fulfillments, already provides us with a clue. If the Clinton years mimic the twenty-two years of Ahab, and the years of Hillary, the twenty-two and fourteen years of Jezebel, and the Obama years, the twelve years of Joram, what do they all hold in common? Each was a leader and standard-bearer of the same political organization—the Democratic Party.

PARTY OF THE GODS

It was not always as it would become. The Democratic Party did not always hold to or champion the agendas it

House of the Gods 119

would come to champion. In fact, in earlier times, it vehemently opposed them. But in positioning itself as the party of change at a time when the principal change transpiring in America was that of apostasy, it became increasingly joined to the causes and movements that were turning America away from God. It did not consciously intend so, but it would end up serving the agenda of Baal, in his turning from God; Ishtar, in her bending of sexuality; and Molech, in his destruction of children. And thus it would become the party of the gods.

ASCENDANCY

From the rise of Bill Clinton to the reelection of Barack Obama, there had been six presidential elections. In that span of time the Democratic Party won the popular vote five of six times while the Republican Party won only once. At the same time, the future of the American electorate as represented by the younger generation was leaning strongly to the Left and toward the Democratic Party. Analysts on both sides of the political spectrum began speaking, celebrating, or warning of an increasingly leftward American future dominated and ruled by the Democratic Party. As was the house of Ahab in the days of King Joram, the Democratic Party was, in the early twenty-first century, positioned to decisively dominate the nation's future.

DOMINION

It was all converging: the political realm, the cultural realm, and the spiritual realm. A radical, anti-biblical, anti-Christian ethos was on the verge of cementing its ascendancy over a once decidedly Christian nation. The cultural revolution, with its creeping soft totalitarianism, was now vying for the total conformity of speech, behavior, and, increasingly, thought, even when it meant a blatant denial of reality. And as it had in ancient times, the house of Ahab was increasingly demanding that those who dissented from its agenda suffer the consequences.

CONVERGENCE

As in the ancient pagan world the realms of the gods and kings, spirits and kingdoms, were typically merged, so now, in America, in its fall from God, the two were again coalescing. And as the gods were, by nature, possessing spirits, they would seek to gain control of the American political and governmental realms, by which the nation would be ruled, and to rule America was to rule much of the world. With the approach of a presidential election, it was all set to converge. But then something happened.

It had happened to the ancient house of Ahab; it would happen again to the modern—even twice. No one expected it. It came suddenly, as if out of nowhere. And yet it was all part of a mystery that began nearly three thousand years earlier, a mystery ultimately rooted in and touching the realm of the gods.

PART VII

THE RETURN OF JEHU

Chapter 23

THE MAN ON THE STAIRS

H E WAS A man cloaked in mystery, an enigma. Thousands of years after his rising, commentators are still divided over his motives, his methods, his ways, and his legacy. He was a man of contradiction and paradox. To many of his contemporaries, he would have appeared especially ill-suited for the mission to which he was called—and yet he was uniquely suited for it. He invoked controversy, and controversy surrounded him. His name was *Jehu.* Jehu was the ancient biblical prototype for a modern leader, a man likewise of contradiction and paradox, and one who invoked and was surrounded by controversy. The world would know him as *Donald Trump.*

THE FIGHTER

Jehu was not born of the royal house but was a military commander.[1] He was a fighter. After being given a prophetic charge, he would launch a campaign to take the throne by force. The campaign began on top of a staircase. The Book of 2 Kings records,

> ...he spoke to me, saying, "Thus says the LORD: 'I have anointed you king over Israel.'"[2] Then each man rushed to take his garment and put it under him on the top of the stairs...saying, "Jehu is king!"[3]

123

Upon hearing that God had called him to become king, Jehu's soldiers, his most devoted core of supporters, placed their garments under his feet as he stood on top of the stairs and proclaimed him king.[4] It was after that proclamation that Jehu descended the staircase, mounted his chariot, and set off on his campaign to take the throne.[5]

ON TOP OF THE STAIRWAY

Could the rise of Donald Trump to the presidency be joined to the rise of Jehu to the throne? The rise of Trump began on June 16, 2015, with the announcement of his campaign for the White House at Trump Tower in New York City. The most iconic image from that event was that of his entrance. He made his appearance standing *on top of a staircase*, a moving staircase especially chosen to be part of the event. As Jehu began his rise to power by descending the stairs and beginning his campaign for the throne, Trump descended to the bottom of the stairs to begin his campaign for the presidency.[6]

THE WILD ONE

Jehu was wild, impulsive, and unpredictable. His methods were often unorthodox, and his actions often questionable. He was hot-blooded, combative, and, at times, merciless. And yet it was that very nature that would be used in the fulfillment of his calling. So the American Jehu, Trump, was wild, impulsive, and unpredictable. His methods were likewise often unorthodox, and his actions often questionable. He was hot-blooded, combative, and, at times, merciless. And yet his nature would be used to fulfill his calling.

The Man on the Stairs 125

In the history of Israel's kings, Jehu was unprecedented. In the history of America's presidents, Trump was likewise unprecedented.

TO DRAIN THE SWAMP

Seeking to reach the royal city before the word of his revolt could reach the king, Jehu's campaign for the throne is described in the ancient account as *furious* or *crazy*. During that campaign, he would encounter a man of piety and abstinence, a leader of religious conservatives in the land, Jehonadab. Through Jehonadab, Jehu forged an alliance with the religious conservatives of the land. He would invite Jehonadab into his chariot, and the two would ride together for the remainder of the race and would together enter the nation's capital, Samaria, where Jehu would seek to put into effect his mission to *drain the swamp*.[7]

ALLIANCE OF THE HOLY

So too the American Jehu embarked on a campaign for the White House that many observers would describe as *furious* and *crazy*. During that campaign, as had his ancient prototype, he would forge an alliance with Evangelical Christians and religious conservatives of the land. He would even have his own antitype to Jehonadab, a religious conservative known for his piety and abstinence, Mike Pence.[8] As did Jehonadab, Pence would become the American Jehu's partner in the race and would enter the nation's capital city, Washington, DC, where Trump would seek to put into effect his mission to *drain the swamp*.

AGAINST JORAM

Jehu could only become the leader of his nation by supplanting the current king, Joram. It would happen violently:

> Then Jehu drew his bow with his full strength and shot Joram between his arms; and the arrow went through his heart, and he sank in his chariot.[9]

And so by the arrow of Jehu the reign of King Joram and King Ahab's dynasty would come to its end.

AGAINST OBAMA

It was thus ordained that the American Jehu, Trump, would set himself against the American Joram, Barack Obama. Trump would become an outspoken critic of the Obama presidency. Trump's campaign for the White House was, indeed, a repudiation of the Obama administration. His victory in that campaign, though much less violent than Jehu's, would effectively bring an end to Obama's agenda and many of his policies. Any hope of their continuance in the next administration was dashed. As Jehu dealt the final blow to King Joram when Joram had been on the national stage for twelve years, Trump dealt the final blow to Obama's presidency in 2016 when Obama had been on the national stage for twelve years.

AGAINST JEZEBEL

And yet Jehu's ultimate nemesis was not the nation's king but its former first lady, Jezebel. Their conflict would come to a head with Jezebel looking down disdainfully

The Man on the Stairs 127

on Jehu from her palace window and Jehu calling to her attendants.

> Then he said, "Throw her down." So they threw her down.[10]

And so Jezebel's violent reign came to a violent end.

AGAINST BAAL

As Jehu was ordained to come head-to-head in a showdown against Israel's former first lady, so it was no accident that Trump would come head-to-head in a showdown against America's former first lady—the American Jehu against the American Jezebel.

When Jehu came against Jezebel, he was coming as well against the cult of Baal that Jezebel had so zealously championed, the cult of child sacrifice. When Trump came against Clinton, he would likewise come against the sacrificing of children in abortion, which Hillary Clinton had so zealously championed.

As the election neared, poll after poll showed that Clinton would inflict a crushing victory over Trump. But the ancient template said otherwise: It ordained that in a battle of Jehu and Jezebel, Jehu would emerge victorious and the nation's former first lady would be defeated. And so the American Jehu emerged victorious, and the American Jezebel was defeated.

AGAINST THE HOUSE OF AHAB

What was Jehu's calling? When he was first hailed as king as he stood on top of the stairs, it was just after the prophet

128

THE AVATAR

had given him a prophetic word that would reveal what he was called to do:

> I have *anointed you king* over the people of the LORD, over Israel. *You shall strike down the house of Ahab* your master, that I may *avenge the blood* of My servants the prophets, and the blood of all the servants of the LORD, at the hand of Jezebel.[11]

Thus Jehu was called not only to become king but to avenge the blood of the innocent and bring an end to the house of Ahab.

THE DYNASTY KILLER

Could the prophetic message given to Jehu to reveal his calling and purpose hold the secret to the calling and purpose of Donald Trump with regard to America? If so, it would mean, first of all, that Trump was indeed anointed to become president. Second, it would mean he was to come against the shedding of innocent blood. He would do so in the stands and actions he took against abortion. But it also would mean that he was called to *strike down the American house of Ahab.*[12] That would signify the ending of the Clinton dynasty. That he fulfilled it is attested to by the headlines that appeared after his victory. When we juxtapose this with actual Bible headings concerning Jehu, the result is striking:

Ahab's Dynasty Is Ended[13]

The Clinton Dynasty Has Come to an End[14]

The Man on the Stairs 129

Jehu Wipes Out Ahab's Royal House[15]
Donald Trump, Dynasty Killer[16]

The media had no idea. But what was taking place on the American political stage was the replaying of an ancient mystery. The American Jehu was fulfilling his calling, even if unknowingly.

But the American house of Ahab was, as we have seen, more than a political dynasty; it was a movement, an agenda, an ideology, and a power overtaking the institutions and culture of American civilization. Its striking down began in the American Jehu's first administration. But the battle was far from over. The American house of Ahab would fight back against the American Jehu. And the American Jehu would rise again to the American throne. It was in his second rising that the striking down of the house of Ahab would most dramatically manifest. And the ancient mystery would again play out and again explain and reveal what was to come.

Chapter 24

RETURN OF THE WARRIOR

WHAT WE ARE now about to see is that the return of Donald Trump to the White House and all that would follow was not an accident or a quirk but another dimension and outplaying of the ancient mystery. The dynamics of the biblical template would again kick in and determine exactly what was to happen. The names would change, others would rise to fulfill the ancient roles, but it was all ordained in the ancient template.

THE OPPOSED

As a military commander, Jehu came to the throne not by inheritance but warfare. Never in American history was a campaign for the presidency so much a fight, so much a battle, if not a war, as that of 2024, which would bring the American Jehu back to the White House.

When he began his rise to the throne, Jehu only had the support of those in his camp, those who hailed him as king. But arrayed against him was the house of Ahab. That meant the kingship, the government, with all its powers and the machinery of state, the ruling class, the cultural elites, the priesthood of Baal and the gods, and every major institution of the land. So it would be for the American Jehu. No major presidential candidate in American history had so many forces, so many institutions, organizations, movements, and strategies so arrayed against him

130

Return of the Warrior 131

and aimed not only at keeping him from the White House but seeking his imprisonment, if not his total destruction.

THE ONSLAUGHT

It was an unprecedented onslaught, an all-out existential war waged by all that constituted the American house of Ahab. The Democratic Party pumped well over a billion dollars to ensure his defeat.[1] The American mainstream news media produced a torrent of overwhelmingly negative coverage concerning him while producing a symphony of praise and adoration for his opponent.[2] The American entertainment industry, Hollywood, the music industry, and its celebrities all used their platforms and resources to attack and defeat him. The abortion industry waged an all-out war against him, as did the organizations and agents representing the LGBT agenda, as did the leaders of academia, as did the rest of what comprised the realm of the woke.

THE UNVANQUISHED

But that was only part of it. Legal challenges were filed to prevent his name from appearing on the ballot *in over thirty-five of America's fifty states.*[3] The legal war waged against him was so massive and, in the eyes of many, so biased that it would be called *lawfare*, a war waged by weaponizing the legal realm.[4] A single felony conviction could have led to his imprisonment. But he was charged with a total of ninety-one felony counts.[5] The New York court would convict him of thirty-four.[6] There was a real prospect that the one seeking the presidency could end up in prison. How anyone could have held up under such a massive onslaught, much less continue his campaign for the presidency, was a wonder to many. But as with the ancient Jehu, the American Jehu was, if anything, a fighter. And yet even all this wasn't the worst of it.

THE UNSLAIN

On July 13, 2024, while Trump was speaking at an open-air campaign rally in Butler, Pennsylvania, shots rang out from a gunman stationed on a nearby rooftop. One of the shots grazed Trump's right ear. It would be the first of *two assassination attempts* made on his life during that one campaign.[7] Rising from the chaos, blood streaming across his face, he stood defiant, raised his fist in the air, and shouted, "Fight, Fight, Fight." It was an iconic image.[8] Never had the world witnessed such a response from a leader who had just survived an assassination attempt. But it was the mystery of Jehu as manifested in Donald Trump. It was Jehu's nature to fight, to defy the odds, the powers that be, and whatever onslaught was set against him.

THE WARRIOR KING

In *The Paradigm* I introduced Jehu as the *warrior* and then, upon his ascent to power, as the *warrior king*. It was years later, in Trump's return to the presidency, that the mystery of the warrior king would fully manifest. It was his response in the wake of the attempt to assassinate him that especially invoked the word *warrior* to describe him. A television commentator would call him the *warrior president*,[9] and the headline of a major American newspaper would read,

Trump Just Proved That He's a Pure *Warrior*[10]

Return of the Warrior 133

And yet it was over a year before the attempt on his life that Trump himself would use the word as if speaking as Jehu. Addressing a campaign rally, he told his supporters,

I am your *warrior.*[11]

The campaign of 2024 was the return of Jehu—the return of the warrior.

THE MORTAL THREAT

But Jehu's war was waged not only against rulers of flesh and blood. Lying behind the political, social, and cultural realms of ancient Israel was the spiritual realm. Behind the house of Ahab were the gods of Ahab and Jezebel. So to war against that house was to war against the gods that indwelled the house. In the same way, Trump's war against the American house of Ahab was a war against the gods and spirits that had come to indwell and dominate American culture. What would we then expect to happen?

We would expect that Trump would represent an existential threat to every force, movement, institution, and individual led by those spirits. We would expect, then, that he would become a target. We might even expect the shedding of blood.

Most of those used by the gods or spirits have no idea of it. But some do. These also took part in the war against the American Jehu. They were of a more mystical nature than his other enemies. But when he returned, so did they.

Chapter 25

RETURN OF THE WITCHES

THE ROOTS OF witchcraft run deep and ancient. They go back to the rites and rituals of ancient paganism.

HER WITCHCRAFT

In their confrontation King Joram asks Jehu if he has come in peace. Jehu responds,

> What peace, as long as the idolatries of
> your mother Jezebel and her *witchcraft*
> are so many?[1]

The actual word used by Jehu for *witchcraft* is the Hebrew *kashaf*, which refers to the casting of spells and incantations. Such things were typical of ancient pagan worship, as practiced by Jezebel, along with sympathetic magic, fortune-telling, and the invoking of spirits. The rites and rituals of ancient pagan worship have survived into the modern world under the heading of *witchcraft*.

WAR OF THE WITCHES

So Jehu warred not only against the house of Ahab but against witchcraft, the pagan practices championed by Jezebel. And the witches of the land would have seen Jehu as their enemy. They would have undoubtedly sought to employ everything in their arsenal against him, to cast their spells and issue their curses.

One would not expect witches to be an issue in a modern

Return of the Witches   135

American presidency. But witches played a part in the ancient template. So is it possible that the mystery of Jehu would ordain that the rise of the American Jehu would be accompanied by the work of witches?

UNDER THE CRESCENT MOON

The answer is, strangely, yes. As Jehu and the witches of the land stood as enemies on opposite sides of the ancient culture war, so the American Jehu, in his rise to the presidency, was warred against not only by political and cultural enemies—but by witches. It was a sign of the times. As America fell away from God, it fell increasingly to the dark side. And as it became empty of the things of the Spirit, it opened itself to spirits of another kind. The number of witches in America exploded, surpassing even the number of Presbyterians.[2]

So as the witches of Jehu's time would have seen in him their enemy, so the witches of America and around the world saw Trump as their enemy. They decided to launch a campaign against him, a witches' campaign. They gathered across America and the world under the crescent moon to cast their spells, incantations, and curses against Donald Trump and his presidency.[3]

RETURN OF THE WITCHES

This was noted and chronicled in Trump's first ascent to the White House. Could then the return of the modern Jehu invoke the return of the witches? It could and it did. As Trump waged his campaign to return to the presidency, witches throughout America and the world again gathered together under the crescent moon to cast their spells against him. And again strange headlines appeared in the media:

Can Witches Defeat Donald Trump? They're Trying[4]

Their convocations included tarot cards and orange candles as well as Trump's image. The latter was used in rituals of sympathetic magic in which his image would be burned or otherwise destroyed. Meanwhile, the participants would chant in unison the words "You're fired!"[5]

WITCHES FOR KAMALA

As the witches of the land were overwhelmingly against Donald Trump's campaign, they were noticeably in favor of another. A number of journalists noted that the rise of Kamala Harris as Trump's political opponent had *reenergized the witches of America* to again cast their spells and curses. The words "Witches for Harris" and "Witches for Kamala" began appearing on signs, websites, and bumper stickers.[6]

JEZEBEL THE WITCH

But Jehu's war against witchcraft had a focal point: Jezebel. To charge her with promulgating witchcraft was to call her a witch. So is it possible that the American counterpart to Jezebel, the first opponent of the American Jehu, Hillary Clinton, could herself be accused of that which Jehu accused Jezebel of? It is and she was.

As strange as the war of the witches waged against Donald Trump is the fact that his first major opponent,

Return of the Witches

the one who fulfilled the prototype of Jezebel, was herself accused of being a witch. Some pointed to her laugh, which mimicked a witch's cackle.[7] Others pointed to her consultations and channeling sessions with New Age mystics and those who believed in spirits and, specifically, goddesses.[8]

THE HALLOWEEN MESSAGE

But even more strange was what Hillary Clinton did in the midst of Trump's campaign to return to the White House. It was October 31, 2023, Halloween, the night of witches, spirits, and dark magic. Clinton posted a photograph of herself online in celebration of the holiday. In the photograph she was dressed in a black witch's outfit, laughing as she touched the brim of the black witch's hat that rested on her head. The American Jezebel had, for some reason, decided to post a picture of herself as a witch. And if that wasn't enough, she added the words

Witches get stuff done.[9]

The posting did not prove that Clinton was a witch but was again in perfect and strange accord with the mystery. Clinton had walked in the mystery of Jezebel. Jehu accused Jezebel of being a witch. It was not that Clinton had any idea. But the mystery manifests nevertheless.

"I'VE BEEN CALLED A WITCH"

When Hillary Clinton issued her endorsement of Kamala Harris in her presidential campaign against Donald Trump,[10] she chose to include the words

I've been called a witch.[11]

The words of the American Jezebel could have been written by another. For with regard to Jehu's words against her, Jezebel herself could have written the exact same words: "I've been called a witch."

"HE HAS A SHIELD"

With all that was arrayed against him in the natural and the spiritual Trump was not overcome but prevailed. Why? For one, the mystery ordained it. But the witches themselves alluded to something more at work. So on the eve of the election, a strange headline appeared:

Witches Report Their Spells Against Trump
Aren't Working[12]

According to the article and others, witches who had been casting spells and curses against Trump were now "publicly bemoaning the failures of their spells."[13] Why were their spells failing to stop him? One of the witches quoted in the article said, *"He has a form of protection surrounding him."* Another witch said, *"He has a shield."* More specifically, it was believed among the witches that his shield was there because many people were praying.[14]

Jehu had the support of the faithful, the religious conservatives, of his land. It was with that support that he prevailed. So too it was with the support of the faithful of the land that, against all odds, the American Jehu would likewise prevail.

Return of the Witches 139

In the American Jehu's return to the White House, the ancient template would again play out with the same dynamics. But the role of Jehu's adversaries would be played by others—beginning with that of the king.

Chapter 26

RETURN OF THE KING SLAYER

JEHU'S RISE TO the throne centers on two figures, two adversaries. He would deal with them in two stages. The first was the king.

THE SUPPLANTER

Jehu could not strike down the house of Ahab without dealing with the king who sat at its head. So Jehu would go to the city of Jezreel, draw his bow, and strike down the son of Ahab, King Joram.[1] Joram was not the only king that Jehu struck down. Jehu was the king slayer. His rise would mark the end of Joram's reign, the death of three monarchs, and the fall of the house of Ahab.

So the American Jehu, Donald Trump, was likewise a slayer of kings—or presidents. On his first rise to power, as we have seen, he came against the current president, Barack Obama, brought an end to his agenda, and supplanted him as president. But he would rise to power a second time. We would therefore expect the ancient template to play out a second time, but now with different players fulfilling the ancient roles. Therefore for the second rise of Jehu, we should expect a second Joram.

THE SECOND AMERICAN JORAM

When Trump began the journey that would return him to the White House, the one who sat as president in the White House was Joe Biden. As Jehu began his campaign

140

Return of the King Slayer

for the throne with his focus set on the current king, it was inevitable that Trump would begin his campaign for the White House with his focus set on the current president, Biden. Jehu's focus on Joram represented only the first part of his campaign for the throne. It would soon change. So too Trump's focus on Biden would represent only the first part of his campaign for the White House. That too would soon change.

THE CONFRONTATION

The fall of King Joram would come quickly and dramatically. The fall of Biden's presidency would likewise come quickly and dramatically. Joram's fall would happen in a face-to-face confrontation with Jehu, each of them in their own chariots, close enough to each other for the two to carry on a conversation. So the end of Biden's political career would likewise come in a confrontation with the American Jehu, Donald Trump, face-to-face and close enough for the two to carry on a conversation—in fact, a debate.

FALL OF THE KING

It would happen on June 27, 2024, before the eyes of the nation and the world. In place of the two chariots were two podiums. The field of battle was the stage of the 2024 American presidential debate. When Joram came face-to-face with Jehu, he came unprepared. When the American Joram, Joe Biden, came face-to-face with the American Jehu, Trump, he too came unprepared. In the ancient account Joram was taken by surprise, outbattled, confounded, weak, and overcome.

In the modern confrontation, Biden was taken by surprise, outbattled, confounded, weak, and overcome.[2]

Jehu ended the reign of King Joram in one day, one encounter, one confrontation. Trump likewise ended Biden's presidency in one day, one encounter, one confrontation. Jehu dealt a mortal blow to Joram's kingship. Trump dealt a mortal blow to Biden's presidency. The event and the blow were again unprecedented. But Trump was the American Jehu. And Jehu was unprecedented—and the slayer of kings.

In the ancient template, the striking down of the king was the first of two acts. The second act would require the entrance of another. So too the mystery that unfolded on the American stage could not be complete without the entrance of another.

Chapter 27

RETURN OF THE QUEEN

WITH THE DEATH of King Joram, the mantle of Ahab's dynasty shifted to Jezebel.

THE STANDARD-BEARER

During the reign of King Ahab, Jezebel occupied the kingdom's second seat of power. After Ahab's death she functioned as queen mother and would have occupied a similar seat of power and influence behind the throne. But when Jehu killed her son Joram, Jezebel's position was no longer secondary. She was now the primary representative and standard-bearer of the house of Ahab and its agenda. It all rested on her. She now stood as the last obstacle and point of resistance in the way of Jehu's ascent to the throne.

FROM KING TO QUEEN

For the ancient template to continue to manifest, we would expect that in the first stage of the rising of the American Trump, the American house of Ahab would put its hope of resisting him in an American Joram, its current leader, the president. But in the second stage, it would shift its hope to another—an American Jezebel. According to the template, that other leader would be one who had served alongside the king in a position of power and influence within the royal palace. The ending of the king's reign would move that one from the sidelines of the national stage and into the spotlight.

143

FROM OBAMA TO CLINTON

And so in the first stage of Trump's first ascent to the White House, the focus of the American house of Ahab was on the American Joram, the functioning president, Barack Obama. But in the second stage of Trump's rising, it was focused on the one running to take Obama's place, Hillary Clinton. As with Jezebel, Clinton had served alongside Obama in a position of power and influence in the White House. As with Jezebel, she would become the standard-bearer of the American house of Ahab and her husband's political dynasty. And as with Jezebel, she too would stand as the center of resistance and battle against the American Jehu.

FROM BIDEN TO HARRIS

In the second rising of the American Jehu to the White House, the mystery would again manifest with a new player in the role of Jezebel. At the beginning of Trump's rise, the American house of Ahab placed its focus and hope on the nation's current president, the second to fulfill the template of Joram, Joe Biden. Though, unlike Obama, Biden was eligible to run for a second term and tried to do so, the template ordained that his run would be cut off.

After his political slaying on the stage of the presidential debate, the focus would likewise shift to another who would stand in his place. It would have to be one who served alongside the fallen leader in a secondary position in his government but who would take on his mantle. That one would then become the standard-bearer of the fallen leader's house to fight against the rise of Jehu. That

Return of the Queen 145

one would be Kamala Harris.[1] She would now move from the sidelines to the spotlight and would take up the mantle of Joe Biden to battle against Donald Trump for the office of the presidency—an American Jezebel against the American Jehu.

JEHU AND THE AMERICAN QUEEN

Never in American history had a woman run as the presidential candidate of a major party—until 2016, when Hillary Clinton ran against Donald Trump. Her candidacy was not ultimately the result of feminism or even the influence of the Clintons. It was, ultimately, because of the ancient template. The template ordained that when Jehu rises to the throne, his last opponent will be female. She will oppose his rising; he will oppose her rule. It was no accident that, in 2016, Trump was the only president in American history to come to the White House by contending against and defeating a female leader. For Jehu was the only king in the history of the northern kingdom of Israel who came to the throne by contending against and defeating a female leader.

In the case of Kamala Harris, she was not chosen to run against Trump because she was deemed the most competent or qualified of candidates, nor was it that her candidacy was the most well planned or well-thought-out. It happened, rather, because it had to happen; the template ordained it. The fall of the American Joram had to lead to the focus shifting onto an American Jezebel to contend for the throne against the American Jehu.

THE ZEALOT

Jezebel was not only interested in power; she was a zealot, a radical, an ideologue. She was committed to promulgating and enforcing a radically anti-conservative and anti-biblical agenda. She would thus seek to overturn traditional, conservative, and biblical values. And so the mystery would ordain that the one who walks in the template of Jehu will not only contend for the throne against a female leader of the king's house, but also against one who represents and promulgates a radical agenda, who seeks to overturn traditional, conservative, and biblical values.

THE RADICAL

So the woman commissioned to battle the American Jehu in each of his ascents to the White House would have to represent and promulgate a radical agenda. And so she would be. In his first ascent Trump's opponent, Hillary Clinton, was a woman who saw traditional, conservative, and biblical values as a threat to her agenda. In his second, the template would replay itself in Kamala Harris. Harris was likewise an agent of a radical agenda. Just before becoming Biden's vice president, she was ranked as among the most radically left-wing American senators. And as with Jezebel and Clinton, the agenda she promulgated warred against conservative and biblical believers and traditional values. As had Jezebel and Clinton, Harris saw those values as hindrances and threats to her agenda.

Return of the Queen

AGENT OF THE GODS

However, Jezebel was acting not only as an instrument of radical change but as an agent of the gods. Her agenda could not be understood without them. It was aligned with the agenda of ancient paganism—whether in the realm of life and child sacrifice, in sexuality, in marriage, in the bending, breaking, and merging of gender, and in the way it viewed those who upheld biblical values. In this, as with Jezebel, Clinton was used as an agent of the same forces, a vessel of the gods.

In the end the candidacies of Hillary Clinton and Kamala Harris were not about either of them, but were the outworking of the mystery of Jezebel and the gods. Both Clinton and Harris assumed the template of the ancient queen as each warred against the rising American Jehu, but were destined, by that same template, to be defeated by him.

Is it possible that the outcomes of three consecutive American presidential elections were not explained by political factors, economic considerations, or social indicators—but by a three-thousand-year-old mystery?

Chapter 28

THE MYSTERY OF RISINGS

IN AT LEAST two of the three consecutive elections in which Trump ran for the White House, the overwhelming majority of media analysts and pundits were caught by surprise and at a loss to explain what had happened. But what if it was all contained in the interplay of an ancient queen and a rising general?

THE MOCKER

In the final showdown between Jehu and Jezebel, the nation's former first lady showed her contempt for the ascending leader as she mocked and disparaged him.

> Now when Jehu had come to Jezreel, Jezebel heard of it; and she put paint on her eyes and adorned her head, and looked through a window. Then, as Jehu entered at the gate, she said, "Is it peace, Zimri, murderer of your master?"[1]

Zimri was an assassin who, after slaying the king, reigned in his place for just days before killing himself in lieu of surrendering.[2] As Jezebel viewed Jehu with contempt, so Clinton and Harris viewed Trump with the same. Both mocked and disparaged him. Both could rest confidently in decisively defeating him. Each was surrounded by polls giving them assurance of victory.[3]

The Mystery of Risings   149

But the ancient template said something else. It would be the one who walked in the mystery of Jehu who would emerge victorious. Is it possible then that this same template could determine the outcome of each American presidential election from 2016 to 2024—in which election he would prevail and in which he would not, and why?

TEMPLATE OF THE OUTSIDER

The template of Jehu's rise to power is not one of peaceful transition or the maintaining of the status quo. It is of shaking, uprising, and revolution. It is not about the preservation of the establishment but its disruption. It involves the coming to power of those who were not in power and the fall from power of those who were. Jehu came to power from outside the throne.

In the election of 2016 Trump rose to power as an outsider to the White House, a disruptor of the establishment and an overturner of the status quo. The dynamics of the election matched the ancient dynamics of Jehu's rise to the throne. Therefore he was victorious.

But in the election of 2020 he ran as an insider. He *was* the president the one who presided over the establishment and the present status quo. The dynamics of that election did not match the dynamics of Jehu's rise to the throne. Therefore he would not prevail.

But in 2024 he came once again as an outsider to the throne, once again as a disruptor of the establishment, and once again as an overturner of the status quo. Thus it again matched the template of Jehu's rising. And therefore he would again prevail and become victorious.

TEMPLATE OF THE SUPPLANTER

Another dynamic related to the campaigns of the American Jehu is that the ancient Jehu begins his rise to power when his adversary is seated on the nation's throne. He comes as the supplanter, taking his adversary's place as king on the throne and undoing his adversary's policies. In the election of 2016 the man who sat in the Oval Office was Trump's adversary, Barack Obama. The dynamics matched that of the ancient template, the rise of the supplanter. Therefore Trump would prevail and succeed Obama as president and undo his policies.

But in the election of 2020 there was no adversary, no other leader occupying the Oval Office. It was Trump himself. He began his race as the nation's leader. Therefore the race was not in accord with the template of Jehu's rising. And thus he would not prevail.

But in the next election he began his race when his adversary, Joe Biden, his opponent in the previous election, occupied the Oval Office. Thus the dynamics were now again in accord with the template of the supplanter. Therefore in the election of 2024 Trump would again prevail, again supplant the nation's ruler, and again undo the works of his predecessor.

TEMPLATE OF THE TWO RULERS

In the template Jehu comes to the throne when the current king is eclipsed by a female leader who bears his mantle.

In the election of 2016 Obama was eclipsed by Clinton, who bore his mantle. The dynamics matched those of

The Mystery of Risings 151

Jehu and Jezebel. Therefore the American Jehu would be victorious.

But in the election of 2020 there was no eclipsed king and no female leader standing in the place of the eclipsed king to contend against a rising Jehu. His adversary was not a woman but Joe Biden, and not a president but an outsider. Therefore it was not in accord with the ancient template. And therefore, Trump would not prevail.

But in the election of 2024 there *was* again an eclipsed king, Joe Biden. And there was again a female leader of the king's house who now bore the mantle of his administration, Kamala Harris. Therefore the dynamics again aligned with the template of Jehu. And therefore, Trump would again prevail.

Thus the ancient template contained, revealed, and explained, if not ordained, the outcome of the presidential elections of 2016, 2020, and 2024.

We have seen the mystery of the American Jehu in his first and second rising. What does it mean? Is it a sign? And if so, then of what?

Chapter 29

THE SIGN OF JEHU

WHAT IS THE meaning of Jehu and his rising? What did it signify for his nation? And could the answer to those two questions reveal the meaning of Donald Trump and the significance of his rising for America? In order to find the answer, we must understand the context, the time and place of Jehu's appearing.

AT THE TIPPING POINT

Israel was called into existence to be a holy nation, to walk in and uphold the ways of God, to be a light to the world. But with that calling came a warning: If the nation ever turned away from and against God and His ways, its blessings would be withdrawn; it would descend into spiritual darkness, decline, and, ultimately, judgment.

By the time Ahab and Jezebel rose to the throne, the nation's fall from God was well underway. But now the national apostasy would plunge to new depths. It was no longer a mere departure from God's way; it was now a war against them, the promotion of other gods and the active persecution, and even murder, of the righteous. By the time of Jehu's ascent, the nation's war against God had encompassed the reigns of no fewer than three kings. An entire generation now knew nothing but apostasy. If there was no change, no turn of the nation's course, there would be no more remedy—only judgment.

152

THE ANSWER TO A FALLEN NATION

Jehu's rise was neither a quirk nor an accident of history. It was an answer. It was, first of all, a response to the prayers and lamentations of a prophet. The name of Jehu first appears in God's response to the prophet Elijah's lamenting his nation's apostasy and fall.[1] The rise of Jehu would be part of God's answer. Thus Jehu was a response to his times, the answer to the fall of a fallen nation. And so the rise of Donald Trump was, as was the rise of Jehu, a response to his times—an answer to the fall of a fallen nation.

THE EXTREME REMEDY

In view of his words, his actions, his nature, his stands, and his ways, many saw Trump as the most extreme of all the occupants of the Oval Office. But his ancient prototype, Jehu, was likewise extreme. One cannot read the account of his rising without noting the extreme nature of his methods and actions.

There is a reason for Jehu's extremity; it was the answer to the extremity of the depth to which his nation had fallen; so with Trump. The extreme nature of Donald Trump was an answer to the extreme nature of America's fall. America had become a nation whose elites could no longer tell the difference between male and female, whose leaders had brazenly championed the killing of millions of unborn children, and whose leading institutions thought it a good idea to surgically remove the organs of children to make them appear as the opposite sex. It had lost its sense of normalcy. As the house of Ahab could see nothing in Jehu but a danger to its status quo, so too the elite of America and the West could see nothing in Donald Trump but the same. And though they could never fathom it, Trump was the response to their fall, the extreme answer to the extremity of a nation's spiritual and moral descent.

THE APOSTASY DISRUPTOR

In the case of ancient Israel, the apostasy had become so ingrained in the nation's perception, institutions, culture, and ways that it could never be dislodged without a massive disruption. Jehu was therefore the nation's agent of disruption. He was the great disruptor to Israel's political establishment, its religious cult, and its cultural status quo. So too in the case of America, the apostasy had become so ingrained in the nation's perceptions, ways, institutions, and culture that it could only be dislodged by a massive disruption. Trump, the American Jehu, was the nation's agent of disruption. He disrupted the nation's political realm, its cultural realm, and the leadership of its elite, the old guard of the American house of Ahab. Trump would overturn the dogmas, the precepts, the mantras, and the sacred cows that had for so long dominated American and Western civilization.

A REDEMPTIVE CHAOS

The American Jehu would be noted for his unique ability to invoke chaos with a single word or act—an agent of chaos.[2] But so too was the ancient Jehu. There was a reason for it. The order by which Israel functioned and lived had become so corrupted that the only hope of remedy would come in disordering it. Chaos was the sign of that disorder.

The Sign of Jehu 155

And yet it possessed a redemptive potential. So too the order by which America in the twenty-first century now lived and functioned had become so spiritually and morally corrupted that the only hope of remedy would involve disordering its order in a redemptive chaos.

THE BATTERING RAM

Jehu was a hammer, an axe, a battering ram. It is no accident that one of his first recorded acts upon entering the nation's capital was the pulling down of Baal's temple.[3] Many of Jehu's day would undoubtedly have viewed it as a reckless act of disruption, disorder, and destruction. But it was the Temple of Baal and its cult that had enabled the sacrificial killing of the nation's children on the altars of its new god. Jehu's destruction of that temple was, therefore, an act of redemption that would save the lives of the innocent. Trump was likewise a blunt instrument, a human hammer, an axe, and a battering ram. He too would set out to pull down the many dwellings of the American house of Ahab and the many American temples of Jezebel.

VESSEL OF JUDGMENT

From the words given to him by the prophet, it cannot be overlooked that Jehu was also called a vessel of judgment. It was not only that his rising would bring judgment and a decisive end to an evil dynasty but that it would constitute a sign to a fallen kingdom, a message and warning given to a kingdom under the judgment of God.

So too Trump was a vessel of judgment. His rising brought reckonings and judgments to the vessels and institutions at war against the ways of God. And yet it was more than that. His rising was a sign to a fallen culture, nation, and civilization under the judgment of God. That a former casino owner, a man not known for piety or godliness but worldliness, could shame a nation over its sins—the killing of its children, the overturning of God's ways and order, and the mutilation of its young—is not a contradiction or an accident. It is a sign of judgment.

And yet the template of Jehu is one of potential, of hope and redemption. We will open that up, as well. But now we begin the uncovering of another realm in the ancient template—one that will give us new and clear revelation concerning the people and events of our time.

PART VIII

THE MYSTERY OF JEHORAM

Chapter 30

THE OTHER KINGDOM

FOR BARACK OBAMA and Hillary Clinton, their primary part in the ancient mystery was in the fulfillment of the templates of King Joram and Jezebel to Trump's Jehu. Obama had been on the national political stage for the same amount of time as Joram, and Clinton, for the same amount of time as Jezebel. But for Joe Biden and Kamala Harris, their fulfillment of the same two templates to Trump's Jehu in his second rising was secondary. They would each play another role in the template, unique to them and primary.

THE OTHER KING

Jehu struck down not one king *but two*. He had only planned on striking down the one, King Joram, but would end up striking down another, King Ahaziah of Judah, the southern of Israel's two kingdoms.[1] Ahaziah, like Joram, was an evil king. He and Joram had formed an alliance. At the time of Jehu's rising Ahaziah was paying Joram a visit, in the wrong place at the wrong time.[2]

TWO KINGDOMS AND TWO RISINGS

So the rise of Jehu would mark the end of two kings, two administrations, and two dynasties, one in the north and the other in the south. The rise of the American Jehu would mark the end of two administrations and two presidencies. The only way for that to happen in the context of

160

THE AVATAR

the American political system would be for Trump to rise twice to the White House.

The mystery now leads us to Israel's southern kingdom, where the template will play out against a different backdrop. Here we will find two other figures, a man and a woman, who will each reveal a mystery of our time.

Chapter 31

JEHORAM THE APOSTATE

HE WAS A relatively obscure king. Most readers of the Bible would be hard-pressed to recall any of his accomplishments if not his very name. But his template will play out in the forty-sixth presidency of the United States.

THE AMERICAN JEHORAM

One was king of the north, and the other, of the south. They both bore the same name. The name appears in Scripture in two forms, *Joram* and *Jehoram*. To avoid confusion, we will continue to refer to the king of the north, the son of Ahab, as *Joram* and will refer to the king of the south as *Jehoram*. The two were contemporaries. They were brothers-in-law. Jehoram had married Joram's sister. Joram reigned in the north before Jehoram reigned in the south and was thus the more experienced of the two and thus more influential in their relationship.[1] Through Joram and his sister, now Jehoram's wife, the ways of the northern kingdom and the house of Ahab would penetrate the south.

It is King Jehoram of Judah that will most centrally contain the mystery of the American president Joe Biden.

THE APOSTATE

Jehoram was raised to know the ways of God. He was born of the house of David, and his father, King Jehoshaphat, was among the most righteous of those who sat on the throne of Judah.[2] And yet Jehoram turned away from the ways of his father and the ways of God.

Under the influence of his wife and brother-in-law, Jehoram was apostatized from God and led his nation to do likewise. So it is written:

> And he walked in the way of the kings
> of Israel, just as the house of Ahab had
> done, for he had the daughter of Ahab
> as a wife; and he did evil in the sight
> of the LORD.[3]

Jehoram's story is one of spiritual weakness, moral compromise, and, ultimately, the total abandonment of the foundations and truths in which he had been raised. Though Jehoram was born of the house of David, he would surrender to the house of Ahab.

THE ABANDONER

So it was for the American Jehoram. Biden's story was likewise one of spiritual weakness, moral compromise, and, ultimately, the abandoning of God's ways. Exemplifying this was his stand on life. At the beginning of his political career he voiced his disagreement with *Roe v. Wade*. He would vote to ban the use of federal funds to subsidize abortion.[4] He would even author legislation banning federal funding of abortion or abortion research overseas.[5] And yet in his rise to the presidency he would give in to the most radical factions and ideologies of his party. The

Jehoram the Apostate

stands he had once taken, he would abandon; the policies he had once championed, he would reverse.[6]

"HE HAD FORSAKEN THE LORD GOD"

Jehoram departed from the God of his father, Jehoshaphat; Biden was raised to believe in the God of Scripture. But though he would profess to be a Christian, his acts and policies would war against biblical values, truths, and practices. What was written of King Jehoram could have been written of Joe Biden; *he had forsaken the Lord God of his fathers.* And what was written of Jehoram as a result could now have been written of Biden—*he did evil in the sight of the Lord.*[7]

Jehoram's apostasy would bring misfortune to his kingdom. His reign would be characterized by defeat, diminishment, and failure. The presidency of Joe Biden would likewise be characterized by defeat, diminishment, and failure—for himself and for his nation. The first major misfortune of Biden's presidency was birthed thousands of years before in the days of King Jehoram.

Chapter 32

THE RETREAT

KING JEHORAM'S FIRST recorded major mistake and disaster would set the stage for the rest. So it would be for Joe Biden—except in the latter case the ramifications would touch the world.

THE EDOM RETREAT

Jehoram's calamity took place in the land of Edom. The Edomites had been conquered by the armies of Israel under the leadership of King David.[1] They were, for years, subject to the kings of Jerusalem. But in the days of Jehoram, they revolted and appointed one of their own as king.[2] Jehoram responded. He launched an attack on the territory of Edom:

> And he got up at night and struck the
> Edomites who had surrounded him
> and the captains of the chariots.[3]

His military campaign ended in catastrophe. Jehoram and his troops were surrounded by the Edomites and in danger of being wiped out. Jehoram had to fight his way out of the trap.

> But his army fled to their tents.[4]

His men fled for their lives in humiliation before their enemies as Judah's long reign over the Edomites came to an end. It was an unmitigated disaster.

The Retreat   165

THE AFGHANISTAN RETREAT

As Jehoram's first defeat involved a hostile people who had come under his nation's dominion, so the first defeat of the American Jehoram, Biden, would likewise involve a foreign land and a hostile people that had come under American dominion. The majority of Edom's descendants would, in later times, become Muslim. So the people and land of Biden's defeat were Muslim. The land of Afghanistan was, for Biden, his land of Edom.

It happened in the first year of his presidency. Biden decided to withdraw the American troops stationed in Afghanistan. He was warned by military advisers that the withdrawal would be catastrophic, bringing America's enemy, the Taliban, back to power. But they reported that Biden appeared "determined to withdraw."[5] The withdrawal was a disaster, with American troops, American citizens, and American allies fleeing in panic and horror before the advance of the Taliban.[6] It was ill-advised, ill-planned, and ill-executed. The situation descended into chaos. The Taliban came into possession of billions of dollars' worth of American military equipment, along with helpless American allies who were now left behind and at the mercy of their enemies.[7]

It would be deemed "the biggest foreign policy disaster since Suez" and "the greatest debacle that NATO has seen since its foundation."[8] Faith in American power and leadership would be shaken, and trust in Biden's competency as president, irreparably damaged. Biden's popular approval plummeted. Though many would not see it at the time, it was the beginning of the end of his presidency.

"HIS ARMY RETREATS IN DEFEAT"

Jehoram lost Edom; Biden lost Afghanistan. As Edom again became, for Israel, enemy territory, so Afghanistan again became enemy territory for America. As Jehoram's troops fled before their enemies, the Edomites, so Americans were now fleeing before their enemies, the Taliban.

Note the words used to describe Biden's calamity and those used in Bible commentaries to describe that of Jehoram:

> Jehoram manages to escape under the cover of night, though his army *retreats in defeat*.[9]

So the news reports on Biden's Afghanistan debacle would use the same words:

> ...the US *defeat* and chaotic *retreat* in Afghanistan.[10]

THE DISASTROUS WITHDRAWAL

Another Bible commentary describes Jehoram's defeat in this way:

> [Jehoram] was forced to *withdraw from the country*, and *to leave* the natives to enjoy that independence.[11]

So too articles describing the first major crisis of Biden's presidency would speak in the same terms:

> President Biden's disastrous *withdrawal* from Afghanistan...[12]

The Retreat 167

The Taliban saw Biden's unconditional *withdrawal* as an invitation to ramp up their offensive.[13]

House Republicans blamed the Biden administration for the chaotic and deadly US *withdrawal* from Afghanistan.[14]

THE GROWING WEAKNESS

Jehoram's humiliating defeat was only the beginning of his problems. It was both a sign of things to come and the trigger that brought about their coming. One Bible commentary on the king's retreat put it this way:

> His army retreats in defeat. This verse highlights the *growing weakness of Judah under Jehoram's leadership* and marks a *significant loss of power for the kingdom*.[15]

In the same way, Biden's disastrous withdrawal would highlight the growing weakness of the United States under Biden's leadership. Compare the words of the Bible commentary with those of a news article written at the time of the Afghanistan retreat:

> The *debacle of the US defeat* and *chaotic retreat* in Afghanistan is a *political disaster* for Joe Biden, whose *failure* to orchestrate an urgent and orderly exit will *further rock a presidency* plagued

by crises and *stain his legacy*.[16]

As it had for Jehoram's kingship, the event would weaken Biden's presidency. But the repercussions of the American retreat would extend far beyond the borders of Afghanistan.

LIBNAH

The Scriptures reveal what happened after King Jehoram's retreat:

> At that time Libnah revolted against his rule, because he had forsaken the LORD God of his fathers.[17]

Seeing the weakness of Jehoram and his army as evidenced by their being routed in Edom, others would rise up to challenge his authority over them. Libnah would be the first. So too Biden's retreat from Afghanistan would produce similar dynamics and repercussions but on a much greater scale, triggering a chain reaction of conflict and calamities around the globe.

THE CHAIN REACTION

One article put it this way:

> More broadly, the *Afghan withdrawal marked the end of credible American deterrence* during the Biden presidency. You can *draw a straight line from the withdrawal* to Vladimir Putin's decision to roll into Ukraine,

The Retreat

or why the Iran-backed Houthis in Yemen aren't afraid to fire missiles at commercial ships in the Red Sea.[18]

A report from the House Foreign Affairs Committee said this:

> *Our adversaries*, like Russia, China, and Iran, *saw weakness* during *the chaotic and deadly evacuation, emboldening them.* Less than one year later, Russia launched a full invasion of Ukraine....And China continues to ratchet up aggression in the Indo-Pacific, including against Taiwan and the Philippines.[19]

And another:

> It Started in Afghanistan: *The Disastrous American Withdrawal* from Kabul *Triggered a Wave of Instability the World Over*[20]
>
> It's evident that *within weeks* of the August 20, 2021, *withdrawal*, Vladimir Putin began amassing troops on the Ukrainian border.[21]

WORLD IN FLAMES

The ramifications of Biden's disastrous retreat in the political and geopolitical realms cannot be overstated. One article put it this way:

170   THE AVATAR

> *Four years of Biden have left the world in flames*: Afghanistan, the Middle East, Ukraine: the US president's blunders have made us all less safe.[22]

The following is one Bible commentator's description of Jehoram's retreat from Edom. It was not a

> victory of Jehoram's, but his *desperate escape*.[23]

Now compare the description of Jehoram's withdrawal from Edom with a modern analysis of Biden's withdrawal from Afghanistan. Note the use of the same exact expression, and note as well what it leads to:

> The *desperate escape* of the Afghans from Kabul is a strategic misstep which *signifies the end of US global hegemony*.[24]

In this the playing out of the ancient template carries ramifications for the entire world.

We now move to what became a defining issue of Biden's presidency and that which would play a part in bringing it to an end. This too appears in the ancient biblical template.

Chapter 33

THE BREACHABLE KINGDOM

JEHORAM'S LEADERSHIP WOULD invoke conflict not only in enemy lands but in his own.

THE ANCIENT INCURSIONS

In the reign of King Jehoram, foreign peoples living just beyond the borders of his kingdom crossed over those borders to infiltrate the land.[1] From the extent of their penetration as evidenced by a hostile incursion recorded in Scripture, it appears that Jehoram did little or nothing to stop it. He was either unable or unwilling. As a result, the incursion of foreigners would reach as far as the nation's capital, Jerusalem.[2]

THE MODERN INCURSIONS

As in the ancient template, the Biden presidency would be marked not only by retreat in a foreign land, but by incursion in his own. As with Jehoram, so with Biden. The issue of foreign peoples crossing over the nation's borders would define his days in power. During the Biden years the number of illegal immigrants crossing the nation's borders reached unprecedented levels. Millions were now illegally entering the land.[3] Many were stunned by the president's lack of response while millions crossed the nation's southern border.

HUMAN TRAFFICKING ANCIENT AND MODERN

But those who crossed the borders of Jehoram's kingdom did not do so simply to get in. They came to take the kingdom's riches, its goods, and its people. They took captives. We know from other scriptures that they profited from their captives. Today, it would be called *human trafficking*.

So too in the days of the American Jehoram, the crossing of borders would lead to an explosion in human trafficking. In one study it was found that about 60 percent of Latin American children who set out to cross the border alone or with smugglers would be forced by their smugglers or by those who had likewise crossed the border into the sex trade, child pornography, or drug trafficking.[4]

A GROWING DISCONTENT

So the days of Jehoram's kingship were of retreat, defeat, weakness, the crossing of borders, and human trafficking. So too were the days of Biden. The biblical account implies that Jehoram's rule provoked a growing discontent among his people. So too Americans would grow increasingly discontent with the presidency of the American Jehoram.

But the ancient template would manifest even more specifically in an event that would unfold thousands of miles across the world.

Chapter 34

THE ARABIAN–PHILISTINE INVASION

AFTER JEHORAM'S RETREAT from Edom and the subsequent rebellion of Libnah, the nation's enemies saw in Jehoram's weakness their opportunity to strike. So they invaded the land.[1] The attack would alter the kingdom's history and would leave a lasting trauma on the house of Jehoram.

THE INVASION

As the ancient invaders raided the land of Israel, is it possible that one of the template's manifestations would be a modern invasion into the land of Israel? And if so, could that invasion take place in the reign of the modern Jehoram, President Biden? It could and it did. In the third year of Biden's presidency the land of Israel was invaded. The event would constitute the worst day in Jewish history since the Holocaust.

THE KING'S WEAKNESS

It was the perception of Jehoram's weakness in the wake of his disastrous retreat from Edom that invited the invasion of Israel's enemies. So it was believed by many geopolitical analysts that the perception of Biden's weakness encouraged Hamas to invade Israel on October 7, 2023.[2]

174　　　　　　　　　　　　　　　　　THE AVATAR

Believing there would be no strong American response or massive repercussions, they invaded the land.

THE ARABIANS

Who was behind the invasion of Israel in the days of Jehoram? The Bible identifies them. They were the Arabians and the Philistines.[3] Could then the modern-day invasion be fulfilled by the modern counterparts of the ancient invaders?

What people would now correspond to the Arabians of Jehoram's day? *Arabian* is another way of saying *Arab*. And so in accord with the template, those who launched the October 7 invasion were the modern equivalents to the Arabians of Jehoram's day—Arabs.

THE PHILISTINES

The other ancient invaders were the Philistines. The Philistines were ancient Israel's archenemies. Is there any people group in the modern world who correspond to the ancient Philistines? There is. They even call themselves by the same name.

They are known today as the *Palestinians*. The word *Palestinian* means *Philistine*.[4] In the language of the Palestinians, the word *Palestinian* is pronounced "Filastini" or "Filastin."[5] As I shared in *The Dragon's Prophecy*, they constitute the modern-day resurrection of the ancient Philistines.

So it was in the reign of the ancient Jehoram that an invasion was launched against the nation of Israel by the

The Arabian–Philistine Invasion   175

modern-world counterparts of the Arabians and Philistines in the presidency of the modern-day Jehoram.

THE GAZAN CAPTIVES

From where did the ancient invasion begin? The Philistines would have launched their attack from the region known as *Philistia*. Today Philistia has a different name—the *Gaza Strip*. So the invasion began in the Gaza Strip, the land of the Philistines. The ancient invaders took Israelite civilians as captives back to Philistia. So the modern-day invaders took Israeli civilians as captives back to the Gaza Strip, modern-day Philistia.[6] As Jehoram was helpless in bringing the captives home, Biden appeared equally helpless.

The weakening of King Jehoram would lead to the end of his reign. It all began with the gods.

Chapter 35

JEHORAM AND THE GODS

IN FOLLOWING THE ways of the house of Ahab, Jehoram was worshipping and serving the gods of that house. And so the gods infiltrated the southern kingdom, even Jerusalem itself, the Holy City.

THE HIGH PLACES OF KING JEHORAM

Jehoram's apostasy would not stop with his falling away from the faith and ways of his fathers. We will now see how he went from an apostate to a zealot on behalf of the gods. He would now attempt to lead his nation into the same transition he himself had undergone, away from God and into the worship of the gods and goddesses of the pagan world. So the Bible records that Jehoram

> made high places in the mountains of Judah.[1]

The *high places* comprised the mountains and hilltops on which pagan worshippers would typically build shrines, altars, and sanctuaries to the worship of their gods. Now Jehoram himself was building them on the mountains and hills of the Holy Land.[2]

The idols of the pagan world were the antithesis to the worship of God. If one could mold and fabricate one's god, one could mold and fabricate one's own truth, one's own morality, one's own reality. Jehoram was thus promoting an ideology that exchanged God for the gods, the truth for

Jehoram and the Gods 177

truths, the absolute for the relative, and objective reality for subjective and alternate realities, one's own god, one's own truth.

THE HIGH PLACES OF THE AMERICAN JEHORAM

We don't know when the American Jehoram transitioned away from God and His ways to a subjective and bendable morality more indicative of paganism. It undoubtedly happened in increments. But by the time Biden came to the White House, he had thoroughly embraced the proposition that one could bend age-old standards, absolutes, and realities. And though he would never use such terms as *gods*, *idols*, or *paganism*, he, nevertheless, championed their agenda.

As did King Jehoram, Biden would work to undermine biblical absolutes and traditional morality. He would ally himself with the ideologies and movements of wokeism and advocate for the alteration of biblical values. He was, in effect, erecting new altars and fashioning new sacred cows on the high places of American culture. Once fashioned and erected, he demanded that they be followed, revered, and bowed down to.

CHAMPION OF THE GODS

It was not only that Jehoram had fallen away from the ways of God but that he now actively contended on behalf of the gods. He was more than an apostate; he was now actively contending for the gods and enforcing their agenda.

The same could be said of the American Jehoram. He not only abandoned his original views against *Roe v. Wade*

178

and the federal funding of abortion, but now he vowed to strike down the Hyde Amendment, which banned the federal funding of abortion, and to sign legislation to make abortion the law of the land.[3] Further, he would weaponize the Department of Justice to wage war against those who upheld the sanctity of life.[4] He would thus become a zealous servant on behalf of the gods of child sacrifice.

JEHORAM AND THE GODDESS

King Jehoram would have also worshipped on the high places of Ashtarte, or Ishtar, goddess of sexuality and the bending of gender. How Jehoram, raised in the knowledge of God, could have embraced such things is stunning. And yet the American Jehoram underwent the same transition.

Before his rise to the White House, Biden had made it clear that marriage could only be defined as the union of a man and woman. But now he would make transgenderism, the physical alteration of gender and identity, a central priority of his presidency.[5] So passionate was Biden's embrace of radical transgender ideology that his administration would work to strike down state restrictions against the sexual transitioning of children.[6]

"HE COMPELLED THEM"

The ancient chronicler records that Jehoram "caused the inhabitants of Jerusalem to go after other gods, and led Judah astray."[7] Not content with his own apostasy, Jehoram made apostasy his national agenda. Behind the phrase "and led Judah astray" is something much stronger. The original word used in the account is the Hebrew *nadach*.

Jehoram and the Gods 179

It can be more literally translated as *he drove Judah away*, or *he compelled them to go astray*. Of Jehoram's championing of the gods, one Bible commentary writes,

> The people were not only allowed,
> *but compelled to take part in the new*
> *rites.*[8]

Jehoram thus forced the worship of other gods upon his people.

ENFORCER OF THE GODS

So too the American Jehoram would not only allow for apostasy but would seek to compel it. He would seek to force American schools to merge genders in competitive sports, that young men would compete against young women.[9] He would seek to force hospitals, particularly religious-based hospitals, to perform abortions and gender-mutilation surgeries against their will, their conscience, and their faith.[10]

We will now open one of the most striking cases of the American Jehoram's war against biblical values and his attempt to compel the nation's apostasy—and yet, as we will see, God would have the last word.

Chapter 36

THE TWENTIETH DAY OF KISLEV

Unlike the apostasy in the northern kingdom, Jehoram's apostasy would involve the desecration of Jerusalem and the Temple of God, the Holy City and the most holy of grounds and vessels. So the American Jehoram, Joe Biden, would likewise take part in the desecration of a most holy vessel—the covenant of marriage.

DAY OF THE RAINBOW

As late as 2006 Biden publicly declared that "marriage is between a man and a woman and states must respect that."[1] But as did King Jehoram, Biden would end up warring against the things he had once upheld. In December of 2022, in an outdoor ceremony on the South Lawn of the White House, amidst great celebration, drag queens, and rainbow flags, Biden signed the Respect for Marriage Act.[2] It was the exact opposite of its name and of what Biden had publicly proclaimed. Marriage was *no* longer to be defined as the union of a man and a woman. Further, every state in America would now be forced to *respect that it was not*. The nation was now to be compelled to accept that which warred against the ways of God.

THE ENSHRINEMENT

And though a religious exemption clause was included in order to ensure the bill's passage through Congress, religious liberty analysts warned that it was little more than

The Twentieth Day of Kislev 181

window dressing.[3] And as far as individuals were concerned, the religious convictions and liberty of Christians and those who upheld the biblical and traditional definition of marriage were now placed in danger. With the stroke of his pen, Biden enshrined same-sex marriage into federal law. The word *enshrined* is, of course, derived from the word *shrine*. Jehoram set up *shrines* on the high places of his kingdom. So the American Jehoram was now setting up a shrine on the high places of American culture, before which all were to bow down.

EZRA'S REBUKE

There is only one place in the Bible where marriage became the means of a mass rebellion against the ways of God. It happened in the days of Ezra when the people of Israel began mixing and merging with the surrounding pagan peoples and thus with the ways of paganism. The merging was sealed with the marriage of Israelite men with pagan women. When Ezra heard what had happened, he called for an assembly in the capital city. There Ezra exposed the marriages they had forged in transgression. The people repented. It took place in

> *the ninth month, on the twentieth of the month.*[4]

The ninth month of the Hebrew year is Kislev. So the twentieth of Kislev became the day when, in the capital city, God exposed the marriages born of rebellion and defiance.

THE TWENTIETH DAY OF KISLEV

To seal what he had done, the American Jehoram had the White House lit up in the colors of the rainbow. The rainbow, as we have seen, was one of the signs connected to Ishtar, the goddess who bent and transformed gender. It was the night of the gathering, December 13, 2022.[5] But on the Hebrew calendar it was *the twentieth day of the month of Kislev*—the very day specified in the Book of Ezra. The American Jehoram had sanctified and enshrined marriages formed in defiance of God's will on the very day when God judged the marriages formed in defiance of His will. So the American Jehoram had signed into law the Respect for Marriage Act on the ancient day that specifically identified the marriages forged in rebellion and defiance of God's will—the marriages God could never respect. As with the desecrations of the ancient Jehoram, God would have the last word.

We will now see how the ancient mystery touches not only the public acts of the American Jehoram—but his personal life.

Chapter 37

THE MYSTERY OF AHAZIAH

THE MYSTERY WILL now take us from the public square and into the house of King Jehoram and the personal life of Joe Biden.

THE KING'S TRAGEDY

King Jehoram would suffer a massive tragedy in his personal life. It happened during the attack of the Philistines and Arabians. According to 2 Chronicles 21, the enemy "carried away all the possessions that were found in the king's house, *and also his sons and his wives.*"[1] In a single tragic act his family was taken from him. He would never see them again.

Could the ancient template contain any connection to Joe Biden and his personal life? Biden is unique in modern presidential history in that he suffered a massive tragedy early in his political career. His first wife, his daughter, and his two sons were involved in a car crash. His wife and his daughter would not survive the accident. His two sons, Beau and Hunter, would be hospitalized but would survive.[2] As it was for King Jehoram, in a single act, Biden's first family was taken from him.

THE YOUNGEST SON

But King Jehoram did not lose every member of his family in the invasion. His preeminent wife, the daughter of Ahab

183

184 THE AVATAR

and Jezebel, remained in the palace. So did one son. The account notes,

> Not a son was left to him except Ahaziah, the youngest.[3]

At the end of his reign King Jehoram had only one son left, one royal heir, Ahaziah. So it was that by the time Biden became president, as it was for Jehoram, it was for him: *There was not a son left to him except one.* His name was *Hunter.* According to the Scripture, Ahaziah was "the youngest of his sons."[4] So the American Jehoram was left with one son, Hunter, likewise *the youngest of his sons.*[5]

TO HIS DESTRUCTION

According to the account in 2 Chronicles, Ahaziah did not follow the ways of righteousness but "did evil in the sight of the LORD."[6] Hunter Biden would likewise not be known for his virtue or moral integrity but rather for his proclivity for drugs, prostitutes, and scandal.[7] Of Ahaziah it was written that his path and counselors would lead him "to his destruction."[8] So too the actions, decisions, and ways of Hunter Biden would tend toward self-destruction.

AHAZIAH AND HUNTER

In Hebrew the word meaning *to seize* is *ahaz.* *Ahaz* is the root word from which comes the name *Ahaziah.* So the name of the last surviving and youngest of Jehoram's sons comes from the Hebrew root word meaning to seize.

The Old English word for *to seize* is *hentan.* Connected to the root word *hentan* is the name Hunter.

The Mystery of Ahaziah 185

So though the one name came from the Middle East and the other from Europe, the last-born and last-surviving son of the ancient Jehoram, Ahaziah, and the last-born and last-surviving son of the modern Jehoram, Hunter, would each bear the name with the exact same meaning as the other—*to seize.*

———————

And now we come to the mystery of Biden's end—a mystery hidden in the end of King Jehoram.

Chapter 38

JEHORAM THE FEEBLE

IN THE MIDST of his reign Jehoram would receive a letter containing a prophetic message and last word on his kingship. It said,

> Because you…have walked in the way of the kings of Israel and have enticed Judah and the inhabitants of Jerusalem into whoredom…you yourself will have a severe sickness.[1]

The prophecy would come to pass. The king's physical well-being, his health, and his infirmity would become an unavoidable issue in the last years of his reign.

THE KING'S INFIRMITY

As Jehoram's infirmity would become increasingly evident in the last two years of his kingship, so too the American Jehoram's. The president's physical well-being, his health, and his infirmity would increasingly become the central issue surrounding the last years of his presidency. Though the concerns were there early on, it was in the latter part of his presidency that the issue would become unavoidable.

It would appear that King Jehoram's infirmity came upon him with relative suddenness. In the case of Biden, his infirmity was related to his age. But the end result was the same. How Jehoram was able to reign while suffering from such a debilitating condition is not known. The

Jehoram the Feeble 187

functions of the throne most likely fell increasingly on others. So too it was reported that the functions of Biden's presidency would increasingly fall on others.[2]

THE WEAKENED KING AND KINGDOM

The weakness of Jehoram's physical condition mirrored that of his moral and spiritual condition. This would, in turn, weaken his kingdom and embolden its enemies to rise up in defiance. The dynamic relationship does not escape the commentaries. One states,

> By compromising with the evil rulers of Israel, Jehoram displeased the Lord and *weakened the nation*.[3]

And another,

> *The perceived weakness* of...Jehoram prompts Edom in the southeast and Libnah in the west to rebel.[4]

So of the American Jehoram it was written,

> His critics charge he has *diminished US power* in a crucial region, and *weakened American global leadership* in the process.[5]

THE ENFEEBLED

A striking word is used in the commentaries to characterize the kingship and kingdom of Jehoram:

> Judah, divided and *enfeebled*, and

188

THE AVATAR

under the rule of a Jehoram, could not
withstand their onset.[6]

The days of Jehoram are characterized by the word
enfeebled. His kingship tended toward enfeeblement,
and in the latter part of his reign it would manifest in
the enfeeblement of his physical being. He would thus
become the feeble king of a feeble kingdom. The word
feeble is defined as

> lacking physical strength, especially as
> a result of age or illness;[7]

> lacking in physical or mental strength;
> frail; weak;[8]

> deficient in qualities or resources
> that indicate vigor, authority, force, or
> efficiency.[9]

Each one of these definitions describes the presidency
of the American Jehoram. They describe as well the state
of the man himself, the increasing signs of his enfeebled
mental and physical condition that came to the fore in the
latter part of his presidency. It was in those days that an
op-ed writer for the left-leaning *New York Times* wrote:

> What a degrading finale for Biden's
> *feeble, forgettable, and frequently
> foolish presidency.*[10]

Jehoram the Feeble 189

THE END

There would be no healing for Jehoram's infirmity. It would ultimately bring to an end his reign and his life. So too in the last months of Biden's presidency the issue of his physical infirmity and growing enfeeblement elicited increasing calls that he bring his campaign for reelection to an end. He would resist them until it became impossible. Finally, on July 21, 2024, he announced that he was bringing his campaign and thus his presidential and political career to an end.[11] As it was physical infirmity that brought an end to King Jehoram's kingship, it was physical infirmity that would bring an end to Biden's presidency.

TO NO ONE'S SORROW

Of King Jehoram's demise the Scriptures record:

> And his people made no burning for him, like the burning for his fathers.... He reigned in Jerusalem...and, to no one's sorrow, departed.[12]

In other words, Jehoram's people would not even perform the rites and rituals traditionally performed in honor of the deceased. *He departed to no one's sorrow.* His people did not mourn his passing. They did not weep and were not sorry to see him go. He would not even be afforded a burial in the tombs of the kings.[13]

So it was for the American Jehoram. By the time of Biden's political death his own party was relieved and even rejoiced to see him go. No one mourned his departure. As

was true for the ancient Jehoram, so it was for the modern—
he departed to no one's sorrow.

It was not long after the passing of Jehoram that another
would rise to the throne, a rising that would defy all
precedent and bring the kingdom of Judah the closest it
would ever come to the reign of Jezebel.

PART IX

THE MYSTERY OF ATHALIAH

Chapter 39

JEZEBEL'S DAUGHTER

JEZEBEL HAD A daughter. She would walk in her mother's footsteps.[1]

ATHALIAH

In the second rise to power of Donald Trump's Jehu, Kamala Harris would fulfill the role as his adversary, Jezebel. But for Harris the role was secondary. As with Biden she would fulfill another role in the mystery, a role exclusive to her and primary. What was it?

It was Jezebel's daughter—*Athaliah*. It is because Jezebel and her daughter were so similar that Harris could fulfill both roles—but her primary and unique role in the mystery was that of Athaliah.

AT THE KING'S SIDE

The bond of Athaliah and Jezebel extended beyond that of blood. Each would function as the number-two regent of her land, Jezebel of the northern kingdom and Athaliah of the southern.[2] So both Clinton and Harris would serve as the number-two leader in America—Clinton as the other half of what many viewed as the Clinton copresidency and Harris as vice president to Joe Biden. Both Jezebel and Athaliah operated in the royal palaces of their kingdoms and greatly influenced the kings of those palaces. So both Clinton and Harris operated in the White House and greatly influenced the presidents who governed in that house.

THE OVERTURNERS

Both Jezebel and Athaliah would for a time lead in the shadow of their partners and then would stand on their own as the chief standard-bearer of the house of Ahab. So too both Clinton and Harris would for a time lead in the shadow of their political partners, Barack Obama and Joe Biden. After that both would stand for a moment as the standard-bearers of the ideological and political Left, the Democratic Party; of the American house of Ahab; and of their former political partners. Both Jezebel and Athaliah stood at the helm of an agenda that would actively seek to overturn and nullify their nation's traditional and biblical values. So both Clinton and Harris stood at the helm of an agenda that actively sought to overturn and nullify America's traditional and biblical values.

LADIES OF THE GODDESS

Athaliah, through Jezebel, was born of a culture that worshipped goddesses along with gods, especially Ashtarte, or Ishtar, the goddess who defied male authority and the patriarchy of the gods. To worship the goddess was to venerate female power. Both Jezebel and Athaliah would, by their acts and nature, embody that spirit.

So Hillary Clinton, in her rise to power, became the most prominent advocate and embodiment of American feminism and female power. As Athaliah followed in the footsteps of her mother, Jezebel, so Kamala Harris, in her rise to power, would follow in the footsteps of Hillary Clinton and would, as had her predecessor, become, in her

Jezebel's Daughter

time in the national spotlight, the foremost embodiment of American feminism and female power.

THE PASSING OF THE TORCH

Athaliah would take up her mother's torch and expand her mother's agenda into new realms. So Kamala Harris would take up the torch of Hillary Clinton and expand her agenda. As Athaliah was Jezebel's daughter, Harris was Clinton's political daughter. Thus it was no accident that when Clinton publicly endorsed Harris at the Democratic National Convention,[3] the headlines read:

> Hillary Clinton Passes the Torch to Kamala
> Harris at DNC[4]

It *was* indeed the passing of the torch, on one hand, from one Jezebel to the other, and, beyond that, from the American Jezebel to her political, ideological, and spiritual daughter, the American Athaliah.

———

Could the origins of Athaliah hold the key to the origins of Kamala Harris?

Chapter 40

CITY ON THE SEA

THE ROOTS OF Athaliah's worship and belief system went back to the Phoenician city of Tyre.

THE TYRIAN MATRIX

Tyre was located on the sea. So the roots of the American Athaliah, Kamala Harris, were likewise centered on a city by the sea. Tyre was located on Phoenicia's western shore, to the north of Israel's western shore. So too Harris's roots were to be found on America's western shore and to the north. As the daughter of Jezebel, Athaliah would have been inculcated in the religious beliefs and practices of Tyre.

Tyre was a city of pagan gods, pagan practices, and pagan values in conflict with and hostile to the values and ways of Israel. Athaliah's origins would determine her agenda. So too Harris's origins would determine her agenda. She came from a region especially known for its leftist and radical views and values: San Francisco, Oakland, and Berkeley.[1] San Francisco was, of course, central in the LGBT movement and agenda. As Tyre had molded the agenda of Athaliah, San Francisco and its surroundings would mold the agenda of Kamala Harris.[2]

BROTHER AND SISTER

Athaliah and Joram were brother and sister, the children of Ahab and Jezebel. With Obama as the American Joram and Harris linked to Athaliah, we might expect there to be

196

City on the Sea   197

a connection between the two. The childhoods of Harris and Obama would hold much in common. Both were born in the first half of the 1960s, three years apart. Each came from a multiracial marriage. Both their fathers were born outside America and would leave them when each was a child.[3] Each would then be raised largely by their mother.[4] And in their adulthood their two paths would converge.

It was in 2004, just as Obama was about to step onto the national stage to begin his rise to the White House, that he met Kamala Harris. Later, when Obama announced his run for the presidency to a crowd in Springfield, Illinois, within the crowd was Harris. Harris would assist Obama in his run for the White House and serve as his California campaign cochair. They would each endorse the other in their campaigns for public office. Harris would, in fact, be called "the female Barack Obama."[5]

A HOUSE OF FOREIGN GODS

Athaliah's mother, Jezebel, was born of a foreign land given to the worship of gods and goddesses. After relocating to her husband's land, she would continue practicing the pagan rites to the gods of her native land. She would undoubtedly do so in the palace and before her children. Kamala Harris's mother was likewise born of a foreign land given to the worship of gods and goddesses, India.[6] As Athaliah was raised in the knowledge of the Phoenician gods, Harris was raised in the knowledge of the Hindu gods and, as a child, would frequently travel to India, where she would take part in the rites and celebrations of the Hindu gods.[7]

DAUGHTER OF THE PRIESTS

Athaliah, through her mother, Jezebel, was born of the line of Ethbaal, king of Tyre. The ancient historian Josephus records that Ethbaal was also the priest of Ashtarte/Ishtar. Athaliah was thus born of the priestly line of pagan gods and worship. Could, then, Kamala Harris likewise be connected to a priestly line? The answer is yes. Harris was born of the priestly caste of Hinduism.[8] So as the ancient Athaliah was born of the priesthood of the Phoenician gods, the American Athaliah was born of the priesthood of Indian gods—both of the priestly house of pagan gods.

Had Athaliah only been a princess in the house of Ahab, history would have taken little note of her. But events would transpire to change the trajectory of her life and catapult her into a nation's spotlight. So too it would be for Kamala Harris.

Chapter 41

ATHALIAH AND JEHORAM

As had her mother, Jezebel, Athaliah would accomplish her ends in partnership with another. Together, they would form an unholy duo.

A POLITICAL UNION

When the Phoenician princess Jezebel journeyed to Israel to marry Ahab, son of King Omri, it was undoubtedly for the purpose of strengthening the alliance between their two nations. So too and for the same purpose, her daughter would journey to the southern kingdom of Judah to marry Jehoram, son of King Jehoshaphat. So the marriage of Jehoram and Athaliah would have been one of many marriages arranged by neighboring kingdoms, forged for political and geopolitical considerations, a political union for the binding together of kingdoms. The American Athaliah and the American Jehoram would likewise be joined together. Joe Biden would enter into a political marriage with Kamala Harris, as Biden chose Harris as his vice presidential running mate in his campaign for the White House. It was likewise a marriage based on political considerations, a political union.

QUEEN OF JUDAH

Jezebel's daughter was now suddenly catapulted to a place of power she could have hardly dreamed of attaining. Athaliah was now queen of the kingdom of Judah. As with her mother, she would not be content in a domestic role in the king's house. She would play an active political role in her husband's administration. As Jezebel had done in the northern kingdom, Athaliah would attempt to do in the south. While Jehoram was the number-one ruler in the land, Athaliah would function as the de facto number two. The impact of her taking on that position would alter the course of her adopted nation.[1]

SECOND TO THE THRONE

Many would see the American Athaliah as ill-prepared and ill-equipped for the position the American Jehoram had chosen her for. As was Athaliah, Harris was suddenly catapulted to the heights of national power. Athaliah would end up exceeding the role given to Jezebel. So Harris, as the nation's first female vice president, would exceed the role given to Hillary Clinton. As was Athaliah, Harris was now the number-two leader of the land.

THE MORE RADICAL

The Scriptures make it clear that it was Athaliah whose influence was most critical in causing Jehoram to sin against the Lord and cause his nation to do likewise.[2] Athaliah was of a more radical nature than Jehoram. So too Harris was of a more radical nature than Biden. As Athaliah represented the house of Ahab to Jehoram, so Harris represented the radical left wing of the Democratic Party. Her elevation to the White House would represent the mainstreaming of a radical leftist and, in effect, antibiblical agenda.

Athaliah and Jehoram

THE JUDEAN MARRIAGE

There would be another manifestation of the ancient template. In marrying Jehoram, Athaliah was joining herself to the nation and people of Judah. It is worthy of note that Harris married Doug Emhoff. Emhoff was Jewish.[3] The word *Jew*, or, in Hebrew, *Yehudi*, means one born of the nation of Judah. Athaliah's husband was born of the nation of Judah. So Harris's husband was likewise born of the nation of Judah. The American Athaliah joined herself through marriage to the people of Judah just as the ancient Athaliah had done thousands of years before.

Could Athaliah's influence over Jehoram to the altering of the nation's course give us insight into what happened to America in the years of Biden's presidency?

Chapter 42

DAUGHTER OF THE GODS

MORE THAN QUEEN or ruler, Jezebel was a zealot, a devotee, a fanatic. She would serve as an agent of the gods of Phoenicia. So too would her daughter.

ATHALIAH IN THE COURTS OF BAAL

Athaliah was now the prominent member of her husband's government to zealously champion the worship of Baal. It was undoubtedly her influence that caused temples and shrines of Baal to be built in Jehoram's kingdom, upon which the sacrifice of children would be performed.

So too the American Athaliah would become the most prominent member of the Biden administration to zealously champion the killing of the unborn.[1] As Baal worship would have been preeminent in the agenda of Athaliah, abortion was preeminent in Harris's agenda. Her rise to the vice presidency coincided with the radicalization of Biden's stand on abortion.

There can be no doubt that Queen Athaliah would have entered the temples and shrines of Baal and worshipped at the altars on which the children's blood had been shed.[2] So too the American Athaliah would enter the American courts of Baal. Harris would become the first vice president in American history to walk through the doors of an abortion clinic. As her ancient prototype would have done, she went there to legitimize, promote, and hallow the altars on which the blood of children had been shed.[3]

DAUGHTER OF THE GODDESS

Athaliah would have also advocated for the goddesses of the Phoenician pantheon, the worship of female power, and the altering of sexuality and gender. So Harris's followers would boast that she worked with Biden to promote the Respect for Marriage Act to enshrine same-sex marriage into federal law.[4] So too Harris was known for radical championing of surgical gender transitioning even for prisoners and those supported by government funding.[5] And as Athaliah would have undoubtedly joined in the worship and rites of the goddess Ashtarte, which included processions and parades celebrating the bending and confusion of gender, so the American Athaliah would become the first vice president in the nation's history to take part in an LGBT Pride parade in celebration of the bending and confusion of gender.[6]

THE MERCILESS WARRIOR

As did her mother, Athaliah would take part with Jehoram in an all-out war against the people and ways of God. The American Athaliah would likewise take part in a merciless war against the people of God and those who upheld His ways. The war would involve federal agents raiding the home of a pro-life father with pointed guns and apprehending him in front of his horrified family.[7] It would involve the arrest of pro-life grandmothers for their peaceful resistance against the killing of the unborn. The government would then seek to sentence them to years in prison.[8] At the same time, when pro-life churches and ministries were vandalized, the administration would do next to nothing to protect them or to prosecute their attackers.[9]

But the marriage of Athaliah and Jehoram would come to an end. Its ending would lead to an era that had no precedent in the kingdom of Judah. Those events and that chapter of the nation's history would contain an ominous warning concerning America's future.

Chapter 43

KING ATHALIAH

THE END OF King Jehoram's reign would set in motion a train of events that would lead to a reign of terror.

ON HER OWN

For a brief moment the king's son would ascend the throne. He would do "evil in the sight of the LORD, like the house of Ahab."[1] The Scriptures tell us why:

> He also walked in the ways of the house of Ahab, *for his mother advised him to do wickedly.*[2]

As Athaliah had influenced her husband to do evil, she would now influence the royal heir. But his reign would be fleeting. Before the year was out, he would be gone, slain by Jehu upon his visit to the northern kingdom.[3] That would leave Athaliah in a precarious situation, like that of her mother, Jezebel, when Jehu rose to the throne.

TO RULE THE LAND

But unlike Jezebel, Athaliah acted swiftly to seize the moment. She would take the throne for herself. She who had functioned as the nation's number-two monarch would now crown herself lord of the kingdom. The ancient template would ordain that when the days of Jehoram came to an end, Athaliah would vie to sit on the throne as ruler of the land.[4] So after the political death of the American

Jehoram, Joe Biden, the American Athaliah, Kamala Harris, vied to become the ruler of the land, America's new president.[5]

BLOOD IN THE PALACE

Athaliah was born of a blood-drenched culture and family. Beyond the practice of child sacrifice her family had a history of murder. Her grandfather had come to the throne by murdering the preceding king.[6] Her mother had maintained her power by shedding the blood of those she saw as standing in her way. And her husband, perhaps influenced by her counsel, killed all his brothers to secure his throne.[7] Now she would apply her family tradition to secure her own claim to the throne. And so as the Scriptures record, Athaliah "arose and destroyed all the royal heirs."[8] Behind those few words was a scene of almost unimaginable evil and horror. Athaliah was a grandmother. She was now murdering her own grandchildren and presumably her nephews, grandnephews, and their cousins—all the royal heirs. She saw them not as her children but as rivals and threats to her power. The reign of Athaliah would thus begin with a river of blood flowing from her own house.

AGAINST THE CHILDREN

As Athaliah rose to the throne on the blood of innocent children, so did Harris. Her ascent to power was supported by the enthusiastic backing and funding of the nation's foremost abortion organization, Planned Parenthood.[9] And in her attempt to become president, she would make the killing of unborn children the clearest and most salient

King Athaliah

issue of her campaign.[10] She would become the most brazenly and zealously proabortion presidential candidate of any major party in American history. The convention that nominated her for the presidency was the most radical in the history of the Democratic Party. It vowed to strike down the Hyde Amendment so that taxpayer funds could go directly to funding the killing of the unborn and to make abortion the law of the land with virtually every restraint removed.[11]

The American Athaliah would seek to avoid saying it out loud, but her agenda embraced the killing of unborn children up to the moment of birth. And true to the spirit and nature of her ancient predecessors, Harris vowed that with regard to abortion, she would remove all religious exemptions.[12] If she became president, she would force Christian hospitals to kill unborn children against their will, their conscience, and their God.

GIFTS TO THE GODS

It was no accident that her running mate, Tim Walz, was the one who accompanied her when she became the first vice president to walk through the doors of the abortion clinic.[13] In fact, it was that event that laid the foundation for the Harris–Walz ticket. It all began in an abortion clinic. It all began with Baal. Beyond that Walz was the first governor to enshrine abortion into state law after the striking down of *Roe v. Wade*.[14] The law removed the requirement of doctors to save the life of a child born alive.[15] Though Walz and his allies sought to deny it, it allowed for the killing of children born alive. In this he was perfectly

208 THE AVATAR

aligned with the American Athaliah, who, when presented with a bill to save the life of a child born in a failed abortion attempt, voted against it.[16] In the rise of the American Athaliah and her partner, the killing of the unborn *and the born*, practices of the pagan world, and gifts to the gods were again in play.

Athaliah's war against the children was unprecedented. So too was the war waged by the American Athaliah and her party against the nation's children. And so it was no accident that a modern-day altar was erected outside the convention that nominated her to the presidency, an altar for sacrificed children.

Chapter 44

JEHOSHEBA

I F ANYONE HAD any doubt as to what Kamala Harris's campaign was all about, that which took place in the shadow of the convention that nominated her to run for the presidency would make it unmistakably clear.

ALTARS AT THE CONVENTION

While Harris was being nominated for the presidency at the Democratic National Convention, outside the convention hall children were actually being killed. It was another unprecedented occurrence in American history. A mobile unit was set up in conjunction with the convention for the purpose of performing abortions;[1] Athaliah's rise to power was accompanied by the killing of children. So the attempted rise to power of the American Athaliah was accompanied by the same.

BREAKING INTO THE HOUSE OF GOD

For those who followed the ways of God, the possibility of Athaliah becoming ruler of the land was a terrifying prospect. If she gained the throne, she would then be able to act with unrestrained powers to carry out her agenda. So too for the American believers who sought to follow the ways of God, the idea of Kamala Harris becoming president was likewise a terrifying prospect. It would mean that she would act without the restraint of the vice presidency. The reign of Athaliah gives clear warning:

> For the sons of Athaliah, that wicked woman, had broken into the house of God, and had also presented all the dedicated things of the house of the LORD to the Baals.[2]

As had her mother, Jezebel, Athaliah had no aversion to the use of force and violence against those who opposed her agenda and against the worship of God. As had her mother, Jezebel, Athaliah would wage war against the ways and people of God.

THE USE OF FORCE

Whether the "sons of Athaliah" refers to flesh-and-blood children or those who followed her ways, it was Athaliah's people who broke into the Temple of God, stole all the sacred vessels, and repurposed them for the worship of Baal. It could not have happened without her blessing. Athaliah was a warrior of the gods. As she promulgated their worship, she warred against the worship of God.

The rise of the American Athaliah promised the same. If she gained the presidency, she would not only end all religious exemptions with regard to abortion,[3] but as made clear in the platform of her party, she would seek to end all religious exemptions with regard to the LGBT agenda.[4] So now those who sought to follow the ways of God would be forced to oppose it in this realm as well. Beyond all that both Harris and Walz made troubling comments regarding the limiting of free speech.[5] No matter how much she and her allies sought to sanitize it, her candidacy foreshadowed a coming war against religious freedom.

JEHOSHEBA

Athaliah's shedding of the children's blood would set her at war as well against those who sought to save them:

> She arose and destroyed all the royal heirs. But Jehosheba, the daughter of King Jehoram, sister of Ahaziah, took Joash the son of Ahaziah, and stole him away from among the king's sons who were being murdered; and they hid him and his nurse in the bedroom, from Athaliah, so that he was not killed. So he was hidden with her in the house of the LORD.[6]

Athaliah had not slaughtered *all* the royal heirs. One was saved. Jehosheba, herself of the royal family and wife of the high priest, Jehoiada, grabbed the baby Joash, Athaliah's grandson, and hid him away from the massacre.[7] She then brought the baby and his nurse into the Temple to be raised there among the priests and worshippers of God.[8]

AGAINST THE PROTECTORS

The fact that Jehosheba had to hide the baby's nurse as well implies that her life was likewise in danger. And had Athaliah known of those who saved the baby and who were now protecting him, she would have viewed them as mortal threats to her reign. She would have sought to kill them as well.

The mystery would, therefore, ordain that the American

Athaliah would wage war not only against the lives of children but against those who sought to save the lives of children from her destruction. And that is exactly what the American Athaliah would do. She would wage war not only against the children but against those who sought to save the children's lives, as in those who stood for life.

To see what was in store for America had Harris won the presidency, what she would have done if unrestrained by the office of vice presidency, we need only to look at what she did before the vice presidency, when she acted unfettered.

AT WAR WITH LIFE

Crisis pregnancy centers exist for the purpose of giving mothers an alternative to aborting their unborn child, to support the mother in the birth of their child, and to help both after the child's birth. In other words, they do the work of Jehosheba, seeking to save babies from the slaughter. It was not enough for Harris, as California attorney general, that abortion was legal and widely practiced; the fact that some babies were being saved from abortion in crisis pregnancy centers was too much. Therefore she launched a legal war against them. She would use her office and the machinery of state to restrain and encumber them. It was unprecedented. It opened the door for similarly pro-abortion members of government in other states to wage similar wars against crisis pregnancy centers across the nation.[9]

Jehosheba

THE VESSELS OF GOD FOR BAAL

In her zeal Harris would go still further. She ordered that every crisis pregnancy center in the state be compelled to post signs advertising abortion clinics. She was, in effect, attempting to force pro-life centers and ministries to direct their people to get abortions. So radical and brazen was her act that it was overruled by the Supreme Court itself.[10] It was also a fulfillment of Athaliah's template. It was the children of Athaliah who sought to take the vessels from God's house and repurpose them for the purposes of Baal—or, in other words, to take that which was devoted to the purposes of God and redirect it for the purposes of death, the child sacrifices of Baal. So Harris was seeking to take that which was dedicated to saving the lives of children and repurpose it for death.

And yet the American Athaliah's war against life and those who sought to save it would be plunged to even greater depths.

Chapter 45

THE HOUSE OF DAVID

THE DANGER IMPLICIT in the template of Athaliah and of a Kamala Harris presidency can be dramatically seen by what she did in the spring of 2016.

THE UNCOVERER

David Daleiden was a pro-life activist who went undercover to expose the abortion industry's trafficking of baby parts for profit.[1] Though abortion advocates claimed he wasn't able to prove that this was an issue, his recordings caught abortion industry executives speaking of this very thing, the sale of baby parts for profit.[2] Later investigations would reveal that the practice was indeed taking place.[3] One might expect that an investigator who exposed such a thing or even opened the door of inquiry into the possibility that such a thing was happening would receive accolades for his work. But that is not what happened. Instead of praising Daleiden's work and opening an investigation into the abortion industry in her state, Kamala Harris opened an investigation *against David Daleiden*.[4]

THE MEETING

As Athaliah and the priests of Baal would have been in close communion, so too were Kamala Harris and Planned Parenthood. As Athaliah was an agent of Baal, so Harris was, in effect, an agent of Planned Parenthood. In March 2016 Harris met with six executives of Planned

The House of David 215

Parenthood.[5] Shortly after that meeting, Harris would set in motion an action that would shock even her allies.

On April 5, 2016, Harris set in motion a raid on Daleiden's apartment.[6] Agents of the California Department of Justice seized four of his computers and hours of video footage.[7] Harris had successfully removed Daleiden's evidence against the abortion industry. The evidence, over five hundred hours of video recordings, would then be sealed off from public viewing and access.[8] Harris's campaign against Daleiden would result in his becoming the first journalist ever to be criminally prosecuted under the state's recording law.[9] Harris's successor, Xavier Becerra, would charge Daleiden with *fifteen felony counts* and would attempt to sentence him to years in prison.[10]

RAIDING THE HOUSE OF DAVID

The royal line of the kings of Judah began with King David. Athaliah was not of that line. When she targeted the royal heirs, she was targeting the house of David. For those of the house of David had a legitimate claim to the throne as opposed to Athaliah's claim, which was illegitimate. Thus the house of David posed a special threat to Athaliah's claim to the throne. Therefore Athaliah waged war against the house of David. And so it is of note that the epitome of the American Athaliah's war against life and those who sought to protect it was focused on a man named *David* and, further, that it involved breaking into the *house of David*.

Harris's intense and seemingly obsessive war against unborn children and those who sought to save them appears puzzling. But the ancient mystery explains it. For Athaliah it was those who sought to save the life of an infant, as in the royal heir, Joash, that posed the greatest threat to her rule. So according to the mystery, the American Athaliah would view those who sought to save the lives of babies as existential threats and would wage war against them. In this she was fulfilling the role of the ancient queen in the unfolding of the ancient mystery.

In the end it would be Joash who would prove to be Athaliah's undoing and her end. Athaliah's end would hold the key to a mystery that would unfold in our time.

Chapter 46

ATHALIAH'S END

ATHALIAH'S BLOODY REIGN would come to a dramatic end. Her downfall would be brought about by one of the babies she had sought to kill.

CROWNING THE CHILD

The future looked hopeless. Athaliah had an iron grip on the nation's throne. She was promulgating the worship of Baal and the gods of Phoenicia and had wiped out the heirs of David's house—or so she thought. The one child saved from her slaughter and kept hidden in God's Temple was now seven years old. It was time. The high priest, Jehoiada, gathered the nation's elders and Levites to Jerusalem and prepared them for what was going to take place. The Book of 2 Chronicles reveals what happened:

> And Jehoiada the priest gave to the captains of hundreds the spears and the large and small shields which had belonged to King David, that were in the temple of God. Then he set all the people, every man with his weapon in his hand, from the right side of the temple to the left side of the temple, along by the altar and by the temple, all around the king. And they brought out the king's son, put the crown on him,

218 THE AVATAR

gave him the Testimony, and made
him king. Then Jehoiada and his sons
anointed him, and said, "Long live the
king!"[1]

TREACHERY!

So the child, Joash, who had lived his entire life hidden
from public view, was suddenly revealed to the nation as
alive and then crowned as king in the Temple of God. The
resulting commotion and celebration reached the ears of
Athaliah. The account goes on:

> Now when Athaliah heard the noise of
> the escorts and the people, she came
> to the people in the temple of the
> LORD. When she looked, there was the
> king standing by a pillar according to
> custom....So Athaliah tore her clothes
> and cried out, "Treason! Treason!"[2]

Athaliah's last recorded words echoed the last recorded
words of her brother King Joram who, in the face of Jehu
and death, shouted, "Treachery!"[3]

THE HOLY AND THE UNHOLY

The high priest then ordered that the queen who had shed
so much blood should now herself be executed:

> And Jehoiada the priest brought out
> the captains of hundreds who were
> set over the army, and said to them,
> "Take her outside."[4]

Athaliah's End 219

And so the reign of Athaliah would come to its end. It was especially fitting that the end would begin in the Temple, the same house her sons had broken into and pillaged for the worship of Baal, and the house of the God she had sought to cast out of Israel. The ending of her most unholy reign began in the most holy of places, the Temple of God.

THE SIGN OF JEZEBEL'S END

She had come to the throne in violence and bloodshed, so in violence and bloodshed her reign would come to an end. It had been the same for her mother. As Jezebel had shed blood, so at the rise of Jehu, her blood would be shed.

On the day that Hillary Clinton, who walked in Jezebel's template, was to receive the nomination of her party to run against Donald Trump for the presidency, a prophetic word was given. The man who gave it had no idea it would be prophetic. He had intended to deliver a speech lifting up the party's presidential candidate. But he kept repeating a particular phrase over and over again. He said, "They threw her down....They threw her down....They threw her down," over and over and over again.[5]

If one had taken that central mantra of his speech that night and typed it into a search engine on the internet, the result would reveal how it would all end and who would win the presidential election. The typed-in words would pinpoint a scripture, 2 Kings 9:23. It is the one verse in the Bible that contains Jezebel's downfall. For her end would come when *they threw her down* to her death. So the very words spoken at the convention with the intent of lifting up the American Jezebel to contend against the American

Jehu would pinpoint the very scripture in which Jezebel, contending with Jehu, was defeated, as *they threw her down.*

As is often the case in the Bible, the end is prophesied at the beginning. What about the American Athaliah? Could there have been a prophetic message or sign given likewise at the beginning of her candidacy, foretelling the end?

THE SIGN OF ATHALIAH'S END

Harris was nominated as the Democratic presidential candidate on August 5. The next day, she and her running mate, Walz, launched their campaign with their first joint appearance. It took place in Pennsylvania and was hosted by the Democratic governor of that state, Josh Shapiro. It was impossible to miss the most passionate issue of that event. It was again the killing of children, in accord with the template of Athaliah, whose rise to power was built on the killing of children. All three—Harris, Walz, and Shapiro—raged against the overturning of *Roe v. Wade*.[6] The American Athaliah would proclaim:

> After *Roe* was overturned, he [Walz] was the first governor in the country to sign a new law that enshrined reproductive freedom as a fundamental right. And with Tim Walz by my side, when I am president of the United States...we will pass a bill to restore reproductive freedom, and I will proudly sign it into law.[7]

Athaliah's End 221

Harris had declared what she would do when she was president. But the event in which she declared it contained a prophetic sign. It would foretell a different ending—a sign of her end.

THE TEMPLE DOWNFALL

Jezebel's end was summed up in the words *they threw her down*. So the prophetic sign given of the American Jezebel's end was the declaration on the day of her nomination that *they threw her down*. But Athaliah's end was connected to the Temple. It was in the Temple that her end began. It was in the Temple that she was overthrown. It was in the Temple that another would be declared the leader of the land. It was in the Temple that the agenda of Baal she had championed would be overturned. And it was in the Temple that her ambition to rule over the land was brought to an end. So as prophetic words are often manifested at the beginning of an epoch, and since Athaliah's end began in the Temple, could the sign of the Temple, of Athaliah's end, have manifested at the beginning, at the first event of her campaign for the presidency?

SIGN OF THE TEMPLE

That very first event of the campaign, which took place the day after she received the nomination of the Democratic National Convention for president, happened at a university in Pennsylvania. Could the place in which the event was held be significant? Could the sign of the Temple manifest there?

The name of the university in which the event took place

was *Temple*. As Athaliah's defeat began in the place called the *Temple*, so the American Athaliah's defeat began in a place called *Temple*. The very first event of the Harris–Walz campaign took place there, and it was there that the sign was given—*the sign of the Temple*.

The giving of the sign of Athaliah's downfall meant that the American Athaliah would not prevail. It prophesied that her plan to become leader of the land would be brought to an end. It foretold that another would be proclaimed leader of the land. The sign of the Temple meant the American Athaliah would be defeated.

As the sign of the Temple was given on the first day of her campaign, another sign would manifest on the last.

Chapter 47

THE YARD AND THE VALLEY

THE TEMPLE IN which Athaliah's reign was overthrown was not as most think it was.

THE TEMPLE COMPLEX

When one hears the word *temple,* one most often pictures an enclosed building with four walls and a roof. But that was not the Temple of Athaliah's end. The Temple of Jerusalem did have such an enclosed building. But only the priests were allowed to enter therein. Athaliah would not have been allowed inside. But the enclosed building or sanctuary was only part of what the Bible refers to as *the Temple.*

The events that ended the reign of Athaliah, as described in 2 Chronicles 23, took place not in the enclosed building but in the surrounding area known as the *Temple complex* or *Temple compound.* One writer observes:

> From a semantic standpoint, the various names given to the compound— *hatser* (courtyard) in Hebrew, or the Greek *peribolos* and *temenos*—describe a space that surrounds another architectural element. The Temple, then, was perceived as an architectural complex containing different components. Just as the altar was part of the Temple structure, so were the surrounding elements—courtyards and galleries.[1]

223

THE COURTYARD

The Temple was thus a complex consisting of an enclosed building and a large courtyard made up of several smaller courtyards. The entire complex was called the *hatser,* or the *courtyard.* The word *yard* is defined as a piece of ground adjoining a building or house, or an area of ground surrounded by walls or buildings. The word *courtyard* is defined as an unroofed area that is mostly or completely enclosed by the walls of a large building. So Athaliah's overthrow took place in the hatser or courtyard, also known as the Temple complex.

THE VALLEY

When the high priest Jehoiada ordered Athaliah to be taken outside, he was referring to the boundaries of the Temple courtyard. He didn't want her execution to take place on holy ground:

> "Take her outside...." For the priest had said, "Do not kill her in the house of the LORD." So they seized her; and she went by way of the entrance of the Horse Gate into the king's house, and they killed her there.[2]

Athaliah was killed *by way of the entrance of the Horse Gate into the king's house.* The king's house was the palace. Most scholars place the palace just south of the Temple complex, bordering and overlooking the Kidron Valley. The Temple Mount itself borders the Kidron Valley. The first-century Jewish historian Josephus identified the site

The Yard and the Valley   225

of Athaliah's execution as being the Kidron Valley.[3] The Kidron Valley would be a fitting place for the queen's end, a place where idols, altars, and other unclean things would be cast out, and a place of death.[4] Whether she was killed *in* the valley or *at* the valley, her death was connected to the valley—as it has been for ages.

THE YARD AND VALLEY OF HER END

So Athaliah's defeat, downfall, and end were connected to two places—the Temple courtyard and the Kidron Valley, the *courtyard* and the *valley*. It was in the courtyard that she was defeated and overthrown. It was there that she witnessed her overthrow, her downfall, and the victory of the king who would sit on the throne she coveted. And it was in the valley that her rule was judged and her reign and life were brought to an end.

NIGHT OF THE YARD

For the night of the presidential election, the American Athaliah had chosen that Howard University would serve as her campaign headquarters. Her campaign staff set up camp inside the university's buildings. It was to be a night of triumph and celebration. But there would be no triumph or celebration. The site she had chosen for her victory would instead be the site of her defeat.[5]

Athaliah's downfall began in the Temple courtyard. The part of the campus that Harris chose as her headquarters on election night had long been known by a particular name. It was called *The Yard*.[6]

So as the downfall of the ancient Athaliah had taken

place in the *courtyard*, the downfall of the American Athaliah would take place in *The Yard*. As it was for the ancient Athaliah, it was there in The Yard that she would be defeated, there that she would receive the news that another would become leader of the land in her place, and there that her agenda would be brought to an end.

NIGHT OF THE VALLEY

Athaliah's defeat took place not only in the courtyard but in the valley, and in the courtyard that overlooked the valley. The defeat of the American Athaliah, Kamala Harris, took place on the ground called *The Yard*. But as the Temple courtyard was connected to another ground that was likewise connected to Athaliah's downfall, so The Yard of Harris's defeat was connected to another ground. It was called *The Valley*.[7] As in the fall of the ancient Athaliah, *The Yard* bordered *The Valley*.[8] So the American Athaliah met her defeat, as had the ancient Athaliah, in *The Yard* and *The Valley*.

It had all been foreshadowed on the first official day of her campaign, as it was held in the place called *Temple,* and it all came to an end on the last official day of her campaign, as it was held in the place called *The Yard* and *The Valley.*

We have seen the defeat of the American Athaliah. We must now look at the victory of the American Jehu. What happened *after* Jehu came to the throne and began to reign? And could that reveal what his modern counterpart would do, what lies ahead, and what it means?

PART X

THE STORM KING

Chapter 48

KING JEHU

THERE IS MUCH in the template of Jehu that became most evident in Trump's return to the White House. It was as the American Jehu rose to power a second time to begin his second administration that these other dynamics of his ancient prototype most powerfully manifested.

THE MAD RACE

After being given the charge of the prophet, Jehu mounted his chariot and with his troops began a race to the royal city of Jezreel. Upon seeing him approach in the distance, the watchman of the city reported,

> The driving *is* like the driving of Jehu the son of Nimshi, for he drives like a *madman!*[1]

The word used by the watchman to describe Jehu is the Hebrew *shiggaon*. It can be translated as *wildly, crazily*, and *like a madman*. The words describe both of Trump's races to the White House, the second race as crazy as the first, as it now defied not only the onslaught of the mainstream media and culture but an array of legal cases, a multitude of felony convictions, two assassination attempts, and more.

229

JEHU'S FURY

But the word can also be translated as *furious*. This, along with the account itself, conveys as well the sense of speed, intensity, and force. One translation renders the watchman's words this way:

> Their *force and speed* is as fierce as the
> *crazy driving of Jehu*.[2]

The speed with which Jehu acted was key to his success in taking the throne and then in securing it. As one commentary puts it, Jehu would fulfill his mission with

> a *hot* and *hasty*, and *unrelenting*
> *energy*.[3]

So fast and so furious was Jehu's execution of his goals that it left his enemies in the house of Ahab unprepared and overwhelmed:

> The rapidity and decisiveness of Jehu's
> movements gave no opportunity to his
> victims to protect themselves.[4]

The same exact strategy and dynamics employed by Jehu would be employed by the American Jehu.

"HIS SPEEDY PACE WAS CEASELESS"

What followed the return of Donald Trump to the White House stunned his enemies and supporters alike. The speed with which he acted was unprecedented. On his first day as president, he signed far more executive actions than any president had ever done on any

King Jehu 231

inaugural day in American history.[5] In his first week and then in his first hundred days,[6] he issued far more executive orders and actions than any president had ever done in the same period of time.[7] He was enacting so much change in so short a time period that his critics and opponents could not begin to keep up. By the time they issued their criticism of one action, he had set in motion several more. The following was written of Jehu's nature and speed:

> His fast driving was characteristic.... Having formed a purpose, he rushed to its realization. He brought things to pass. He combined energy with tenacity, and was capable of rapid decision....He had a strong personal magnetism that coerced his associates into willing and even eager subservience....He was not only rapid but persistent. He never tired. His speedy pace was ceaseless.[8]

The same words written of Jehu could just as accurately have been written to describe the modern American leader who walked in his footsteps.

THE STORMER

Jehu took the throne of Israel by storm. He was himself a living storm, throwing all around him, a decadent system and apostate institutions, into chaos and upheaval. One writer summed up the rise and reign of Jehu this way:

> *Jehu storms his way* through 2 Kings 9 and 10 with fury and reckless abandon.[9]

It was characteristic of Jehu. And it was characteristic of Trump. He was a living storm. When he defeated Kamala Harris to return to the White House, *The New York Times* published the news with a massive front-page headline reading,

TRUMP STORMS BACK[10]

So *The New York Times* was now using the same words to describe the rise of the American Jehu that were used to describe the rise of his ancient prototype.

THE RETURN OF THE KING

Jehu could act with absolute authority; he was king. But Trump was president. And yet even that aspect of the ancient leader would manifest especially in the latter's second administration as the mainstream media bestowed on him a new title. The *New York Times* headline put it this way:

"The Return of the King": Trump Embraces
Trappings of the Throne[11]

To understand what Trump would do upon returning to the White House, one must understand the charge given to Jehu by the prophet at Ramoth-Gilead.

Chapter 49

THE DECONSTRUCTOR

IT WAS ONLY a matter of hours for Trump's return to the White House to trigger a tsunami of reactions from the mainstream media and public opinion. To some, he was a threat to democracy and would destroy the nation. To others, he was saving the nation from destroying itself. But what was actually happening was something different, something that transcended both interpretations. It was, rather, the outworking of a mystery begun thousands of years before he was born.

"YOU SHALL STRIKE DOWN"

The prophecy given to Jehu contained this central command:

> You shall strike down the house of Ahab...[1]

The fulfillment of that command would mean not only the ending of a royal house but the striking down of the establishments, systems, cults, conventions, and institutions connected to the house of Ahab. Only by doing so could the lingering effects of the reign of Ahab and his house be removed from the land.

DISMANTLING THE TEMPLE

Thus, as we have seen, one of Jehu's central campaigns was to remove the cult of Baal, with its child sacrifices, from

234   **THE AVATAR**

the land. The defining moment of that campaign was his destruction of Baal's temple in the capital city. Note the words in the scriptural account that record it:

> Then they *broke down* the sacred pillar of Baal, and *tore down* the temple of Baal and made it a refuse dump to this day. Thus *Jehu destroyed* Baal from Israel.[2]

Broke down, tore down, destroyed. One commentator puts it this way:

> One of Jehu's signal achievements is *to dismantle the house of Baal* in Samaria.[3]

So Jehu's calling to strike down the house of Ahab and the Temple of Baal would involve breaking down, tearing down, dismantling, and destruction.

THE OTHER TEMPLE

The acts of Donald Trump have continually mystified friends and foes alike. But in order to understand them, one must understand the calling of Jehu. The American Jehu would take up the same mission, to *break down, tear down,* and *dismantle* the American house of Ahab, the American Temple of Baal—its establishments, its systems, its cults, its conventions, its ideologies, and its institutions. So upon his return to the presidency, Trump especially set out to dismantle the establishments and ideologies of the radical left and the institutions and houses of the woke that had taken over much of

The Deconstructor   235

American society. Thus, upon returning to the White House, he wasted no time in breaking down the systems and ideologies that warred against traditional American and biblical values. The American Jehu returned to the White House with the fury and ferocity of his ancient prototype to strike down the American house of Ahab and dismantle the American Temple of Baal.

THE ACTS OF JEHU

And so it was no accident that the headlines describing the first acts of the new administration would echo the first acts of King Jehu:

> Trump Set to *Dismantle* DEI Within Federal Government in First Day...[4]

> Trump Has Said the Education Department Should Be *Dismantled*...[5]

> President Trump's Plan to *Dismantle* the Deep State[6]

> How Much of the Government Can Donald Trump *Dismantle*?[7]

The headlines now bore unwitting witness to the mystery of Jehu. For to *strike down* a house is to dismantle it.

Upon his return to the White House, Trump embarked on a campaign that went back not only to the acts of Jehu but to a reality television show.

Chapter 50

THE PURGER

JEHU REALIZED THAT he could never change the course of his nation if the old guard remained in control in its government and on the high places of its culture. So he began a merciless campaign to remove it.

AHAB'S LORDS AND PRINCES

The first to be removed were King Joram and Jezebel. But it didn't stop there. He then turned his focus to the lords and princes of the house of Ahab. So the ancient account records:

> Jehu killed all who remained of the house of Ahab in Jezreel, and all his great men and his close acquaintances and his priests, until he left him none remaining.[1]

Jehu removed the heirs, agents, and rulers of the house of Ahab from the nation's government. Though his methods were questionable and brutal, he had purged the nation's government. The house of Ahab and its impact on Israel's future was nullified.

THE AMERICAN LORDS AND PRINCES

The American Jehu likewise knew that he could never change America's trajectory if the old guard and what many would deem the *deep state* remained in place in the

The Purger 237

nation's government. As long as the American house of Ahab remained in the highest echelons of the American government—in its agencies, branches, and departments—it would be impossible for the nation to change its course.

So just as Jehu had done, Trump set out to remove the old guard from the American government. Those who had used their positions to promulgate an ideology that Trump saw as inimical to American values, traditional values, and biblical values were now to be dismissed, put on leave, fired. He removed bureau heads, agency leaders,[2] generals and military commanders,[3] and those who championed radical ideologies and agendas within the American government. The massive removals would trigger an uproar, but the American Jehu was again doing as the ancient Jehu had done thousands of years before, as he executed a massive purge of his nation's government.

JEHU PURGES ISRAEL

The following are headings used in Bible translations and articles to sum up the acts of Jehu at the outset of his reign as recorded in 2 Kings 9 and 10. Note the word that continually appears:

Jehu *Purges* Israel[4]

Jehu's Coronation and *Purge* of Israel[5]

Jehu Continues *Purging* the House of Ahab[6]

Jehu's *Purge* of Baal Worship in Israel[7]

TRUMP PURGES AMERICA

Compare now the Bible headings describing the acts of Jehu to the headlines describing the actions of the American Jehu at the outset of his second administration:

Donald Trump Ramps Up His War on "Woke" with *Purge* of Federal DEI Workers[8]

Unprecedented Policy *Purge*: Trump's Single Order Attempts to Dismantle Biden's Legacy[9]

Trump Administration *Purges* Military Leadership[10]

Purges at FBI, DOJ Trigger "Battle" for Career Staff[11]

Trump's Unprecedented *Purge* at the Department of Justice...[12]

A Sweeping *Purge* Is Taking Place Throughout America[13]

JEHU ON REALITY TELEVISION

In the purge of the ancient Jehu, the removal of the agents and heirs of Ahab was accomplished by execution. In the purge of the American Jehu, the removal was accomplished through less violent means—by the termination of their employment. One article summed up one of the early purges of Trump's second administration with this headline:

Trump Announces *Purge* of over 1,000 Biden Appointees: *"You're Fired!"*[14]

The Purger 239

The headline alluded to the words Trump placed at the end of his written notice of termination, "You're fired!" Trump was employing the two-word catchphrase he had used on the reality television show *The Apprentice.* In fact, Trump had become famous for those two words long *before* his first rise to the White House.[15] Could it be that even that was part of the mystery as well? For those words would become central in the modern parallel to Jehu's purge of the house of Ahab. The mystery was so all-encompassing that it could even involve something as seemingly innocuous as the catchphrase of a reality television show.

There would be another side to the ancient king's template in which Trump walked. It would connect the prophet Elijah with an inaugural ball.

Chapter 51

SWORD OF JEHU

JEZEBEL HAD VOWED to kill the prophet Elijah.[1] Elijah fled for his life. He made his way to Mount Sinai. There he would be given a word from God.

ELIJAH'S PROPHECY

> Also you shall anoint Jehu the son of Nimshi *as* king over Israel....It shall be *that* whoever escapes the sword of Hazael, Jehu will kill; and whoever escapes the sword of Jehu, Elisha will kill.[2]

This first prophecy given of Jehu in Scripture contains a significant phrase—*the sword of Jehu.*[3] Jehu was one of three people Elijah was called to anoint, each one connected to the sword. *The sword of Jehu* spoke of the ancient king as an instrument of judgment, the vessel by which a corrupt kingdom would be pulled down.[4] It was implicit as well in the word given to Jehu by the prophet, the charge to strike down the house of Ahab and avenge the blood shed by Jezebel. So Jehu was a vessel of justice, vengeance, and retribution. He would avenge the blood of the innocent, the righteous, and the servants of God.

Sword of Jehu 241

JEHU'S VENGEANCE

One of the charges leveled against Donald Trump by his critics upon his return to the White House was that he was acting out of a spirit of vengeance. So such headlines appeared as:

A Spirit of Vengeance in Trump's First Week[5]

Trump II: Back with a Vengeance[6]

And yet the same headlines could have been written of Jehu. As Trump's nature or motives may have lent themselves to such an agenda, the same could have been said of Jehu. As one Bible commentary puts it:

> Jehu was an instrument of divine vengeance, even when fulfilling the projects of his own ambition.[7]

"I AM YOUR RETRIBUTION"

Jehu was a vessel of retribution on a government and culture that had grown perverse in its apostasy and deadly in its shedding of innocent blood. In the words of one commentary,

> Jehu would be the instrument of divine retribution.[8]

Retribution is not a word one typically expects to be raised in a discussion of a modern American president. But Trump was not a typical American president. He was the modern equivalent of the ancient king. And so the headlines would read:

Trump Has Moved Quickly to Exact
"Retribution"[9]

Trump 2.0: Bans, Purges and Retribution[10]

Trump himself would say,

> I am your *justice*. And for those who
> have been wronged and betrayed, I
> am your *retribution*.[11]

THE SWORD

The sword of Jehu would have an even more dramatic manifestation. On the night of his return to the presidency, Trump made an appearance at the Commander in Chief Ball, an inaugural gala dedicated to the nation's Armed Forces. There he was presented with a large object—a *sword*. Trump took the sword, lifted it above his head, and began dancing with it.[12] It was another unprecedented moment—an American president appearing before the American people, dancing with a sword. But it was in accord with the mystery. For it was only fitting that the American Jehu should wield the *sword of Jehu*.

The defeat of Athaliah and Jezebel, the return of Jehu, what did it all mean—for America, for the world, and for the future?

Chapter 52

THE MEANING OF JEHU

IN ORDER TO uncover what the return of the American Jehu portends for the future, we must look to the past to see what the ancient radical king meant for the future of the northern kingdom.

MAN ON A MISSION

In the early days of his second term as president, Trump put up a post on the internet that caused a massive uproar in the mainstream media. It was a picture of the president walking down a city street at night dressed in a long black coat. On the top of the picture in big, bold, and capitalized letters were the words:

HE'S ON A MISSION FROM GOD.[1]

And on the bottom of the picture were the words:

& NOTHING CAN STOP WHAT IS COMING.[2]

Never had an American president put forth such words in reference to himself. The media accused him of holding delusions of grandeur, claiming infallibility, and believing himself divine. And yet the words were in complete alignment with the mystery and template of Jehu.

THE PURPOSE OF THE ANOINTING

With all his quirks and contradictions, Jehu, of all the kings of Israel, was unquestionably a man *on a mission from God.* It is worthy of note that it was ordained that

244 THE AVATAR

Jehu would first be anointed with oil and then given the mission he was to fulfill. In other words, even if for a moment, he knew he was anointed before knowing why or for what purpose he was being anointed. So it was with the American Jehu; he likewise knew he was anointed before knowing what he was anointed for. For just as Jehu had been drawn into a mission from God above and beyond anything he had planned or imagined, so too it was with the American Jehu. What then was the purpose of Trump's mission? The mystery is found in the meaning of Jehu.

A BRUTAL MERCY

The northern kingdom's descent into apostasy had long been underway by the time Jehu was commissioned by the prophet. The nation's first king, Jeroboam, set it all in motion when he erected two golden calves for his people to worship.[3] With the subsequent rise of the house of Ahab and the ascendancy of Baal, the nation descended to still greater depths. Unless its trajectory was altered, unless it turned back to God, its future would end in judgment and destruction.

In view of the kingdom's long and progressive descent, the reign of Jehu is all the more striking. It would represent the first time since the days of King Jeroboam that its apostasy was halted. In fact, of all the kings who reigned over the northern kingdom, the Word of God would commend just one—Jehu. Though, to the house of Ahab and the nation's apostate culture, Jehu brought judgment, he brought hope to the nation. For only by turning back

The Meaning of Jehu   245

the kingdom's long descent from God could there be any chance for redemption.

As the kingdom's fall involved the worship and serving of gods and idols, to reverse that fall its gods would have to be cast out and its idols struck down. That was the meaning of Jehu. Though his work was often brutal and merciless, only by removing what he removed, purging what he purged, and dismantling what he dismantled, could the nation's fall be given pause and reprieve and the chance to turn back.

THE AMERICAN FALL

It was in the 1960s that America's departure from God would become unmistakably evident. At the beginning of that decade, the nation began removing God from its public life, starting with the banning of prayer in its public school system.[4] Though, at the time, the ruling appeared to be of limited context, it would set in motion a metamorphosis that would touch every realm of American culture and would, over time, intensify, deepen, and gain increasing momentum and critical mass. America was emptying itself of God, and according to the ancient warning, its house would not remain empty; others would come in, gods and spirits. And unless its trajectory was altered, the nation would progress to calamity.

THE RADICAL SHOCK AND HOPE

Never since it began had the course of the nation's apostasy been in any substantial way halted or turned back. It was perhaps because of Trump's radical nature, as it was of

Jehu's, that he could be used to shock the system and alter that trajectory. With all his quirks and contradictions, the American Jehu would initiate the first massive rolling back of the American apostasy. In this, the nation was being given a chance. What it would do with that chance was an open question—just as it was an open question as to whether that chance would be the last it would be given.

Could the days of Jehu and the time he was given on the national stage have determined the days and time given to his modern counterpart?

Chapter 53

THE TWENTY-EIGHTH YEAR

WE NOW OPEN an ancient mystery behind the time ordained for Donald Trump to preside over the American political stage.

THE TEMPLATE PROPHECY

After Trump's failure to retain the presidency in the 2020 election, many predicted that his time was over. Even his own party, it was said, was looking to move on from him. It was during that time, in between his departure from the White House and his announcement to again run for the presidency, that I was asked by many if I believed that Trump would again be president. I answered that what would align with the template of Jehu would be that Trump would again run and win the presidency in 2024. How did the three-thousand-year-old template of the ancient king foretell that?

TIME OF THE KINGS

The template ordained the rise and fall of the American leaders of our time—and, specifically, the time given to ancient kings of Israel and the time each American leader would have on the *national political stage*. But Trump's case is different. He did not start out in government or as a politician but as a real estate developer and entrepreneur.[1] It was for this and, later, for his career as a reality television star that he became famous. Unlike the other

247

248   THE AVATAR

figures in the template, he was on the national stage long before he entered the political or governmental realm. So does the mystery still apply?

THE FIRST CAMPAIGN

When was Donald Trump's first campaign for the presidency? Most people would answer that it was the campaign for the presidential election of 2016. But the answer is incorrect. It began long before that. Trump first entered the presidential realm in the year 2000. In September 1999 he wrote an article that appeared in *The Wall Street Journal* titled "America Needs a President Like Me." In it he argued that he would be "the kind of president America needed in the new millennium."[2] On October 7 Trump announced the formation of an exploratory committee for a presidential run on a third-party ticket as the Reform Party candidate.[3] It was the beginning of his first presidential campaign and his entrance onto the national political stage. The campaign would be named *Trump 2000*.[4]

TRUMP 2000

As presidential candidate, Trump appeared in the media and at numerous campaign events throughout the country. But on February 14, stating that the infighting within the Reform Party was not conducive to his winning the presidency, Trump officially withdrew.[5] Still, Trump won the Michigan primary on February 22. And on March 7 he won the California primary.[6] Though he ended up withdrawing from the race, Trump 2000 was the precursor to

The Twenty-Eighth Year 249

Trump's campaign for the White House sixteen years later and thus to his presidency.

THE YEARS OF TRUMP

On November 5, 2024, Trump won the presidential election and returned to the White House for his second term. He was elected to serve as president for four years, his last full year in office as president being 2028. At the end of that year an election would be held to determine the next president and administration. Trump entered the presidential realm and the national political stage with *Trump 2000*, his first presidential campaign. From the election of 2000 to the election of 2028 is a span of *twenty-eight years*. The year will even bear the number *twenty-eight*.

THE YEARS OF JEHU

In 2 Kings 10:36 the years of Jehu's reign are summed up. Jehu, it records, reigned over Israel for a period identified in three Hebrew words: *Esrim U'Shmoneh Shannah*. *Esrim* means *twenty*. *Shmoneh* means *eight*. And *shannah* means *years*. So the time given to Jehu from the beginning of his rise to the end of his days on Israel's national and political stage was *twenty-eight years*.

As for the American Jehu, the time given him from the beginning of his entrance into the presidential realm with his first campaign for the White House to the end of his days on America's national and political stage, from the year 2000 to the year 2028, is *twenty-eight years*. At the end of his second term the days of Trump will have been *Esrim U'Shmoneh Shannah*—the exact time given to the ancient king in whose footsteps he walked.

THE PARAMETERS OF THE TEMPLATE

Had Trump succeeded in retaining the White House in the election of 2020, *the mystery would not have been fulfilled.* In other words, in order to fulfill the mystery of Jehu, he had to *not retain the White House in 2020.* Further, Jehu rose to power in the twelfth year of the previous king, Joram. So the American Jehu had to rise to power in Obama's twelfth year on the national stage, 2016—which he did. But he also had to be elected to a term that would end in the twenty-eighth year. The only way that could happen was if there were two risings, two terms, and two presidencies. Trump had to *win* the White House in 2016, *depart* from the White House in 2020, and *win* the White House again in 2024. And so according to the biblical template, that is exactly what he did. The American Jehu rose to power in the *twelfth year* of the previous ruler in 2016 and returned to power in 2024 to a presidency set to end in the *twenty-eighth year.*

Before we come to the answer and the hope of redemption, we must go one step deeper. We must pull away one more veil or mask. What we will find lying beneath it will be a mystery of stunning ramifications. It will open up, in unmistakable clarity, how critical and relevant is the mystery of the gods—and how dangerous its potential. And it will reveal how close we came to the total ascendancy of the gods, how close we still may come, and where it is all taking us. It will represent a convergence of mysteries, that of gods and kings, of spirits and governments—*the mystery of the avatar.*

PART XI

AVATAR

Chapter 54

AGENTS OF THE GODS

WE HAVE SEEN the interplay of gods and kings, spirits and governments, deities and dominions. What we are now about to see is how all these converged on American soil in a play for the nation's future and that of the world.

We have noted how close the American apostasy came to the point of being sealed, the point of no return. But could there still be more to the story? Could there have been a sign given on America's national stage? Could the agenda of the gods and spirits have manifested in plain sight in real time? And did we miss it?

If the mysteries of Jehu, Ahab, Jezebel, Joram, Jehoram, and Athaliah are of an explosive nature, what we are now about to see will be all the more explosive. Because of this we must reaffirm the balance. The revelations involve individuals but are not ultimately about them. The individuals are only vessels, instruments, agents, and avatars with little or no idea as to how they are being used, just as Gospel writers record that the disciple Peter was unwittingly used as an instrument of Satan. Those who follow the ways of God are not to hate or condemn but love and pray for all, even for their enemies, even those who would persecute them, and even those used as vessels in the war against them. The righteous must seek their redemption.

We now direct our focus on one such instrument and avatar. It is not that this one is, of course, an actual manifestation of

253

a god. Nor is it to say that this one is indwelled by a particular spirit. Rather it is that this one has served as an instrument, an unwitting vessel, a representative, and a living image and is, in that sense, a type of avatar. It is also not to say that there are not other such ones but that this is the most prominent and the one that came closest to attaining dominion over America.

The mystery we have thus far opened—a mystery of gods, spirits, kings, and avatars—will now converge on the American national stage and before the world.

Chapter 55

THE GOD-KINGS

I N ORDER TO remove the final veil, we must open the phenomenon of the *god-kings*.

THE REIGN OF THE GOD-KINGS

In the ancient pagan world the king or ruler was often taken to be the actual living representation and embodiment of deity—a god-king. The god-kings could be found on the thrones of Egypt, Babylon, Persia, Africa, Asia Minor, China, India, Southeast Asia, and beyond.[1] Those under their rule saw them as the flesh-and-blood manifestations of the gods. In Egypt the pharaohs would reign as incarnations of Amun-Ra,[2] Re,[3] and Horus.[4] In Indian and Southeast Asian culture the concept and phenomenon of the god-king had its own name—*devaraja*, from *deva*, meaning god, and *raja*, king.

LIVING IMAGE OF THE GOD

In Egypt and Mesopotamia the king was believed to emanate the very image of deity. In the writings of ancient Egypt the pharaoh was addressed by his respective god as "my living image on earth."[5] Even royal titles would often bear the names of the embodied god and the king's role in bearing his image. The name of Pharaoh Tutankhaten means the *Living Image of Aten*, the sun god.[6] Later on, his name would be changed to *Tutankhamun*, meaning the *Living Image of Amun*, god of the air.[7] In Mongolia the king was believed to have actually descended from heaven in order to rule on earth.[8] In such kingdoms and civilizations it was not a king only who sat on the throne but an avatar of the gods.

THE CONDUIT

The god-king was believed to have special access to the realm of the deities and so was to function as a channel, a conduit, between people and their gods and goddesses. He would often officiate over the festivals and sacred days of the gods. In some of these, the king would even act out the part of the god as his incarnation. So it was in the "sacred marriages" of Mesopotamia, where a high priestess would assume the part of the goddess Ishtar and the king, her consort, Dumuzi or Tammuz.[9] The god-king functioned as a divine agent on earth, representing the gods to his people, and his people to the gods.

RETURN OF THE GOD-KINGS

What happens when we apply the biblical truth of the shedim and daemonia, the reality of active and volitional spirits behind the gods, to the phenomenon of the god-king? It leads us to the conclusion that the god-king would not simply be a king or leader associating himself with a god but a god or spirit associating itself with a leader or king. For the shedim and daemonia are, after all, *possessing spirits*.

And what happens if we then add the parable of the spirits into the equation? It would lead to the conclusion and warning that if any nation or civilization that has

The God-Kings   257

known God, having been delivered of the gods by the power of His Spirit and Word, should ever turn away from God, it would open itself up not only to the return of the gods *but to the return of the god-kings.*

RETURN OF THE AVATARS

It is therefore no accident that those nations and cultures that most dramatically turned away from God to embrace such post-Christian ideologies as communism, fascism, and Nazism are the same that most dramatically and passionately endowed their governments and their rulers with godlike authorities, godlike auras, and godlike powers. Indeed, their leaders have ruled as the god-kings of the post-Christian age.

As America and the West are not immune to the phenomenon of the gods, they are not exempt from the phenomenon of the god-kings. In fact, they are especially vulnerable. Is it possible then that the turning of America away from God could manifest in the return of the god-king—a leader bearing the image and likeness of a deity, a representation of a god, or goddess—an avatar?

We now open the mystery of the American avatar.

Chapter 56

THE AVATAR

AVATAR IS A Sanskrit word deriving from two Sanskrit root words: *ava*, meaning downward, and *tara*, meaning across or to cross over. It refers to the downward journey by which a god crosses over into another form or manifestation, the descent of a god to earth. It is a central tenet of Hinduism.

THE EMBODIED GOD

In the parable of spirits the disembodied demon must find a "house" to inhabit, an individual to possess.[1] We have seen in the worship of the gods—as in Cuba, South America, Nigeria, and India—the belief in the possession as well as its manifestations. In these cases as the spirit or god indwells the body of the worshipper, the worshipper takes on the identity of the god or spirit. The worshipper assumes the god's characteristics, mannerisms, and psyche—acts like the god, speaks like the god, moves like the god, becomes like the god. The possessed individual becomes, in effect, a vessel of the possessing spirit, an avatar of the indwelling god or goddess. In the case of a god-king, in his total identification with the deity, he reigns as an avatar of the god he embodies.

THE AVATAR ENTHRONED

What makes the god-king especially dangerous is, first, that he operates with godlike authority and, second, that

The Avatar 259

his identification with or possession by the god functions in the realm of government. Thus it impacts an entire people, kingdom, or nation. And if behind the gods are spirits, then he becomes a vessel through which the spirits exercise dominion over a people, a nation, or a civilization.

Is it possible then that a modern-day equivalent of the god-king could be raised up by the gods and spirits to rule a nation that had once known God but turned away? Is it possible that they could use a flesh-and-blood vessel to implement their agenda and attain their dominion? Is it possible that the possessing spirits could, through such a one, seek the possession of America?

PHARAOHS, QUEENS, AND DICTATORS

When the pharaoh stood against Moses and the Hebrews, he did so as an agent of the gods of Egypt. When Ahab and Jezebel persecuted Elijah and the prophets, they did so as agents of the gods of Phoenicia. Indeed, one can see this in Jezebel, an avatar of Ishtar, goddess of immorality and fierce destroyer of those she saw as her enemies. When the post-Christian dictator Fidel Castro warred against God and His people on the island of Cuba, he did so while unwittingly mimicking the Santerian god Chango, even up to the day of his burial. If there were to rise an American equivalent of the ancient god-kings, one who would manifest their image, implement their agenda, and serve as their agent, what would that rising look like?

THE CHOSEN VESSEL

The gods, in their vying for dominion, would seek one who was likewise vying for dominion. They would attempt to raise up and place that one in the highest seats of power. They would seek one who would serve their agenda and oppose the purposes of God. Whether that one served the gods knowingly or unknowingly was irrelevant, only that the vessel was open to being used.

And if already connected to the realm of the gods, that one would be especially suited to become, as the ancient god-kings, a representation, an embodiment, an agent, and an avatar.

Has such a one appeared? And if so, who?

Chapter 57

THE HOUSE OF BRAHMIN

WHAT IF THE template of the ancient kings that lies behind the modern American political leaders goes deeper still? What if behind the one mask lies another? And what happens if we remove it?

BEHIND ATHALIAH

In Kamala Harris's battle against Donald Trump was the template of Jezebel. But behind that was Harris's more primary role of Athaliah. But what if behind the mystery of Athaliah lies something even deeper? Athaliah, like her mother, was deeply joined to the spirits and gods of ancient Phoenicia. She served as their agent, their advocate, their vessel, and their avenger. What if the modern-day Athaliah was likewise connected to the gods? And what if she was connected to a particular god?

THE GOD OF AVATARS

The word *avatar* is associated with one god more than any other—the god Vishnu, the second of Hinduism's three preeminent deities. Vishnu is venerated as the sustainer of the universe. Among all the gods in the Hindu pantheon, Vishnu is especially known for manifesting in the form of avatars.[1]

Beyond his avatars of spirit, Vishnu appeared in avatars of flesh and blood. The first of these was named *Vamana*. In Vamana, Vishnu was born into the priestly house of the

261

Brahmins.[2] Vishnu also incarnated himself as the warrior-sage Parashurama. Parashurama was also born into the house of Brahmins.[3] And Vishnu's prophesied last incarnation is to be Kalki. Kalki is also to be born of a Brahmin house.[4]

HOUSE OF AVATARS

The Brahmins represent the highest caste in Hinduism. They serve as ministers of the gods, officiating in Hindu temples, presiding over Hindu rites and ceremonies, and offering up sacrifices to the Hindu deities.[5] They are believed to possess special access to the gods and to serve as mediators between the gods and the people. The Brahmins are said to be especially favored by the gods and their houses, especially chosen for the birthing of avatars. As the highest of Hindu castes, the Brahmins would provide the avatar the greatest platform to exert power and influence on the world. Thus the house of the Brahmins is believed to be most conducive to the bringing of avatars into the world.

CHILD OF THE BRAHMINS

Among those born into the house of the Brahmins, the house of avatars, was Kamala Harris.[6] In Hinduism it is believed that goddesses appear as avatars in the form of women. One of these was Vishnu's own wife.[7] Is it possible then that the child born of the Brahmins, in the house of avatars, and called *Kamala*, could be used as a vessel of the gods? And what would it mean if she were to acquire

The House of Brahmin

the highest seat of power in the land as did, in ancient times, the god-kings?

To uncover the meaning, we must open the mystery of the lotus.

Chapter 58

LOTUS

IN THE STATE of Tamil Nadu in southern India, in the tiny village of Thulasendrapuram, villagers gathered to their temple to fervently pray to their gods.

A PRAYER TO SHIVA

The worshippers offered prayers before their idols as the Hindu priest lifted a flame before one of their gods. They had come together to pray for the outcome of the 2024 American presidential election. They prayed to the gods to grant victory to Kamala Harris. An article recorded the words of the Hindu priest who led the prayers:

> Our deity is a very powerful god. If we pray well to him, he will make her victorious.[1]

His "very powerful" god was Shiva, the Hindu lord of destruction.[2]

TEMPLE OF KAMALA

Harris was, in fact, connected to that temple. It was built in her ancestral village. On one of its walls, among the names of the temple's patrons, was the engraving of her name.[3] In the days of Jehu, worshippers of the gods and goddesses would undoubtedly have prayed in their temples on behalf of Jezebel and Athaliah. They would not have prayed for Jehu, the one who opposed the gods and

Lotus   265

idols they worshipped, but against him. So the prayers lifted to the gods in that Hindu temple were to be offered up to procure victory for Harris and the defeat of the American Jehu, Donald Trump. What happened there in the temple of Thulasendrapuram was joined to the mystery of Kamala Harris.

THE EASTERN ENTRANCE

When Israel turned away from God, it turned instead to the gods of the nations that surrounded it. It is no accident then that at the same time America began turning away from God, removing Him from its culture and national life, it began as well to open itself up to the gods of the pagan world. That opening resulted in the reentrance of the ancient gods and spirits of Western civilization, as I wrote in *The Return of the Gods,* but also in the entrance and increasing acceptance of *other gods.* As the West turned away from God, it began turning to the gods of the East. As Israel turned from God to the gods of other nations, so America turned to the gods of other cultures, to those of India, the world's greatest natural reserve of pagan gods.

WELCOMING THE OTHERS

The house, emptied of God, will not remain empty. Others will come into it. So it is no accident that the same decade that saw the driving out of God from American public life, the 1960s, also saw the growing acceptance and popularization of Eastern religion, worship, gods, and ideas in American culture. It was then that belief in such things

266   THE AVATAR

as karma, reincarnation, pantheism, the godhood of the
self, and New Age spirituality, and such practices as yoga,
transcendental meditation, and the chanting of mantras
began taking hold in the Western world. As much as Israel
departed from God, to that same degree it opened itself
up to embrace the gods of the pagan Middle East. And
as much as America and the West departed from God, to
that same degree they opened themselves up to embrace
the gods, beliefs, and practices of the pagan East.

FLOWER OF THE GODS

In India the lotus flower is revered as sacred, a symbol of
enlightenment, purity, birth, rebirth, reincarnation, life, fertility, and eternity. The lotus is found throughout Hindu
scriptures. It has thus become the symbol of Eastern religion and spirituality, the symbol of Hinduism, Buddhism,
and Jainism.[4] Several of the most prominent of Hindu deities are portrayed as sitting on and reigning from a lotus
flower. The universe itself is said to have been born from a
lotus growing out of one of the gods.[5] As one of the most
sacred of symbols in Hinduism, the lotus is deeply joined to
the gods and goddesses of the East.

KAMALA

In the Bible a person's given name often carries great significance, often prophetic, foretelling the person's calling
or destiny. The patriarch Abraham would become the pro-
genitor of the Jewish and Arab peoples. His name translates to *father of the many*.[6] The hero Gideon would strike
down the army of Midian.[7] His name means *one who*

Lotus 267

strikes down. Ruth would become the loyal friend of the Israelite widow Naomi. Her name means *friend.*[8]

Lotus is an English word derived from Greek. It does not, of course, appear as such in the language of the gods of Hinduism. The lotus, symbol of Eastern religion and, specifically, of its gods and goddesses, appears in the Hindu scriptures in its original Sanskrit form—as *Kamal* or *Kamala.*[9]

SIGN OF THE DEPARTURE

So as the ancient god-kings represented the gods and pantheons of their kingdoms, the child born into the house of the Brahmins, Kamala Harris, was given the name that represented the gods and pantheon of the East. And just as Jezebel and Athaliah represented the gods of Phoenicia, so the woman Kamala, by virtue of her name, represented the gods of India. She was given the name at birth in 1964.[10] It was a key moment in America's spiritual trajectory. It was just after the beginning of God's removal from American public life and on the verge of the mass entrance of Eastern gods and religion into the nation's mainstream. So to the Eastern world, the name *Kamala*, the lotus, speaks of gods and goddesses, but to the West, a nation's departure from God and its subsequent fall into apostasy. What would the rise of one bearing that name mean?

To find the answer, we must go deeper still.

Chapter 59

GODDESS

THE NAME *LOTUS* encompasses all the Hindu gods and goddesses and Hinduism itself. But could the mystery be even more specific than that?

THE GODDESS LAKSHMI

The avatar would embody a specific god or goddess. Among the most central and preeminent of the Hindu deities is the goddess Lakshmi. Lakshmi is among the most widely revered and worshipped of Hindu goddesses.[1] She is typically depicted as a queen seated on a throne, surrounded by elephants, having four arms, and worshipped as the goddess of fortune, beauty, prosperity, love, fertility, and power.[2]

THE GODDESS OF AVATARS

Like Vishnu, Lakshmi is known for her incarnations and avatars. In fact, Lakshmi and Vishnu, the god of avatars, are lovers. And so Lakshmi is known through her many avatars. When Vishnu comes into the world in the form of an avatar, Lakshmi likewise descends into the world and is reborn as her own avatar. Thus the avatars of Vishnu are often matched by the avatars of Lakshmi. So the goddess was said to have been born as the avatar Dharani to be the wife of Vishnu's Brahmin warrior avatar, Parashurama, and as the avatar Sita to be the lover of Vishnu's warrior-king

Goddess 269

avatar, Rama, among many others. The avatar of the one followed after the avatar of the other.[3]

SHE OF THE LOTUS

Lakshmi is typically portrayed as sitting on a lotus. She reigns from a lotus throne. She wears a garland of lotuses. She is described as the one whose face is like a lotus, whose eyes are as beautiful as the lotus, in whose hands is the lotus, who dwells within the lotus, and who of the lotus is born. So great is the association of this particular goddess with that particular flower that she herself bears the name *Lotus*, or *She of the Lotus*.[4] The goddess is thus known by the name *Kamalatmika*, or *Kamala*. Lakshmi is Kamala, and Kamala is Lakshmi.[5]

So Kamala Harris was named after a goddess, a goddess who rules from the lotus throne, the goddess Kamala. As she rose to power, most Americans had to learn how to pronounce her name. They had no idea that what they were pronouncing was the name of a goddess. When her supporters chanted praise to her name, they echoed the praise and worship of the goddess.

KAMALA THE GODDESS

But there was more. The Sanskrit word for goddess is *devi*. *Devi* is the feminine form of *deva* and means *the shining ones*. Devi can, more specifically, refer to Hinduism's primeval mother goddess Devi, who appears, among other goddesses, as Lakshmi or Kamala. The goddesses of the Hindu pantheon are also identified by the same name, *Devi*.[6]

270 THE AVATAR

At her birth Kamala Harris was given not one name but two. Her second given name was *Devi*. Thus she was named *Goddess*.

The avatar of Hinduism is completely one with the god or goddess he or she embodies. The one who is indwelled by a goddess becomes as the goddess. So too the god-king avatars of the ancient world would often bear the name of the deity they manifested. Kamala Harris bore the name of an ancient goddess who was also known by the name *Devi*. And thus the woman born in the house of the Brahmins, the house of avatars, was named *Kamala Devi*, which translates to *Kamala the Goddess*.[7] The avatar is one with the god it embodies.

As the ancient god-kings were known as *the living image* of the gods they personified and manifested, is it possible the woman known as *Kamala the Goddess* would bear the image of the one whose name she bore? Is it possible that her life would be conformed into the likeness of the goddess?

Chapter 60

THE GOPALAN

COULD THE HOUSE into which Kamala Harris was born hold more secrets linked to the gods and the avatars?

MAYA

The Sanskrit word for illusion is *maya*. The word *maya* stands for the Hindu belief that the world and the self are separated from the underlying unity of reality and thus exist in a cosmic illusion.[1] As the goddess of worldly fortune and desire, Lakshmi, or Kamala, is joined to maya.

Less than three years after Harris was born and given the name *Kamala*, a sister was born. She was given the name *Maya*. As in the pantheon of Eastern gods in which the goddess Kamala/Lakshmi is joined to illusion, maya, so in the house of her birth, Kamala was likewise joined to Maya. And lest the connection be missed, Maya's middle name is *Lakshmi*.[2]

KRISHNA THE AVATAR

As Vishnu was especially the god of avatars, Harris was named after Vishnu's lover, goddess of the female avatars who accompanied the male avatars of Vishnu. The most widely worshipped of Vishnu's avatars is Krishna.[3] Krishna is the trickster god who overturned the four-wheeled vehicle, the same of which I wrote in the account of our near-death experience on the way from Agra to New Delhi.

It was in the year after Harris was born that the International Society for Krishna Consciousness was founded in New York City. The society would become a central channel through which the worship of Krishna would spread to America and the West. The house into which Harris was born would bear a special connection to the trickster god.

THE GOPALA

Hindu writings speak of Krishna playing with and herding cows. Because of this he was given the name *Gopala*. *Gopala* means the *Tender* or *Protector of Cows*.[4] It was from that name given to Krishna that the Indian surname *Gopalan* was derived. Harris's mother was born of the line of the *Gopalans*.[5] And thus Harris was born into a house named after a Hindu god. And so in her Hindu surname, Harris was named after a god, and in her first and second names after a goddess.

Added to this, the goddess after which Harris was named was herself connected to Krishna, the god after which Harris's family was named. The goddess's avatar was Krishna's lover and was known as a gopi, a follower of the *Gopala* god.

HOUSE OF THE AVATAR

But there was more. Krishna was not only a god; he was an avatar, the manifestation on earth of the god Vishnu. So the name *Gopalan* refers to an avatar. And so Harris was descended from the line of *Gopalan*, born in the house of the avatar.

The Gopalan 273

And this wasn't her only connection to the avatars. As Krishna was not only a god but the avatar of another god, so Kamala, whose name Harris also bore, was not only a goddess but was herself the avatar of another goddess. Kamala was Lakshmi's manifestation on earth. And so Harris was both born into the house of an avatar god and given the name of an avatar goddess. She was, from the beginning, infused with the mystery of the avatar.

———————

Is it possible that behind the *origins* and *rise* of Kamala Harris are the *origins* and *rising* of an ancient goddess?

Chapter 61

LADY OF THE WATERS

THE ORIGIN MYTH of the goddess Kamala, the story of her rising, joins her to the *Samudra Manthan,* the *Milky Ocean.* The title holds the key to the story.

ORIGIN OF THE GODDESS

According to the story, the Hindu warrior god Indra was charged with protecting the universe. Through a careless act, he lost his powers, as did the other gods. The universe was taken over by the *asuras,* evil spirits or demons. The gods went to Vishnu seeking his counsel as to how the asuras could be overcome. He told them to churn the waters of the Milky Ocean that they might obtain the nectar of immortal life.

The gods tricked the asuras into helping them churn the waters. Using a giant serpent as their churning rope, the gods and the demons began churning the milky waters. For years and ages they continued churning, seeing nothing but ocean foam and froth. Finally, the ocean began yielding its treasures. Foremost among them was the goddess Kamala.[1] Out of the ocean foam the goddess began to rise, seated on a lotus and with a lotus in her hand. With her help the gods defeated the asuras and the world was restored.[2] It is because of this that the goddess Kamala/Lakshmi became known as *Jaladhija, the One Born of the Ocean* and *Daughter of the Water.*[3]

274

Lady of the Waters 275

CHILD OF THE OCEAN

Could the life of Kamala Harris, as a "living image" of the goddess, reflect the goddess's origins? And if the "birth" of the goddess Kamala was connected to the waters of the ocean, could the same be true of the birth of the woman Kamala? Harris was born in Oakland, California.[4] Oakland is a city set on the waters. It lies on the east of the San Francisco Bay, the Bay itself lying on the east side of the Pacific Ocean. As the entrance of the goddess Kamala into the world was joined to the waters, so the entrance into the world of the woman Kamala was likewise joined to the waters.

THE MILKY WATERS

After coming into the world, Harris spent the first and, then, later years of her childhood in Berkeley, California, not far from Oakland.[5] Berkeley also lies on the waters of the San Francisco Bay. On the San Francisco Bay one can find shells. Among them is the scallop shell. Shells, and particularly the scallop shell, are especially associated with the goddess Lakshmi.[6]

The myth of the goddess's birth involves the churning of the ocean froth and foam from which she emerged and by which she was first lifted up on her lotus throne. So the waters of the San Francisco Bay, by which Kamala Harris first appeared and then grew up, are likewise known for the froth and foam they churn up.[7]

THE OCEANIC RISING

The goddess's origin myth not only speaks of her birth but of her rising. Both began in the waters. Could then the rise of the goddess Kamala lie behind the rise of the woman Kamala? Could Harris's rise to the heights of political power have also been *born of the ocean*?

It was on the San Francisco Bay that Harris would first enter the halls of government, becoming a deputy district attorney, then assistant district attorney, and then, in 2003, San Francisco's district attorney.[8] Her rise to the attorney general's office and then to the United States Senate and then to the White House began in San Francisco.[9] So the rise of the woman Kamala began as it was for the goddess Kamala, in the midst of the waters, as *one born of the ocean*.

The mystery of the goddess involved power. Could it lie behind the strange ascent of Kamala Harris to the highest house of the American government?

Chapter 62

COSMIC QUEEN AND SLEEPING GOD

THE RISE OF Kamala Harris to the heights of American political power was unlikely. Her first attempt at running for the presidency quickly evaporated in the face of fleeting support and funding.[1] And yet just when there seemed no hope of fulfilling her presidential ambitions, she would suddenly be catapulted to the White House. Could there have been another dynamic behind her rising in the realm of the gods?

GODDESS OF GOVERNMENTAL POWER

The goddess Lakshmi was linked to power—governmental power. She was worshipped as the consort to kings, including some of the most powerful of reigning Hindu deities and several lesser ones.[2] If behind Kamala Harris is the mystery of the goddess, then is it possible that the goddess's connection to governmental power lay behind her own unlikely ascent to the heights of governmental power?

SECOND TO THE COSMIC THRONE

It was Vishnu with which the goddess was most associated. According to Hindu mythology, it was through Vishnu that the universe came into existence. He is worshipped as one of Hinduism's supreme beings, the *Preserver*, the *Lord* of the World, sustainer of the universe, and overseer of the cosmic order.[3] Alongside Vishnu's jewel-encrusted throne is the *lotus throne* of the goddess on which she coreigns.[4]

So as the goddess ruled on the highest of thrones, at the side of the Hindu king of creation, is it possible but that the one who bore the name of the goddess was destined to govern at the side of the president, the highest leader of the American government? And as the goddess ruled as the cosmic second-in-command to Hinduism's "Lord of the World," is it possible that the one who bore her name was likewise ordained to become the second-in-command over America?

THE COSMIC MAMALAH

During her vice presidency, and long before she was considered a candidate for the presidency, Harris appeared on a nationally broadcast television program in which a striking exchange took place. The program's host told her, "We need you to be *Mamalah* of the country."[5] She was asking Harris to become the "Mother" of the nation. The use of such words in reference to an American leader was unprecedented. The moment would be seen as especially awkward. But could it have been unintentionally significant?

The goddess was known as the Great Mother or, in other words, the Mamalah. As Vishnu was referred to as Lord of the World, his coregent goddess was addressed as Mother of the World.[6] To the millions who witnessed it, the words of the host appeared strange and out of place. But they

Cosmic Queen and Sleeping God   279

were actually in perfect accord with the deity that lay behind Kamala Harris, the Great Mamalah goddess.

SLEEPY VISHNU

Contrary to what we might expect, in the pairing of the goddess to the ruling god Vishnu, it is Vishnu who appears as mostly passive, and the goddess, mostly active.[7] So in the pairing of Harris to President Biden, it was Biden who appeared to many as passive, and Harris, the more energetic of the two. Trump would refer to him as "Sleepy Joe."[8] In view of the pantheon the label is striking, for Vishnu was known as the sleeping god. He was the deity who fell into the *yog nidra*, the cosmic sleep. While the "king of creation" sleeps, Lakshmi/Kamala, in effect, performs his function as sustainer of the universe, compensating and covering for her "sleepy Vishnu."

And yet the goddess had another side, another persona, and another face dramatically different from the one she displayed as Lakshmi. It was a darker side, and one especially embodied in her manifestation as Kamala.

Chapter 63

THE MAHAVIDYA

WE HAVE REMOVED one mask after the other, one persona and face after the next. Now we remove the mask of the goddess herself.

MANIFESTATION OF THE DEVI

In the pantheon of Hinduism, the goddess behind all goddesses is known as the *Mahadevi*, the *Great Goddess*, or simply the *Devi*, the *Goddess*.[1] The ten manifestations of the Devi are called the *Mahavidyas*. The tenth is the goddess Kamala.[2] Kamala is considered the Devi's final manifestation.[3] As a Mahavidya, she is not called *Lakshmi*, only *Kamala*. It is in this manifestation, as Kamala, that the other and very different side of the lotus goddess is revealed.

THE GODDESS ON HER OWN

As Lakshmi, the goddess is portrayed at Vishnu's side. But as Kamala, Vishnu is, for the most part, gone from the picture. As Lakshmi, the goddess reigns with the god. But as Kamala, she does not coreign but reigns alone on the lotus throne. As Kamala, she moves from being Vishnu's partner, second-in-command, the cosmic number two, and becomes what appears to be first-in-command. As Kamala, the focus shifts from the god and goddess to the goddess alone.[4]

Is it possible that this too lies behind the rise of Kamala

The Mahavidya 281

Harris? Could the mystery have ordained that the woman named after the goddess would start in America's number-two position in the form of the vice presidency, then seek to occupy its number-one position, the presidency?

The goddess Kamala eclipses Krishna to sit alone on her throne. So the woman Kamala would eclipse the president under whom she served and would vie to take his place. As did Vishnu in light of the goddess Kamala, the president would fade from view in light of the woman Kamala. It is noteworthy that this same pattern manifested in the case of Athaliah, who after serving as second-in-command would seize the king's throne—but now it manifests in the realm of the gods.

THE DUALITY OF THE GODDESS

The goddess's transformation is not limited to the political or governmental realms. As Kamala, the Mahavidya, the goddess is separated not only from the king but from her husband and, indeed, from the context of marriage itself. As one writer puts it:

> As a Mahavidya Kamala is...almost entirely removed from marital and domestic contexts.[5]

As Kamala, the Mahavidya, the goddess functions not as a wife or mother but on her own. In this is the goddess's duality. As Lakshmi, she is joined to her husband and performs the function of a wife. But as Kamala, her identity has virtually nothing to do with men or marriage, family or children. She is as one devoid of them.

So in the goddess's duality is the duality of Kamala Harris. On the one hand, Harris was married and part of a family. But on the other, she functioned as one devoid of them. She exemplified the agenda of radical feminism, as embodied by the Mahavidya goddess Kamala, in which men, marriage, family, and children were de-emphasized.

THE REPLACER

As Kamala, the Mahavidya, the goddess was not only separated from the gods; she was over them. So one commentator writes of the Mahavidya goddesses:

> Their power and authority do not derive from association with male deities. Rather, it is their power that pervades the gods....When male deities are shown, they are almost always in supporting roles....and are depicted as subsidiary figures.[6]

As Kamala, the goddess departs from her role as Lakshmi in support of her male partner. We would expect then the woman Kamala to do likewise. Departing from her supportive and subordinate role to a male leader, namely the president, Kamala Harris was now vying for the presidency, subordinate to no one. The men who now surrounded her, as with her running mate, appeared to be, or were, subordinate. And as did the goddess Kamala, she now embodied female governmental power and authority over all.

The Mahavidya

A GODDESS FOR GOD

As a Mahavidya, the goddess Kamala took on the attributes, functions, and roles traditionally associated with men, that of warrior and slayer. So too the woman who bore the name *Kamala* would champion an agenda in which gender roles were reversed, bent, transitioned, merged, or replaced. The bending and voiding of distinctions was typical of paganism, the blurring of God and the universe, man and animal, matter and spirit, male and female, good and evil. The issue of gender was only a symptom. So the rise of the woman named *Goddess* was about more than a woman replacing a man; it was ultimately about a pagan ethos replacing a biblical one, the replacing of God with the gods.

And yet even this hid something deeper. To find it, we must remove yet another mask.

Chapter 64

A NECKLACE OF SKULLS

OF THE TEN Mahavidya goddesses, Kamala would appear to be among the most benign. But appearances can be deceptive.

THE TERRIFYING

Hinduism's "Great Goddess," Devi, who lies behind the Mahavidyas, one of which is Kamala, is also called *Shakti*. The Devi or Shakti is also considered to be the same as the goddess *Kali*. Kali is the terrifying Hindu goddess of death and destruction. She is typically depicted holding a sword in one hand and a decapitated head of her enemy in one of her many other hands. She is portrayed as drunk with the blood of her victims.[1] So behind Kamala is the Devi, also known as Shakti and Kali. So it is written:

> As a Mahavidya, Kamala also has become associated with fearsome qual-ities....Her hundred- and thousand-name hymns in the *Sakta-pramoda*, for example, call her Klartri [Kalaratri] (a fearsome name for Kali).[2]

Therefore behind Kamala's benign and innocuous appearance lies something dark and terrifying.

A Necklace of Skulls

SLAYER OF HER ENEMIES

Could the dichotomy of the goddess Kamala lie behind the dichotomy of the woman bearing the name *Kamala*? It must here be remembered that her given name was not *Kamala* alone but *Devi*. And *Devi* refers not only to *a* goddess but specifically to the *Devi*, the primal arch-goddess of the Hindu pantheon—also identified as Shakti and Kali. There was to Kamala Devi Harris a similar duality; on one hand, she appeared benign, but on the other hand and underneath her innocuous appearance was something very different.

In one of her hymns the goddess Kamala is identified as the "Slayer of Madhu and Kaitabha, Slayer of Sumbha and Nisumbha."[3] The goddess Kamala, like Kali, was a slayer, a fierce destroyer of her enemies. In the same way, the other side of Kamala Harris was fierce. She too was a slayer of her enemies. As a prosecuting attorney, she leveled charges against her enemies and sought their punishment. As the goddess Kamala slew demons, the woman Kamala sought to slay those she had demonized, rightly or wrongly. In her vying for the presidency, she would seek likewise to demonize and, in effect, slay her opponent, Donald Trump.

THE BHIMA, THE TAMASI, AND THE GHORA

Other striking words, titles, descriptions, and names appear in the hymns of the goddess Kamala, several of them especially befitting of the goddess Kali. One of her titles is *Bhima*, meaning *the Terrible One*. Another is *Tamasi*, meaning *the Darkness*. She is also known as *Ghora, the*

Awful One.[4] The dichotomy of such descriptions given to the goddess Kamala under her benign appearance could also be found in the woman Kamala. Underneath Harris's innocuous persona was an agenda that called for the unlimited slaughter of unborn children. No other issue so aroused her passion. In this respect, she had stood for what is *Awful, Terrible,* and *of the Darkness.*

THE MUNDAMALA

The *mundamala* is a necklace made up of human skulls.[5] It is associated with the *Devi* and can be seen in Hindu imagery of Kali.[6] In the hymns of Kamala, the goddess is called *She Who Wears a Garland of Skulls.*[7] A necklace is worn for the purpose of adorning or beautifying its wearer. The goddess Kamala wears the mundamala, a necklace of skulls. So the woman Kamala adorned herself with the cause of abortion as if it were something to be praised and admired. But it involved the destruction of life. It was the jewelry of the Mahavidya, an adornment of death, a necklace of skulls.

———————————

We now open one of the strangest manifestations of the goddess and one of its strangest fulfillments.

Chapter 65

THE LAUGHING ONE

OF ALL THE attributes for which Kamala Harris would become known, one appeared especially strange and incongruous. And yet even this would bear an eerie connection to the ancient goddess.

LAUGHING KAMALA

It became an issue in her campaign for the presidency. It was her laughter. It seemed as if she could not make it through an informal speaking event or conversation without laughing. But it was not only its frequency but the context in which it took place. She would laugh when being asked about the economy.[1] She would laugh when being asked about refugees.[2] She would laugh when it was inappropriate and abnormal to laugh. Her laughing was so incongruous that it would elicit questions from many observers, criticism from her opponents, and concern among her supporters.[3] It was so curious and striking that it became a meme on the internet.[4] She would come to be known as "laughing Kamala."[5]

But could this strange characteristic of a modern political figure be connected to the mystery of gods and avatars?

THE LAUGHING GODDESS

The strange laughter of Kamala Harris can be found in the Eastern pantheon. One of the basic concepts of Hinduism is that of the *Laughing Goddess*. Harris was

287

288 THE AVATAR

given the middle name *Devi*. As we have seen, while the word can denote *a* goddess, it specifically corresponds to the name of one particular goddess, *Devi*. Devi is the primal goddess of Eastern religion who manifests herself in the female deities of the Hindu pantheon. Thus Harris was given the name *Devi*, the one who manifests herself not only in the form of the goddess Kamala but also in the form of the laughing goddess of Hinduism.

ATTAHASA—THE LAUGHTER OF THE DEVI

The ancient Hindu text known as the *Devi Mahatmya*, or the *Glory of Devi*, is more specific. Devi, in the form of the goddess Durga, defeats her enemy Mahashasura. The text describes the Devi's strategy as *attahasa*, meaning *laughter—loud, roaring laughter*:

> She started roaring. She started giving attahasa [laughter], again and again.... The whole sky filled with the loud sound of her attahasa [laughter]. And it echoed. In a big way, her attahasa [laughter] echoed. All the worlds became agitated....Seeing all this— the sky filled with the attahasa of Devi [the laughter of Devi].[6]

Thus the *Devi Mahatmya* identifies Devi as the primordial goddess of attahasa—loud, extreme, and roaring laughter. Thus Kamala Harris bears the name of Hinduism's ultimate and cosmic laughing goddess.

The Laughing One 289

THE TENTH EMANATION

Among the most prominent and frightening manifestations of the *laughing goddess* is *Kali*. The goddess Kamala, as we have seen, was specifically connected to the goddess Kali. The following quote connects each of the mystical dots:

> *Kamala* ("the lotus"):
> The tenth of the ten *Mahāvidyās*....
> The ten Mahāvidyās are the emanations of Mahākālī, the Goddess of time and death.
> She is depicted as a *fearful laughing goddess*.[7]

In other words, the goddess Kamala, as a Mahavidya, is an emanation of the goddess *Mahakali*, or the *Great Kali*. Kali is, in turn, the fearful laughing goddess. Thus Kamala is an emanation of the *frightening, laughing goddess*. And so the woman named *Kamala Devi*, of all people on the American and world stage, would become especially known for this unique attribute—a strange laughter.

THE SOUND OF DESTRUCTION

But what made the laughter of the goddess most striking was not only its immensity but its context. The goddess's laughter was strangely incongruent to its context. And so the laughter of Kamala Devi Harris, in its strange incongruence, followed after the incongruent laughter of the ancient goddess. The sound of the laughing goddess was linked to warfare, terror, and violence. One account describes two warriors who made the mistake of approaching the fearful laughing goddess.

> [They] encountered the *frightfully laughing Goddess* with her outstretched tongue. After they were killed...[8]

The sound of the laughing goddess was, thus, connected to destruction. The last thing her enemies heard as she destroyed them was the sound of her laughing.

THE LAUGHING AVATAR

As district attorney, Harris oversaw and directed the prosecution and conviction of Jamal Trulove on the charge of murder. He would be sentenced to fifty years in prison. It was later ruled that he was innocent, and his conviction was overturned. Strikingly, Trulove would later recount that at the reading of his verdict Harris "busted out laughing."[9] As the laughing goddess laughed at the destruction of her enemies, so the woman who bore her name did likewise. So it was again in accordance with the mystery that the laughing goddess would have a laughing avatar.

We now must go deeper still into the origin of the goddess and that of her avatar. What will be uncovered, in view of the mystery, is nothing less than stunning.

Chapter 66

DAY OF THE GODDESS

IT IS ONE of the most important days in the Hindu calendar, a day of rites and rituals, celebration and worship. It is a day that holds great significance for the present hour and for America.

SHARAD PURNIMA

It is called *Sharad Purnima*. It falls on the first full moon of autumn. On that day, the idols of Hindu gods and goddesses are clothed in white to symbolize the brightness of the moon. While many gods are worshipped on Sharad Purnima, the holiday is especially devoted to one. It is the day of veneration to the goddess Lakshmi/Kamala.[1]

On Sharad Purnima, worshippers bathe themselves in rivers to attain purity. Some fast. Homes are decorated with floor paintings and flowers. Sacred food is distributed and partaken of. Prayers are lifted up, and mantras are recited.

THE IDOL OF THE HOUSE

Sharad Purnima is not complete without the tangible appearance of the goddess. Her idol is central to its rites. Her worshippers adorn her image with opulent clothing and jewelry. It is then typically placed on a specially prepared altar within the worshipper's house. Offerings are then presented to the idol, fruits and sweets of milk and rice. And as Lakshmi/Kamala is the goddess of the lotus,

292   THE AVATAR

her worshippers also present collections of lotus flowers on her altar. Hymns and mantras are offered to the goddess through the night as her worshippers seek her favor,[2] while in some regions of India dances are performed in worship outdoors under the stars.

THE MYSTERY DAY

We have seen the connection between Kamala Harris and the ancient Eastern goddess whose name she bears. We have seen how her life followed after the goddess's mythology and conformed itself to her image. It is time now to lift the final veil that we might know and see what no one knew or saw at the time it happened and long before it would become manifest.

Kamala Harris came into the world on the day devoted to the *gods and spirits.*

The woman who would bear the name *Goddess* was *born on the day of the goddess.*

The woman named *Kamala* entered the world *on the day dedicated to* one specific deity—the goddess named *Kamala.*

Kamala Harris was born on October 20, 1964. She was born on the day of a Hindu festival. She came into the world on *Sharad Purnima.*

The woman who would bear the goddess's name was born on the day of the goddess whose name she bore. The one whose life would follow and bear the image and likeness of a particular goddess would begin her life on earth on the day given to celebrate that very same goddess.

Day of the Goddess 293

DANCE OF THE GOPALA

Sharad Purnima celebrates the *Rāsa-līlā,* the dance of the Gopala, the cowherder god, Krishna.[3] The Rāsa-līlā is the dance of love Krishna performed with the gopi milkmaids led by the chief gopi, his consort, Radha, the avatar of Lakshmi/Kamala. It is a night dance, performed under the stars. As Krishna was the avatar of the god Vishnu and Radha the avatar of the goddess Lakshmi/Kamala, the Rāsa-līlā was a dance of avatars.

Kamala Harris was born of the house called *Gopalan,* after the god called *Gopala,* Krishna. She was born at night, the night of the Gopala's dance with the *gopis* and Radha, the goddess's avatar. So on the night of the dance of the goddess's avatar, a child came into the world who would become, in effect, the avatar of the goddess.

In 1964, on Sharad Purnima, a Hindu mother spoke the name *Kamala* in devotion to her newborn child as worshippers all over the world spoke the same name, *Kamala,* in mantras of devotion to their goddess.

And so it was in accordance with the mystery that the one who would serve as the living image or avatar of the goddess would be born not only on the very day of that very goddess but on the very night of the dance of the goddess's avatar.

It is a night of vigils kept in the hope of ushering in the manifestation of a deity. But it ushered in something else.

Chapter 67

NIGHT OF THE VISITATION

THE HOLIDAY IS known as *Kojagara Puja*. It is not only a celebration or commemoration; it is an event, in and of itself, a happening, or the preparation for a happening—a manifestation.

WHO IS AWAKE?

The name *Kojagara Puja* comes from a question. *Kojagara* means "Who is awake?" On the night of Kojagara Puja it is considered crucial that its observers do not fall into a sleep but stay awake and vigilant. Those who sleep, it is believed, miss the blessing. But those who stay awake are to be given health and prosperity.[1]

So the observers seek to stay awake in all-night vigils. The vigils consist, in some cases, of fasting, praying, singing, the chanting of mantras, and dancing to the gods.[2] Some play games throughout the night in order to avoid falling asleep.[3] Ceremonial lamps are lit to illuminate the night. But it is the light of the moon that is most important. On Kojagara Puja the devotees are encouraged to gaze into the moon and worship under its light—all in preparation for an expected event.[4]

THE VISITATION OF THE GODDESS

The reason it is considered crucial to stay awake that night is because it is believed that on the night of Kojagara Puja, and only on that night, a deity makes a special visitation, a

294

Night of the Visitation   295

descent to earth.[5] The deity is the goddess Lakshmi/Kamala. Kojagara Puja is the night on which she visits the earth. So it is written of this night:

> Goddess Lakshmi [Kamala] descends to
> Earth on the full moon day of Ashwin
> to observe the actions of mortals.[6]

On the night of Kojagara Puja worshippers are to gaze into the moon, as it is believed that when the moonlight reaches the earth, the goddess Lakshmi/Kamala has stepped on the earth.[7]

Upon entering the world, the goddess wanders from house to house to see who is awake and who is asleep on the night of her visitation.[8]

To prepare for her coming, the worshippers clean, decorate, and embellish their homes for the goddess's visitation. To welcome her in, they draw the outline of her footprint on their doorsteps.[9] It is believed that upon entering each house, the goddess asks, "Kojagara?" or "Who is awake?," and thus the name of the holiday. Those who can answer her question are then to receive her blessing.[10]

NIGHT OF DESCENT—NIGHT OF THE AVATAR

What is Kojagara Puja? It is another version of Sharad Purnima. But its name focuses specifically on the goddess's entrance into the world and each house. October 20, 1964, the day Kamala Harris was born, was Kojagara Puja, the day when the goddess Kamala visits the world.

So the child named *Goddess* entered into the world on the night appointed for the goddess to enter into the world.

And as worshippers around the world kept vigil and stayed awake into the night to welcome the goddess into their houses, a young Hindu woman worshipper kept vigil and stayed up into the night to welcome the child named after the same goddess into her home.

And as the goddess named *Kamala Devi*, or *Kamala the Goddess*, is to make her appearance on earth on the night of Kojagara Puja, so it was on the night of Kojagara Puja that the child named *Kamala Devi*, *Kamala the Goddess*, made her appearance on earth.

This brings us back to the meaning of the word *avatar*, the descent, the descending of a god or goddess into the world in a different form.[11] The avatar is the manifestation of that descent. So she who bore the name *Kamala Devi*, *Kamala the Goddess*, was born on the day of the descent of the goddess whose name she bore. And her life would be a manifestation of that descent, the manifestation of an avatar.

And yet there is one more puzzle piece to the mystery of that day.

Chapter 68

BIRTH

THE DAY ON which Kamala Harris entered the world contains one more secret.

BIRTH OF THE GODDESS

The myth of the goddess's birth, her emergence from the waters of the Milky Ocean, her being lifted up on the ocean foam, is told and retold every year. It is part of her birthday celebration. What day is it? It is Sharad Purnima, Kojagara Puja. The day is not only given to the celebration and worship of the goddess, not only to the opening of one's house and the receiving of her night visitation—it is her birthday.

It fell on October 20, 1964.

The goddess's birth was celebrated all over the world. And in the midst of the celebration, the child named *Goddess* was born.

As worshippers recited and told the story of the "birth" of the goddess Kamala and her emergence from the waters, the child named *Kamala* likewise emerged and, by the waters of the ocean, was brought forth into the world.

THE DAY OF KAMALA DEVI

On that day it is appointed that the worshippers are to recite these words:

> Oh Kamala, lotus-like and lotus-dwelling goddess, be gracious,

be gracious....I bow to goddess Mahalakshmi.[1]

The word *Mahalakshmi* is another name for the goddess Lakshmi, another name for Kamala. So all over the world, they lifted up prayers to the goddess Kamala, and the child named Kamala was born.

On that day it is also appointed that this chant be spoken:

> *Kamala Devi* is above and beyond all worlds....
>
> *Kamala Devi* is of golden radiance.
>
> *Kamala Devi*...She is dark; She is the unifier.
>
> *Kamala Devi*...is the conclusion of the universe; She is the core of its destruction.[2]

So the people chanted, "Kamala Devi, Kamala Devi, Kamala Devi," over and over again, and the child Kamala Devi was born.

BIRTH OF THE AVATAR

No one could have planned or orchestrated it. It was all part of the mystery from the very first day.

On October 20, 1964, a child was born into the world and appointed to bear the name of a goddess.

She was born on the day of the goddess whose name she bore. She entered the world on the night appointed for the goddess to enter the world.

The avatar bears the identity and essence of the god or

Birth 299

goddess it manifests. And so on the day that Kamala Devi, Kamala the Goddess, was born, Kamala Devi, the one called *Kamala the Goddess*, was born. In other words, on the day of the birth of the goddess, the avatar was born.

And so the avatar, born into the mystery of the goddess, was born on the day of the goddess's birth.

We now move through the years to the moment Kamala Harris was about to ascend onto the national and world stage—and to the appearing of a strange and significant image.

Chapter 69

IMAGE OF THE AVATAR

OULD THE MYSTERY of the gods join together the engraved images that adorned the walls of ancient Egypt with the digital images of the twenty-first century?

THE IMAGE OF MERGING

As the ancient god-kings of Egypt and Mesopotamia reigned as "living images" of the deities, their imagery was of great import. In their engraved and painted representations, they were portrayed wearing the garments and adornments of the gods they personified.

In ancient Egypt the pharaohs were depicted as falcons or as falcon-headed figures, as the king's image was merged with the image of Horus, the falcon god. So too the images of the Egyptian goddess-queens were merged with the symbols, headdresses, and adornments of the goddesses they embodied, such as Isis and Hathor.[1] Is it possible then that the merging of imagery, that of the gods with those who represent them, would find its way into the modern world and to our day? Could an image appear in the modern world, merging together a modern-day avatar with an ancient goddess?

THE APPEARING

It was October of 2020. Joe Biden had chosen Kamala Harris as his running mate in his campaign for the White House. It was less than one month from the presidential election

Image of the Avatar

and from Harris's rise to the White House. Could a sign have been given at that moment to reveal the *other* realm, that which was taking place behind the political stage?

It did appear—in the form of an image. In ancient times, the images of the god-kings would appear in the form of statues or as engravings on stone walls. But in the twenty-first century, it would appear on the internet. As the images of ancient Egypt merged the representations of the pharaohs with the features, attributes, and symbolism of the gods they embodied, so the image merged a photograph of Kamala Harris with the features, attributes, and symbolism of a pagan goddess. Appearing just before Harris was to be lifted up to the heights of American power, could it have been a warning?

FROM EGYPTIAN TEMPLES TO THE WORLD WIDE WEB

It was a representation of what had already been. From the moment of her birth, Kamala Harris's life was joined to the goddess. But now that joining was manifested in visual form. In the image, Harris's face was juxtaposed onto the body of a deity. The pharaohs were joined to the gods of Egypt, the kings of Babylon with Mesopotamian gods. Harris was merged with a Hindu deity. The image was created, not by an enemy but from Harris's own house, from the daughter of her sister, Maya.[2] It was intended to glorify its subject. But what it did was join to the gods the woman who had been joined to the gods from the day of her birth—it manifested the mystery.

THE AVATAR AND GODDESS

As in the images of ancient Egypt, where the queens were crowned with the headdresses and adornments of the goddesses, so Kamala Harris was crowned with the headdress, jewelry, and garments of a goddess. And it was typical in Hindu imagery; she was portrayed as having many arms. In her hands were the goddess's symbols and weapons: a spear, a shield, a sword, and the *shankha*, the conch shell of the gods.[3] Harris was being portrayed as a Hindu goddess by her own family. In view of all the connections, from her name *Goddess* to the date of her birth, the image was beyond striking. As did the ancient images of the Egyptian pharaohs, the image revealed Kamala Harris as one with the gods—the avatar of a goddess.

WARRIORESS

It was an image of conflict and warfare. It was meant to represent the presidential campaign, but in the realm of the gods and spirits of Hinduism. The image of a warrior goddess was needed. Though the goddess Kamala is described in terms of ferocity and warfare, the slayer of her enemies, images depicting her as such are not common.[4] The closest match would be that of the goddess Durga. So it was with the Hindu goddess Durga that Harris was merged.[5] And yet in Hindu writings, one can find Durga as a manifestation of the goddess Lakshmi/Kamala.

Image of the Avatar 303

GODDESS, LION, AND BEAST

The image portrayed Harris as a Hindu goddess riding into battle on a lion. Such elements are often linked to the goddess Durga, but Hindu imagery also depicts Lakshmi or Kamala riding into battle, mounted on a lion, and wielding an array of weapons in her many arms. In the image, the "goddess" Harris is battling an enemy beast of Hindu mythology. She juts her spear toward his shoulder and neck to vanquish him. But in place of the creature's head was the head of Donald Trump. And as far as the lion on which the "goddess" Kamala was riding, it was none other than Joe Biden, his face replacing that of the lion.[6]

PROPHECY OF THE GODS

As strange as was the image, equally strange was its message. When it appeared, Harris was not contending for the presidency, nor was she directly battling Donald Trump. Biden was. But in the image, Biden, as the lion, was playing a supporting role, enabling Harris to battle against Trump. None of it fit the election of 2020. But it would fit and would come true in the election of 2024. It was only then that Biden would drop out of the race and play a supporting role to Harris's campaign for the presidency. Only then would Harris ride on the back of Biden's presidency to contend directly against Donald Trump and attempt to vanquish him. In that sense, the image was prophetic. Could it then be that this was the plan all along, not of man but of the principalities, the spirits, the gods that lay behind her agenda and for which she served as vessel? For the image was ultimately depicting the merging of a god or spirit with a human being, a goddess-queen, an avatar.

Could the goddess of Kamala Harris's mystery and the goddess of America's apostasy be connected?

Chapter 70

THE EASTERN AND WESTERN GODDESS

AT THE CENTER of the dark trinity of gods to which Israel turned when it fell away from God was Ishtar. It is this spirit, this principality, with its bending and alteration of sexuality and gender, that has likewise become central in the modern apostasy of America and the West. And it was this spirit, at the time of Kamala Harris's campaign for the White House, that appeared to be on the verge of taking complete possession of American culture. Could there then be a connection between the goddess Ishtar, that turned an ancient nation away from God, and the goddess Kamala?

UNDER THE SURFACE

The two goddesses would, on the surface, appear to be very different: Kamala or Lakshmi of the Indian and Hindu world, and Ishtar of the ancient Mesopotamian and Mediterranean world. And yet it is the way of the gods to join themselves and merge themselves with the gods of other lands and ages. Could the goddess Ishtar and the goddess Kamala possess the same characteristics, elements, and dominions?

GODDESS OF LOVE AND WAR

Both Lakshmi or Kamala and Ishtar are among the most widely adored and preeminent of goddesses. Kamala was known for her beauty and was one of India's foremost goddesses of love. Ishtar was also known for beauty and was one of Mesopotamia's foremost goddesses of love. The Hindu goddess had dominion over fertility. So did the Mesopotamian Ishtar.[1] Both goddesses were described as slayers of their enemies. Both embodied duality: love and war, beauty and ferocity, the characteristics and functions of male and female.

GODDESS ON THE LION

From ancient times, Kamala/Lakshmi was associated with lions. Lions were the goddess's *vahana,* the vehicle, mount, animal, or creature that serves to transport the deity.[2] The lion would carry the goddess on its back. The goddess is depicted armed and riding a lion into battle. Ishtar, like Kamala, was associated with lions.[3] Lions were likewise Ishtar's vahana, the vehicle or mount by which she was transported.[4] Ancient Mesopotamian reliefs depict her riding on the backs of lions, her feet by or on their heads. And ancient Mesopotamian mythology speaks of her riding lions into battle.[5]

GODDESS OF OWLS AND SHELLS

Kamala/Lakshmi is also associated with the owl, another of her vahanas.[6] In Hindu mythology, the owl carries the goddess or accompanies her in her travels.[7] Ishtar was likewise associated with the owl. In one of the most famous

The Eastern and Western Goddess 307

of images associated with Ishtar, the goddess is depicted standing on two lions and flanked by two owls.[8]

Another symbol associated with Kamala is the seashell. The goddess is associated with the conch, the cowrie, and the scallop shell.[9] In fact, the goddess's followers use shells in her worship.[10] Ishtar, in her Greek incarnation as Aphrodite, was likewise strongly connected to the seashell.[11] She was often depicted as riding on a giant shell of a scallop.[12] The shell was seen as a symbol of fertility, procreation, and new life.[13]

BORN OF THE OCEAN FOAM

The origin myths of the two goddesses hold in common a very unique element. In Kamala's origin myth she rises up from the waters of the sea. In Aphrodite's origin myth she rises up from the waters of the sea. It is, in part, because of their origin stories that each goddess is associated with the seashell. More specifically, the goddess Kamala was born of the ocean foam. The goddess Aphrodite was likewise born of the ocean foam. In fact, the name *Aphrodite* is believed by many to be derived from the Greek word *aphros,* meaning *foam,* and denoting *one born or risen of the foam.*

THE ISHTAR TERRA AND THE LAKSHMI PLANUM

The second planet from the sun is named *Venus* after the Roman goddess of the same name. But long before the second planet was connected to the Roman goddess, it was connected to the Mesopotamian goddess Ishtar.[14] It was given the name Venus only because that was the name of

Ishtar's Roman incarnation.[15] The most prominent deity in the Hindu pantheon to be joined to the planet Venus is Lakshmi—Kamala.

The planet Venus has three massive, continent-sized highlands, each known as a *terra*. Of the three, one is named *Ishtar*.[16] Within the Ishtar Terra is a massive plain consisting of over one million square miles and known as a *planum*. It is named *Lakshmi*, or the goddess *Kamala*.[17] Even in the heavens, on the planet Venus, the two goddesses are joined together.

THE ONLY TWO

Of all the deities in the world, there are only two that possess *all* of the following attributes: goddess of love, goddess of beauty, goddess of fertility, goddess of duality, of life and death, love and destruction, marriage and its absence, femininity and masculinity, goddess of the seashell, goddess of the owl, goddess of the lion upon which she rides, goddess of ocean waters, goddess born of the foam, and goddess of the second planet from the sun. In the Western world, it is *Ishtar*, also known as *Ashtarte*, *Aphrodite*, and *Venus*. In the Eastern world, it is known as *Lakshmi*, also known as *Kamala*.

GODDESS OF JEZEBEL AND ATHALIAH

In this, two mysteries again converge. We have seen how Harris served as the antitype of both Jezebel and, more specifically, her daughter, Athaliah. Both Jezebel and Athaliah worshipped, promulgated, and were identified with the deities of the Phoenician pantheon. Prominent

The Eastern and Western Goddess

among those deities was Ashtarte/Ishtar. Thus Jezebel and Athaliah would have been associated with that goddess. So the American Athaliah was associated with the goddess Kamala/Lakshmi, Ishtar's Eastern counterpart.

As the ancient Athaliah would have been associated with the Western goddess of lions, the American Athaliah was associated with the Eastern goddess of lions. As the ancient Athaliah would have represented the Western goddess of the planet Venus, the American Athaliah represented the Eastern goddess of the planet Venus. Behind the American counterpart of the ancient queen was the Eastern counterpart of the ancient queen's goddess.

THE WOMAN NAMED GODDESS

Kamala Harris's rise to power paralleled the rise to power of the spirit and movement of Ishtar in American and Western culture. Harris would champion that spirit and its agenda. It was no accident that in the presidential election of 2024, when that spirit, movement, and agenda were poised to take possession of American culture, everything hung on the woman named *Goddess*, the avatar of Ishtar's Eastern counterpart.

But that act of possession would be thwarted, disrupted. There would be a turning. Behind that turning was an ancient day given to turn a nation away from its darkness.

Chapter 71

THE ALTAR OF ISHTAR

I T WOULD HAPPEN on the National Mall, but its origins went back to the Book of Leviticus.

THE YOM KIPPUR GATHERING

A man of God and vision, Lou Engle had long held a burden for a sacred gathering of prayer and repentance on the National Mall with a special focus on women. He asked me to help him in leading it. The event would fall on Yom Kippur, the Day of Atonement, the holiest day of the biblical year, the day of prayer, the confession of national and personal sin, and repentance. So on Yom Kippur 2024, hundreds of thousands of believers gathered at the National Mall to repent and pray for America. I opened the convocation with prayer, the sounding of the shofar, and the ancient words of Leviticus that ordained the day.

ALTAR OF MOLECH

Four years earlier, I stood on the National Mall, on the same spot, for another sacred gathering called *The Return*. *The Return* was likewise a national day of prayer and repentance but with a strong focus on the nation's sin against its unborn children, as in the child sacrifices of Molech. As the prophet Jeremiah had smashed a potter's jar before the valley in which his nation's children were sacrificed, I was led to do the same on the National Mall.

I was led as well to seal the prayers prayed that day with

The Altar of Ishtar 311

the sounding of trumpets. After declaring the sealing of those prayers, I called for the power of God to go forth from that place, then shouted the word *go!* At that moment, the trumpets sounded from the stage, and the multitudes shouted as on the day of Jericho. And something happened. It was on that same day and in that same hour that Trump, standing on the White House lawn, set in motion the nomination of Amy Coney Barrett to the Supreme Court.[1] Barrett would cast the vote that would overturn America's Temple of Baal and altar of Molech, *Roe v. Wade.*[2] The president set it all in motion on that same day, hour, minute, and at the very second that I said the word *go!* The Temple of Baal and the altar of Molech began to crack.

AGAINST THE GODDESS

I was now standing on the same spot on which I had stood for *The Return.* I was again led to perform another prophetic act. It would focus on the goddess. When I had first been asked to minister at that event over a year earlier, I sensed that the spiritual focus of that gathering would concern Ishtar, the goddess and spirit of sexual immorality and the bending of gender. No one could have then known that less than two months before the event, a woman would be lifted up to contend for the presidency and America's future, championing that agenda and *bearing the name Goddess.*

ALTAR OF ISHTAR

In ancient times, when Israel repented of its apostasy and turned back to God, the most tangible sign of its turning was manifested in the breaking of the altars of the gods. So there on the National Mall, I was led to break the altar of Ishtar. The last ordained act of Yom Kippur was the casting out and removal of sin and darkness from the land. So the last priestly act of that Yom Kippur on the National Mall was the casting out of sin and darkness from the land as sealed in the breaking of Ishtar's altar.

THE SMASHING

It was almost sunset, the time of Yom Kippur's end, when the altar was set on the stage before me. I led the gathering in a prayer against Ishtar, to the casting out of the spirit that broke apart marriages; abused children; trafficked young women; twisted sexuality; enslaved multitudes; altered, bent, confused, and destroyed gender; mutilated the innocent; defiled all it touched; and brought destruction to lives, families, and nations. I lifted up a large sledgehammer and brought it down against the altar. Nothing happened. I lifted it up a second time and once more brought it down against the stone. This time, the altar split in two and collapsed on the stage. The sound of the prayers being lifted up on the National Mall now reached a crescendo, a massive roar. The altar of Ishtar was broken.[3]

The Altar of Ishtar 313

THE CHANGE

When the believers gathered on the National Mall, America was at a crossroads. Two opposing visions and agendas were battling for its future. But on the day of Yom Kippur, when darkness was cast out of the land, they prayed and interceded, and the altar of Ishtar was split in two. Less than thirty days later, the woman named *Goddess* was defeated. She had borne the agenda of Ishtar, just as she had borne the name of Ishtar's Eastern counterpart. The altar of the goddess was broken, as was the rise and agenda of the woman called *Goddess*.

THE AVATAR'S PURPOSE

Ishtar's agenda, with its altering of sexuality, marriage, and gender, had only advanced through American culture and had never, in any meaningful way, been turned back or halted. When we prayed on that day of Yom Kippur for the turning back of that agenda and spirit, we did so in faith. But less than one month later, for the first time ever, the massive rolling back of that agenda would begin.

The purpose of an avatar is to accomplish a goal, an end, that could not otherwise be accomplished. To overcome an avatar is to overcome the purpose for which the avatar was sent. To overcome the avatar of a goddess is to overcome the goddess's purposes. So it was no accident that the defeat of the one named *Goddess* brought about the rolling back of those purposes and that agenda.

THE CASTING OUT

As had the altar of Molech four years earlier, the altar of Ishtar had begun to crack. As we had prayed the prayer of casting out on the ancient day of casting out, there would now begin a massive societal and cultural casting out. On his return to the White House, the American Jehu would set in motion a multitude of presidential orders and directives aimed at removing gender ideology from the army, the Department of Justice, the Department of Education, from every realm of government, and every domain under his authority.[4] He would order the purging of thousands of government web pages dedicated to the LGBT agenda and the alteration of sexuality.[5] He would seek a ban on the mutilation of children in gender transition surgeries.[6] And he would make it official government policy that there are only two genders—male and female.[7]

As Jehu had pulled down the temples and altars of the gods, the American Jehu was now pulling down their modern equivalents, rolling back and dismantling the agenda and temples of the goddess in American society.

THE FORESHADOWING

With the defeat of Jezebel and Athaliah, there came a great dismantling of the pagan temples and altars that covered the land. So it is no accident that the defeat of Hillary Clinton led to the overturning and dismantling of *Roe v. Wade*. Nor was it an accident that the defeat of Kamala Harris led to another great dismantling.

What took place on that Yom Kippur gathering on the National Mall was a prophetic act. We had broken the

The Altar of Ishtar   315

altar of Ishtar. It was symbolic, foreshadowing. But now it was happening in reality and across the nation. On the surface, Trump was issuing presidential directives, actions, and orders. But what he was actually doing was something much more profound and ancient. The American Jehu was lifting up a sledgehammer over the nation and smashing the altar of Ishtar.

The rise of the goddess was a sign. What did it mean?

Chapter 72

SIGN OF THE AVATAR

WHAT DOES THE rise of the woman named *Goddess* signify?

THE FIRST WARNING

It was in the early part of the seventeenth century that America's first founders consecrated the new civilization to the will, the purposes, and the glory of God. There was no question as to who that God was. It was the God of the Scriptures, the God of Israel. When the Israelites stood at the verge of entering the Promised Land, their leader, Moses, warned them against turning from God to the gods. So too at the dawn of American civilization, the Puritan leader John Winthrop gave that first generation a message with the same warning. He said,

> But if our hearts shall turn away, so that we will not obey, but shall be seduced and worship and serve other gods, our pleasure and profits...we shall surely perish out of the good land.[1]

THE GOD WITHIN THE NAME

But Israel turned from God; so did America. In its turning from God, Israel opened the door to the gods. So did America. In the case of Israel, the apostasy reached its

Sign of the Avatar 317

critical mass in the days when the gods took dominion of its culture, its institutions, and its government—the days of Jezebel. Contained within the name of Jezebel was the name of the god she represented, Baal. So the nation came under the rule of the gods at the same moment it came under the dominion of a woman bearing the name of a pagan deity.

And now, for the first time in its history, America, a nation that had likewise been consecrated to the purposes of God, had come to the moment of standing on the verge of being ruled by a woman whose name likewise bore the name of a pagan deity. In the case of ancient Israel, it was a sign that the nation was about to come under the dominion of the gods. What then would the same sign mean for America?

THE AMERICAN AVATAR

The idea of god-kings and goddess-queens, living images, avatars, ruling a kingdom or nation was a feature of pagan civilization. The avatar was the manifestation of a pagan deity. Therefore the domain over which the avatar ruled was, by definition, a pagan one.

If a god or spirit can lead a king or queen, if it can rule a ruling avatar, it can lead and rule a nation. But the idea of avatars was completely alien to Judeo-Christian civilizations and nations such as America. Avatars do not rule over Christian civilizations. So the return of the avatar was, in and of itself, a sign of America's state and fall. As the avatar goddess-queen of the ancient world, Kamala Harris had unwittingly become a living image, an uncanny manifestation of the goddess whose name she bore. That she was now being lifted to the heights of power, that she was now being positioned for the Oval Office, and that she was now actively seeking to rule the nation was no accident.

Avatars and god-kings only rule over pagan nations, nations given to the gods. America had turned from God. That a woman called *Goddess* was now on the verge of becoming its ruler was an ominous sign. America was in danger and on the verge of becoming a nation under the dominion and possession of the gods and spirits.

ONE NATION UNDER GODS

So too it was no accident that at one of her campaigns she told those who proclaimed *"Jesus is Lord"* that they were at the wrong rally.[2] Indeed, they would be forcibly removed. The woman with the name of a goddess had become a sign in flesh and blood of the ancient truth: The empty house would not stay empty. America had emptied itself of God; now others would come, gods and goddesses and their avatars, to possess it. In ancient times, they had all been cast out at the declaration that "Jesus is Lord." Now the woman called *Goddess* was vying to rule the American house, and in her rising the declaration that "Jesus is Lord" was cast out.

America, the nation that had once been uniquely given to the will and purposes of God, was now on the verge of giving itself to a woman bearing the name *Goddess*. America, which had once proclaimed itself to be *one nation under God,* was on the verge of becoming one

Sign of the Avatar 319

nation under the *Goddess*—one nation under gods. It was a sign and a warning. For when Israel turned from God to the gods and goddesses, it was a harbinger of a nation heading toward judgment and calamity.

As we have opened the last mystery of the woman called *Kamala*, we must now open the final mystery of the man called *Trump*.

PART XII

MYSTERY OF THE VESSEL

Chapter 73

THE TRUMPET

WHEN WE REMOVED the last veil in the mystery of Kamala Harris, we found a goddess. What then will happen if we remove the last veil in the mystery of Donald Trump? What will we find? Not a spirit or god—but something very different.

THE TRUMPETS OF JEHU

Behind Trump is the mystery of Jehu. But could there be something even deeper and more primary lying behind it? If we are to uncover it, we must go back to the moment of Jehu's rising:

> Then each man rushed to take his garment and put it under him on the top of the steps; and *they blew trumpets*, saying, "Jehu is king!"[1]

The signal and sign of Jehu's ascent was the sound of the trumpets. Of all the kings who ruled the northern kingdom of Israel, Jehu is the only one whose rise to power is recorded as having begun with the sound of trumpets.

SOUND OF REVOLUTION

The sound of trumpets was that of uprising, of revolution, of change and judgment, the ending of reigns and dynasties, and the ascending of a new king. The sound of the trumpets was the sound of Jehu. They set in motion, they trumpeted, everything else that was about to happen. It was the sound of downfall, the end of Jezebel and Joram, the overturning of their kingdom, the tearing down of Baal's temple, and the driving out of his cult—the heralding of a new king, a new dynasty, a new day.

THE TRUMP

So the trumpet was linked to Jehu from the time of his calling and anointing. In the King James Bible, 1 Corinthians 15 is rendered this way:

> ...at the last *trump*: for the *trumpet* shall sound.[2]

First Thessalonians 4 is rendered thus,

> The Lord himself shall descend from heaven...with the *trump* of God.[3]

The surname *Trump* is of German derivation. But in English, the language of the nation he was to lead, *trump* means *trumpet*.

THE MYSTERY OF HIS PURPOSE

It is no accident that, as it was for the ancient Jehu, so the American Jehu was linked to the trumpet. The scriptural principle in which an individual's given name can be endowed with significance as to that individual's calling, purpose, and prophetic destiny could be seen in the case of Kamala Devi Harris—as her given name pointed to the mystery that underlay her life—that of the goddess. So it was with Trump. It was all there from the day of his birth.

The Trumpet 325

Trump's calling, purpose, and prophetic destiny were found in the trumpet. Trump was Jehu, and Trump *was* a trumpet.

SIGN OF JEHU

In Trump was the sign of Jehu, the sign of a coming change, of a revolution, and of an uprising that would shake the American political realm. In Trump was the sign that a new Jehu would ascend to the heights of American power. And in Trump was the sign of the falling of American leaders, dynasties, agendas, and legacies. As the trumpets of Jehu signaled the fall of Jezebel, so Trump signaled the fall of Hillary Clinton and Kamala Harris.

It is worthy of note that even Athaliah's fall was connected to the trumpet. The Bible records:

> When she looked, there was the king standing by his pillar at the entrance; and the leaders and *the trumpeters were by the king.* All the people of the land were rejoicing and *blowing trumpets....*So Athaliah tore her clothes and said, "Treason! Treason!"[4]

SOUND OF OVERTHROW

It was the sound of the trumpets that signaled Athaliah's downfall. The same sound that had set in motion the downfall of her mother would set in motion her own. So with the political downfall of Hillary Clinton, it happened to the sound of Trump. And so too with the defeat of Kamala Harris, it happened to the sound of Trump. As with Jezebel and Athaliah, the downfall of each was linked to the sound of the trump.

As the trumpets of Jehu set in motion the purge of Israel's government, so in Trump was the sign that the American government would be purged. As the trumpets of Jehu led to the overthrow of Baal's temple, so in Trump was the sign that America's Temple of Baal, *Roe v. Wade*, would be overturned.

THE VESSEL BEYOND ITSELF

Many of Trump's critics impugned his motives, his ways, his nature, and his intentions. But that was to miss the point. A trumpet is an instrument, a vessel used to accomplish a purpose. As with Jehu, the point was not the motive or even the man but the purpose for which the instrument was used. The trumpet sounds because of the one who sounds it and because the purpose of the trumpet, or, in this case, the Trump, is to sound.

In the case of Harris the mystery of her life first manifested at the time of her birth. In the case of Trump, the mystery of his life would first manifest likewise at the time of his birth.

Chapter 74

THE APPOINTED SCRIPTURE

O N THE DAY of Kamala Harris's birth, observances were held around the world to celebrate the birth and visitation of the goddess. On the day of Donald Trump's birth, observances were also held around the world, but of a very different nature.

WORD OF THE SABBATH

Every Sabbath, Jewish people gather in synagogues to worship and open the scrolls of the Hebrew Scriptures to the passage appointed from ages past to be read on that specific day. Trump entered the world on a Friday, the day on which the Sabbath begins. That means there was an appointed scripture to be recited. What was the scripture appointed for the Sabbath that began on June 14, 1946, the day of his birth?

The appointed scripture spoke of a *vessel*, an *instrument of God*. The vessel was a *trumpet*. More specifically, it spoke of a sacred and consecrated trumpet to be sounded in the appointed times and purposes of God. Thus, in the wake of the birth of the one who would be known as *Trump*, all over the world, God's ancient people read, recited, and chanted the Word of God that spoke of God's *trumpet,* the *trump* of God.[1]

THE JARRING VESSEL

According to the appointed scripture, the trumpet was to lead the people. At its sounding, they were to gather together. And when it sounded the call to advance, they were to move forward. So the Trump who was born on that day would likewise lead the people. When he sounded, they would gather together. And when he called for them to move forward, they would do so. The sound produced by the trumpet was dissonant, piercing, and jarring. It could not easily be ignored.

So the Trump who was born on that day would likewise produce a sound that was dissonant, piercing, and jarring. It would pierce through the noise of his nation's media and the discourse of his times. One could love him or hate him, but one could not easily ignore him. He was a trumpet—a disrupter. According to the appointed scripture for the Sabbath of June 14, 1946, the trumpet was also to be used as an instrument of war. So the sound of Trump was likewise the sound of a warrior, of conflict and battle. The trumpet was a vessel of power, of kings and kingdoms, armies, revolution, and uprising. So the sound of Trump was the sound of power, of revolution, uprising, and the changing of kings.

THE BRINGING FORTH

The scripture appointed to be read on the Sabbath of Trump's birth spoke specifically of the *making,* the *producing,* and the *bringing forth of the trumpet.* It spoke of the *birth of the trumpet.*[2] So in the wake of Trump's birth, the ancient command to bring forth the trump was read,

The Appointed Scripture 329

recited, and chanted throughout the world. When Kamala Harris came into the world, the worshippers of the gods were heralding the coming into the world of the goddess Kamala. When Trump came into the world, the worshippers of God would recite the scriptures of the coming into the world of the trumpet, the trump. As the woman named *Kamala the Goddess* was born on the day joined to the birth of Kamala the Goddess, so the man named *Trump* was born on the day joined to the birthing of the trump of God.

———————————

Could the mystery of the trumpet lie not only behind Trump's birth but his rising?

Chapter 75

THE APPOINTED TIME

THE TRUMPET OF God was to be sounded at God's appointed times. Could the mystery of those appointed times have determined the time of Trump's rise to power—the exact year?

WHEN THE TRUMPET BLOWS

The same passage of Scripture ordained for the Sabbath of June 14, 1946, says this:

> Also in the day of your gladness, in your appointed feasts, and at the beginning of your months, you shall blow the trumpets.[1]

The trumpet was a sacred vessel to be sounded at the appointed times of God. Among the most prominent of God's appointed times was the Jubilee—the year of restoration, freedom, and return.[2] The connection between the trumpet and the year of restoration is so strong that the Hebrew word for *Jubilee, Yovel,* actually means *trumpet.*

YEAR OF THE TRUMPET

> Then you shall cause the *trumpet of the Jubilee to sound...you shall make the trumpet to sound throughout all your land.*[3]

330

The Appointed Time   331

The ordinance set forth that every fifty years the trumpet would sound to begin the Jubilee. At the sound of the trumpet, that which was lost would be restored, that which was bound, set free, and each would return to their ancestral possession. By the time Trump announced his presidential candidacy in 2015, he was already sixty-nine years old. But could the timing of his candidacy and rise to the White House have been hidden in the passage of Scripture given at the time of his birth?

THE PROPHETIC JUBILEE

As every Jubilee is a year of return and restoration, each Jubilee falls fifty years after the last year of return and restoration. The restoration centers on the land of Israel. For nearly two thousand years, the people of Israel were separated from their ancestral possession, their Holy City, Jerusalem. That separation ended in 1967 when Israeli soldiers entered the gates of the ancient city. It was the year of return and restoration, Israel returning to its ancestral possession, a prophetic Jubilee.[4] What happens then if we count forward from 1967, Israel's prophetic Jubilee? When would the next Jubilee be?

THE TIME OF SOUNDING

Fifty years from 1967 comes to the year 2017. In the Year of Jubilee, the trumpet is lifted up. So it was that in the prophetic Jubilee of 2017 Trump was lifted up before the American and world stage. In the Year of Jubilee, the trumpet sounds throughout the land.[5] So too Trump began sounding throughout the land.

332   **THE AVATAR**

In the Year of Jubilee those who return to their ancestral possession are given the legal recognition and right to possess it. So it was in 2017 that Trump issued the Jerusalem Declaration, giving Israel the legal recognition of its return to its ancestral possession. When the trumpet sounds in the Year of Jubilee, the right to the land returns to its original owner.[6] So in the Year of Jubilee 2017 Trump sounded, and the right to Jerusalem returned to its original owner, Israel.[7]

It would not be the last time the mystery of the Jubilee and the trumpet, or the Trump, would manifest. Both abortion in America and the case of *Roe v. Wade* began in the year 1970. So it was in 2020, the Jubilean year of both, that Trump sounded and the overturning of *Roe v. Wade* began.

At the beginning of this book, we spoke of the trumpet as a vessel of spiritual warfare. Could this other dimension of the trumpet be part of the mystery of the man called *Trump*?

Chapter 76

THE TRUMPET AND THE GODS

BEGAN THIS BOOK with my encounters with the gods, idols, and spirits of the nations. In each case, the trumpet played a critical part. Could the man called *Trump* also play a critical part with regard to the gods and spirits of the age?

TRUMPETS AND DEITIES

In the night gathering of Chennai, India, it was the sound of the trumpet that triggered what took the form of a mass exorcism of spirits. In Cuba, it was the image of the trumpet that struck the head of the goddess and removed its crown. In Nigeria, it was another image of the same trumpet that became the backdrop for another uncrowning of a "god," the Ooni of Ife, former "Lord of the Earth." Each journey witnessed a showdown of sorts between the gods on one hand and the trumpet on the other. What is the connection?

RABBIS, TRUMPETS, AND SPIRITS

The writings of the rabbis are not Scripture, but they give us insight into ancient Jewish beliefs drawn from biblical principles and foundations. In the Babylonian Talmud, the rabbis recount the story of an exorcism:

> He brought forth *trumpets* and had them sounded and *exorcised the*

demonic spirit.[1]

The account records the casting out of a demonic spirit by the sounding of the trumpets. So too the rabbis write that on the Feast of Trumpets, the sounding of the trumpets is to be done in a set and ordained way:

...to *confound the Satan* [the Accuser].[2]

Again the trumpet is seen as an instrument to be used against demonic and satanic powers.

SHOFARS AND SHEDIM

Of the sounding of the trumpets on the Hebrew holy days, the rabbinic sage Rashi writes:

I saw, "one who *blows...{a trumpet}...* ['for a demon']...to *chase away an evil spirit* from upon one's self."[3]

Again the trumpet is shown as a vessel by which spirits of darkness are exorcised. The Hebrew word for the demon at which the trumpet is blown is *shed,* the singular form of the plural *shedim.* It is the same word that appears in the Bible to speak of the *new gods* to which the Hebrews sacrificed:

They sacrificed to demons [shedim], not to God, *to gods* they did not know, to *new gods,* new arrivals.[4]

Behind the gods to which they sacrificed were the shedim. And the shedim, according to Jewish tradition, were cast out by the sound of a trumpet. It all aligns with what I

The Trumpet and the Gods

witnessed in the nations, the mass phenomenon in India at the sound of the trumpet: the striking down of the idol with the image of the trumpet, the removal of the Ooni's crown.

VESSEL OF UNEARTHLY BATTLEFIELDS

The principle comes from Scripture where the trumpet is connected to war, the sign of God's power, by which the enemy is defeated. On earthly battlefields, the trumpet sounds against enemies of flesh and blood, but in the spiritual battles, against enemies of spirit—the shedim and the gods. The scripture given at the beginning in which the trumpet is sounded to bring victory against the enemies of God bears repeating:

> When you go to war in your land against the enemy who oppresses you, then you shall sound an alarm with the trumpets, and you will be remembered before the LORD your God, and you will be saved from your enemies.[5]

This verse was as well in the passage of Scripture appointed to be proclaimed on the Sabbath that began on June 14, 1946, *the day of Trump's birth.* The child born on that day was called to become a vessel against the enemy, an instrument against the spirits, a trumpet, a Trump, against the gods.

TO DRIVE OUT THE GODS

And so in this capacity, the trumpet is to drive out the enemy, a vessel of exorcism. This is critical in understanding the mystery of Trump. He is a vessel of exorcism, an instrument set on driving out what had come into the land but didn't belong. In the spiritual realm, it was the gods that returned to America and the West.

Therefore the Trump sounded against the temples of Baal and the altars of Molech, against the vessels of child sacrifice in abortion. Therefore the Trump sounded against the altars of Ishtar by which sexuality and gender were inverted and by which millions were defiled. The Trump did not need to know how he was being used any more than a trumpet needs to know why it is being sounded. The Trump would sound to drive out the gods, to cast out the shedim, that had come back into the empty house.

THE AVATAR AND THE TRUMPET

Could the avatar and the trumpet share in common a defining attribute? They do. Both the avatar and the trumpet are vessels. The avatar is a vessel of the gods; the shofar, or trumpet, a vessel of God. We have a mystery of two vessels, in which each stands in opposition to the other. For it was no accident that the one born into the mystery of the trumpet would stand against the one born into the mystery of the goddess. The trumpet is, in a sense, the anti-avatar. It sounds forth to drive out the spirits, the shedim, the gods, so it was appointed that he who, at his birth, was given the name *Trump* would sound forth to drive out she who, at her birth, was named *Goddess*.

The Trumpet and the Gods   337

What happens next? Does the mystery give us a glimpse into what the future holds, what is yet to be or can be, and what we are called to do?

PART XIII

REDEMPTION

Chapter 77

THE RETURN OF GOD

WHEN THE SPIRITS are exorcised and the gods cast out, then what?

THE END OF THE STORY

In each of my encounters with the gods there was an epilogue. The cries of mass deliverance in India led to the sharing of the gospel, a mass prayer of salvation, and a mass receiving in of God's presence. The casting out of spirits led to the coming in of God's Spirit. The striking of the goddess in Cuba led to revival in the city below and to the worshippers of the gods coming into the churches, having their idols smashed, and receiving God's presence. And the Yoruba king's renouncing of his godhood would lead to the proclaiming of one God across the land and to revival among millions, and, among other places, in the palace of the king himself.

WHEN THE GODS ARE CAST OUT

It goes back to the Hebrew word for God, *Elohim*. The word speaks of the one true God, but it is also used to speak of the gods of the pagan world. It is thus either one Elohim or the other, if not God, then the gods, and if not the gods, then God. It is the ancient parable in reverse. If God is removed, the gods will come in to take His place. But if the gods are removed, cast out, then the house is open to receive God, and in place of the spirits, the Spirit.

341

And thus we move from *the return of the gods* to *the return of God.*

A NATIONAL RETURN

With Jehu's victory over Joram, Jezebel, and the house of Ahab, with his pulling down of Baal's temple, and his driving out the gods of Phoenicia from the land, Israel was given a chance to turn back to God. With the fall of Athaliah in the south, the kingdom of Judah also set out to drive the gods of paganism out of its midst:

> And all the people of the land went to the temple of Baal, and tore it down. They thoroughly broke in pieces its altars and images.[1]

But it was not only a casting out; it was an ushering in:

> Then Jehoiada made a covenant between the LORD, the king, and the people, that they should be the LORD's people.[2]

So the turning away from the gods was connected to a national return to God. In the driving out of the gods came the receiving in of God's presence and blessings to the nation.

A CIVILIZATIONAL INFILLING

Therefore if there is now to be a mass turning away from the gods, the idols, and the altars of our apostasy, then we stand at the same moment as did ancient Judah at the fall

The Return of God 343

of Athaliah and ancient Israel at the fall of the house of Ahab. It is a most critical moment. But it is not, in and of itself, the end.

The casting out of the gods must open the door to the return of God. The emptying of our government, our institutions, and our culture of the gods and their dominions must usher in the infilling of the presence of God. The rolling back of our desecration must usher in our reconsecration. And the casting out of the spirits must open the door to the coming in of the Spirit of God.

At the defeat of Athaliah, the Temple of Baal was torn down, and then the people reconsecrated themselves to God. So the present moment cannot be one only of tearing down but of building up, not of cleansing and driving out alone but of receiving back Him of whom we had emptied our house. The civilizational exorcism must lead to a civilizational infilling. If we do so, then it will become the greatest of moments. If we do not, it will become something else entirely.

The house must not remain empty. That would be the most dangerous thing. And that brings us to the other side.

Chapter 78

THE WINDOW

THE TRUMPET WAS an instrument of blessings and redemption on one hand, but of warning and judgment on the other. So too was Jehu. So too is Trump.

THE TRUMPET'S DUALITY

In the Jubilee and the feasts and celebrations of the Lord, the trumpet was sounded for blessing, restoration, freedom, and rejoicing. But on the Feast of Trumpets, on Yom Kippur, in the days of war and in the hands of the watchman, the trumpet was sounded for warning, alarm, and judgment. The same duality can be seen in Jehu; he was a vessel of blessing and redemption and yet at the same time a warning of judgment. He came to bring relief, restoration, and deliverance to the oppressed and persecuted. But he also came to bring judgment on the house of Ahab and on the gods it championed. And yet his rise to the throne was even more significant than that.

A WINDOW OF TIME

When Israel descended toward judgment, it was God's mercy to raise up kings to lead the people to repentance and restoration. In the southern kingdom of Judah, He raised up such righteous kings as Jehoshaphat, Hezekiah, and Josiah. In the northern kingdom of Israel, it was only Jehu.

The reign of such a king would represent a window of

The Window 345

time and grace, a chance for the nation to turn back to God. In the case of Josiah, it was a *final* window and the *last* chance to avert judgment. Soon after Josiah's reign was over, the nation entered into judgment and was destroyed.[1] So too Jehu's rise to the throne was a sign. God was giving a fallen and apostate nation a chance to alter its course, avert judgment, and turn back to Him.

REDEMPTION OR JUDGMENT

So too there is to the modern-day Jehu a duality, on one hand, a vessel of relief and deliverance, and on the other, a vessel of judgment. By the time of his ascending, the American apostasy and descent had entrenched itself in the highest houses of power and was only gaining speed and momentum. For a nation to have so known of God and then to have so turned away is a most dangerous thing. It stands on the verge of a total darkening, from which there is no return, or of entering into judgment— or both. It was in the midst of all this that Trump rose to power. With all his idiosyncrasies, contradictions, and controversies, it took someone of so jarring a nature to jar and disrupt the nation's falling. The rise and return of the American Jehu constitutes a window.

As for the window, it represents two things at once—on one hand, of the chance for return and restoration, on the other, of a warning that the time is late, and of the danger that lies ahead if the window is missed. The American apostasy did not disappear in the wake of Trump's election. The fact that it progressed so far and so deep up to

346 **THE AVATAR**

that point meant that it would take something of equal or greater mass to turn it around. Will that happen?

THE GOOD

Jehu was commended of the Lord. In 2 Kings 10, it is written,

> You have done well in accomplishing
> what is right in my eyes.[2]

In this, Jehu was exceptional, the only ruler of the northern kingdom to be given such a word from God. He had brought the house of Ahab to an end, driven out the worship of Baal, lifted up the name of God, and given the nation a reprieve. And yet there was another side.

THE OTHER SIDE

The Scripture also records this of Jehu:

> So Jehu destroyed Baal worship in
> Israel. However, he did not turn away
> from the sins of Jeroboam son of
> Nebat, which he had caused Israel to
> commit—the worship of the golden
> calves at Bethel and Dan.[3]

So while Jehu did the will of God in dramatic ways and critical realms, he did not do so in every way and realm. He failed to turn the nation away from its worship of the golden calves that had been erected by its first king, Jeroboam. Further, the Scripture records,

> Jehu was not careful to keep the law of

The Window 347

the LORD, the God of Israel, with all
his heart.[4]

THE HOPE

Jehu was a mix. So too in many ways is the American Jehu.
Jehu was an imperfect vessel who could be careless with
the ways of God and reckless in his acts. On one hand, he
fulfilled the will of God. On the other, he both exceeded
and fell short of it. The same attributes that proved a
strength when employed for the purposes of God would
prove a weakness when not. So the Bible records of Jehu
that the nation of Israel was decreased in his days.[5]

All this is as well a caution and warning for our day.
While we have this window, we must pray that the
American Jehu and those of his house will prove greater
than his ancient prototype—and will seek, above all things,
to serve the will and purposes of Him who called them.

God will raise up those whom He will raise up to use as
vessels of His purposes. But our hope must never rest in
any vessel, even vessels of God, but only in God Himself.

What then is the answer? And could a sign regarding it
have already been given?

Chapter 79

THE ANOINTING OF THE PRIEST

WHEN IT HAPPENED, it sent shock waves throughout the nation. And yet behind it lay a mystery that went back to an ancient priesthood.

THE FLASK OF OIL

The charge given by the prophet to Jehu could not be fulfilled without the outpouring of oil—the anointing:

> Then take the flask of oil, and pour it on his head, and say, "Thus says the LORD: 'I have anointed you king over Israel.'"[1]

The Scripture records the giving of God's anointing, particularly at key moments in God's plan, the beginning of a king's reign, the commencement of a mission or ministry. The anointing signified that the anointed was chosen and called to serve the purposes of God.

THE ANOINTING OF JEHU

In the story of Jehu, the anointing is crucial. Of all the rulers of the northern kingdom, he is the only one recorded as having been anointed with oil. The command to anoint him was initially given to Elijah in an answer to the prophet's lamentations over his nation's apostasy. The anointing of Jehu was unique as well in that it was joined not only to the office of kingship but to a very specific calling and

The Anointing of the Priest 349

mission of judgment and cleansing. Could there then be a connection between the American Jehu, Donald Trump, and the anointing of God?

THE CONSECRATION OF THE PRIESTS

The first of God's people to receive the anointing as recorded in Scripture were Aaron and his sons, the priests of Israel.[2] In order to begin their ministry, they had to be anointed. The anointing of the priests was not only of oil, but blood. God commanded Moses to anoint Aaron and his sons with the blood of the sacrifice. The blood was to be placed on three specific parts of their bodies. Only after that could they begin their ministry and fulfill their calling.

THE FRACTION

On July 13, 2024, Donald Trump was speaking at a campaign rally in Butler, Pennsylvania, when shots of gunfire rang out.[3] It was the sound of an assassin who had aimed his bullets at Trump's head. Before the bullets could strike him, Trump turned his head to the right. One of the bullets grazed his ear, leaving him bloodied but alive.[4] Had he not turned his head at that exact moment and to that exact degree and no further, he would have been dead. His life was saved by two fractions, a fraction of an inch and a fraction of a second.

A LASTING MARK

What happened that day in Butler, Pennsylvania, would leave a lasting mark on Trump's thoughts and outlook. In its aftermath, he would speak of God and in more personal terms than he had ever before done. Jehu knew he had been anointed of God and given a mission. After Butler, the American Jehu would hold the same conviction and speak of it publicly—that he was anointed for a divine mission and purpose.[5] But could there have been more to what happened on that stage that day?

THE CONSECRATION OF THE EAR

In the priestly anointing, God told Moses to take the blood of the sacrifice and put it

> on the tip of the right ear of Aaron
> and on the tip of the right ear of his
> sons.[6]

It was symbolic. To serve the purposes of God, the priest's ear has to be open to hear His voice, His word, His will, and His counsel. The ear of the priest had to be consecrated to God and so was anointed with blood.

The bullet intended to take Donald Trump's life, instead drew blood from his ear, which then began streaming down his face. In the ancient anointing, the blood had to touch the ear of the candidate for the priesthood. On the stage in Butler, Pennsylvania, the blood now touched the ear of the candidate for the presidency. More specifically, the blood had to touch the priest's *right ear.* So the blood touched Trump's *right ear.* More specifically, the blood had to touch *the tip of the right ear* of the priestly candidate. And so, more specifically, the blood now touched *the tip of the right ear* of Donald Trump.[7]

The Anointing of the Priest 351

Of course, it was his own blood, and it was an assassination attempt. Nevertheless, it would follow the pattern of the priestly anointing.

THE CONSECRATION OF THE THUMB

God then told Moses to place the blood

on the thumb of their right hand.[8]

The hand and thumb of the priest spoke of the acts and works they were being anointed to perform. The minister of God was not only to hear the voice of God but to obey what he heard and perform the works of God. So the ancient anointing proceeds from the ear to the hand. After being grazed by the bullet, Trump raised his hand to touch his bloodied ear. In the priestly anointing, the hand of the candidate must come into contact with the blood. So the hand of the presidential candidate now came into contact with the blood. More specifically, the blood had to touch *the right hand* of the priest. So it was specifically Trump's *right hand* that was lifted up to touch the bloodied ear. And more specifically, the anointing of the priests involved *the thumb of their right hand.* And so Trump specifically lifted up *the thumb of his right hand* to touch the blood of his right ear.[9]

THE CONSECRATION OF THE TOE

One more part of the priest's body was to be touched by the blood of the anointing. Moses was to place the blood

on the big toe of their right foot.[10]

In order to minister for the Lord, the priest had to walk in the ways of God, seek His leading, and follow in His path. So his foot was to be as well anointed with the blood.

The blood from Trump's ear would pour down profusely toward the stage floor. He would then himself be forced down on that floor. While no one can say exactly what happened next, the blood could have only touched his feet if his shoes were removed.

In his descent to the floor, Trump's shoes were somehow removed from his feet. He lay, at first, crouched down on the stage floor, blood running down his face. Then, when he was able, he rose to his feet, standing on the same spot on which he had been pushed down.

The last part of the blood anointing focused on the foot of the priest. So did Trump as he then called out for his shoes.[11] It is believed that the priests were consecrated with their shoes removed and that they ministered for God shoeless. So on that day, on that stage, Trump's shoes were removed; he became shoeless.

THE ANOINTING AND THE OFFICE

As in the ancient anointing, so in Butler, Pennsylvania, it began with blood on the tip of the right ear, then descended to the thumb of the right hand, and then to the shoeless feet of the one to be consecrated. In the days ahead many would become convinced that Kamala Harris would win the presidential election. But in the mystery of the anointing, it was all sealed that day in Butler. For the anointing was for the office. And it was ordained that the one who received the anointing would be the one

The Anointing of the Priest 353

who would likewise receive the office—in this case, the presidency.

But there was more to the anointing—of the priests and of Donald Trump.

Chapter 80

THE INVESTITURE

THE SECOND PART of Trump's anointing would take place before the eyes of the nation and the world.

MASHKEH—THE CUPBEARER

The Bible speaks of one called the *mashkeh,* the *cupbearer.* One can find the cupbearer from the story of Joseph in Egypt to Nehemiah, the cupbearer to the Persian emperor.[1] The cupbearer played a critical role in the royal court. Specifically, he was charged with guarding the king against an assassination attempt. He would bear the cup to ensure it wasn't poisoned.[2]

The word *cupbearer* would become in French, the word *boutellier,* the cup or bottle bearer. From *boutellier,* the word entered into English. It became the word *butler*—as in *Butler,* Pennsylvania. The assassination attempt on Trump's life happened in the place called *Butler,* a word having to do with an assassination attempt against a ruler. More specifically, the word spoke of the one in charge of making sure the assassination attempt would be thwarted and the ruler's life saved. In the case of Butler, that would happen by a fraction of an inch and a fraction of a second. It can be taken then that the "Butler," the one who saved the ruler's life, was not of flesh and blood.

354

The Investiture 355

THE INSTALLATION

The anointing of blood would lead to the installation of the priest into his office and ministry. So the anointing of blood in Butler had to lead to something else. It was not an accident that what happened in that place would lead directly to the Republican National Convention.

Just two days after the event in Butler, the Republican National Convention began. The point of that convention was to nominate Donald Trump so that he might be installed into the office of the presidency. The convention would represent the continuation and second part of the blood anointing of Butler.

The connection between the two events would be unavoidable as Trump appeared on the convention stage with a bandage marking the spot from which the blood had flowed.[3] And as the consecration of the priests took place in public, so both the assassination attempt and Trump's nomination at the convention would take place in public, the latter unfolding before the nation and the world.

IN FRONT OF THE HOUSE OF MINISTRY

> Then you shall bring Aaron and his
> sons to the door of the tabernacle.[4]

The consecration of the priest had to happen at a specific place—before the Tabernacle or Temple of God; in other words, in front of the place in which he was to serve in his given office of the priesthood. Could the dynamics of the installation of the priests have replayed in the installation

356   **THE AVATAR**

of Trump as the Republican presidential candidate in 2024?

When Trump gave his acceptance speech at the Republican National Convention of 2024, he did so with a bandage marking his right ear and against a massive backdrop. The backdrop was an image of the White House.[5] Thus, as with the ancient ordination, his installation would take place in front of the house in which he was to serve upon receiving the office.

IN FRONT OF THE DOORWAY

But the ordinance was more specific than that. The consecration of the priest had to take place *in front of the door* of the Tabernacle. The Hebrew word used is *petakh*, which can signify an entranceway, opening, doorway, or door. Could then the ancient dynamic replay in Trump's nomination for the presidency? Could it have happened in front of a *petakh*, a door or doorway?

The answer is yes. When Trump accepted the nomination for the presidency, he did it *in front of the doorway*.[6] As the priest had to be ordained in front of the doorway of the house in which he would serve, so Trump was ordained in front of the doorway of the house in which he would serve, the White House. In his previous nomination in 2020 he also stood in front of an image of the White House, but of the South Portico.[7] This time, the backdrop was of the North Portico. In this, the doorway was most prominent and central and perfectly framed his body as he received the nomination.[8]

The Investiture   357

IMAGE OF THE TEMPLE

For most of Bible times the priests were ordained in front of the doorway of the Temple of Jerusalem. The section of the White House chosen for Trump's acceptance speech in 2024 strangely mimicked the facade and doorway of the Temple of Jerusalem.

It was a massive vertical rectangle facade of light stone lined with columns—just as was the facade of the Temple of Jerusalem. The door of the backdrop was framed with concentric squares, just as it is in re-creations of the Temple of Jerusalem. The two doors of the backdrop were framed by four massive pillars of stone. The two doors of the Temple of Jerusalem were framed by four massive pillars of stone.[9]

Thus Trump received the nomination and gave his acceptance speech in front of an image of a facade that mimicked the backdrop of the priestly ordination. As the ancient anointed one had once stood with blood on his right ear in front of the door of God's house, so now Trump stood with his ear marked with blood in front of the doorway to the house in which he would serve.

THE SEVENTH DAY

> You are to consecrate them for seven days.[10]

The priestly anointing and consecration took place over the span of seven days, the ordination being sealed on the seventh day. In the case of Donald Trump, it all began when the blood touched the tip of his right ear in Butler,

Pennsylvania. It was Saturday, July 13, 2024. Every Hebrew day begins at sundown and ends the following sundown. The shots rang out at 6:11 p.m., two and a half hours before sundown.[11] At sundown, the second day began. On Sunday at sundown, the third day began. On Monday, sundown, the fourth day, on Tuesday, sundown, the fifth day, and on Wednesday, sundown, the sixth day.

The seventh day, after Butler and the blood anointing, began at sundown, Thursday night, July 18. It is on the seventh day that the anointing and consecration must be sealed. Trump received the nomination for the office of the presidency on July 18, Thursday night, just after sundown. Seven Hebrew days after the blood touched his right ear, on the final night of the Republican National Convention, the consecration was completed—on the seventh day.

THE MEANING OF THE CONSECRATION

In the ancient account, it is only upon his anointing and consecration, and because of it, that Jehu becomes aware of his calling and mission from God. So it would be for the American Jehu according to the ancient template. It was, thus, only upon his anointing and consecration at Butler, and because of it, that Trump would become aware of having been given a calling and a mission from God.

What then does it mean that the nomination of an American president took place according to the pattern of the ancient priestly anointing and consecration? Both the anointing and consecration are given to the one who is called for a specific purpose. The purpose is not of human origin and is above any plan or intent on the part

The Investiture 359

of the one receiving it. That it followed the ancient priestly anointing would signify that the one being called was called beyond the governmental realm and to the spiritual realm, the realm of serving God. The priest ministered as a representative of his nation. Could it be that Trump's narrow escape from calamity was a foreshadowing that the nation would likewise narrowly escape a different kind of calamity, from being sealed to darkness and, ultimately, judgment? And since the calling of the priest was to accomplish reconciliation, to bring his nation to God, could it be that the reason Trump was raised to power was ultimately that he would have a part in turning America back to God?

———————

To these last questions the last mystery will speak.

Chapter 81

THE OBELISK

IT IS JUST under one and a half feet wide and just under six and a half feet high. It is made of black limestone. There is no other object like it in the world.

THE BLACK OBELISK

Of all the figures who appear in the Bible, there is no drawing, painting, carved relief, sculpture, or image created at the time of their existence, or in biblical times, to give us an idea of what they might have looked like—*except one*. It is called the *Black Obelisk*. The Black Obelisk is a neo-Assyrian stone monument commemorating the victories and acts of the Assyrian king Shalmaneser III.[1] Carved into the Black Obelisk is the only known depiction made in ancient times of an Israelite king or any biblical figure. It is the image of *Jehu*.[2]

IMAGE OF THE AMERICAN JEHU

One of the most powerful photographs of the American Jehu was taken on the stage of Butler, Pennsylvania. After the gunshots rang out and the bullet grazed his ear, Trump was surrounded by Secret Service agents who forced him down to the stage floor. At that moment a picture was taken. The resulting image was unprecedented. It showed Trump on his knees, blood streaming down his face, bowed down to the stage floor.

360

The Obelisk   361

IMAGE OF THE ANCIENT JEHU

The stone image of King Jehu was nearly three thousand years old. What did it show? It showed Jehu *on his knees and bowed down to the ground*—the same as in the image of the modern Jehu. Though that which caused the bowing down of the ancient Jehu was different from that which caused the bowing down of the American Jehu, the effect was the same. In the ancient stone image, the face of Jehu is shown in profile. In the modern photographic image, the American Jehu's face is shown in profile. Both Jehus are captured at their moment of prostration.

THE BOWING OF A KING

In the ancient stone image, King Jehu is bent over forward to the point where his face is nearly touching the ground. In the photographic image of the modern Jehu, he is likewise bent over forward to the point where his face is nearly touching the ground. In the photographic image taken in Butler, Pennsylvania, Trump places his hand between his face and the ground. In the ancient stone image of the Black Obelisk, Jehu places his hands between his face and the ground. The ancient stone engraving of Jehu on his knees had waited thousands of years before another Jehu would be conformed to the same image.

THE BOWING OF A NATION

In the case of Trump, the image was linked to the event that corresponded with his anointing. What did it mean? In the Bible, to bow down is an act of humility, an act of worship. The priest was to consecrate himself to God and the king, to humble himself before God's kingship. Each was a representative of his nation. Could then the bowing down of the American Jehu be a sign not only to Trump but to the nation? Could God be calling America to humble itself before Him in worship and reverence, to rededicate and reconsecrate itself to His purposes? And as it was with Trump on that day in Pennsylvania, could it be that only by falling to its knees can America be saved?

We now come to the final questions, the final matter, and the final answer.

Chapter 82

JUDGMENT, REDEMPTION, AND ETERNITY

HOW LATE IS the hour? What will the future bring? And what are we to do?

A WAR OF KINGDOMS

We have witnessed a war of kingdoms. The war touches the realms of government, politics, rulers, society, and culture—and yet transcends them all. It is ultimately a spiritual war and a war of spirits. On one hand is God and the foundations on which America and the West came into existence. On the other are the gods and the spirits and all that comes in their wake. In the war are many battles. In the most recent of battles, the realm of the gods and spirits suffered a defeat, and the sealing of their reign was averted. But the war is not over.

THE PURPOSE OF THE WINDOW

That which has been underway for decades and has so deeply ingrained itself in a nation's culture is not undone in one political election. While Jehu was an instrument of God, he was not, in and of himself, the answer. So the American Jehu, Trump, is likewise an instrument of God, but not, in and of himself, the answer. Even the window now given is not, in and of itself, the answer—but a means to and an opening for the answer. The answer lies in the purpose for which the window was given and that through which it may come. America's problem, and that of the West, is not ultimately political, economic, societal, or even cultural—but spiritual.

JEHU'S OMISSION

Jehu ended the persecution of God's people, dismantled the nation's institutions of godlessness and evil, and drove out the cult of Baal, with its sexual immorality, its perversities, and its sacrifices of the nation's children. He turned away the gods of the nations but never turned the nation back to God. He drove out the spirit of Baal but never opened the doors for the Spirit of God. And in having done all the rest but having not done that one thing, all the rest, in the end, would be undone. After his reign was over, the nation would resume its descent from God until the day of its judgment, when it would be wiped off the face of the earth.

THE WARNING

And herein lies the warning—if we address the fruit, the leaves, the branches, and the stem but do not address the root, then the rest will grow back. If the root of the problem is left intact, then every other effort will be undone. If we change a government but not a people, then the unchanged people will change the government back. If we turn the laws but do not turn the hearts, then the unturned hearts will turn the laws back again. And if we cast out the gods but do not replace their absence with the presence of God,

Judgment, Redemption, and Eternity 365

then we will be left with an empty house, and the house will not remain empty.

For the gods are spirit; they do not die. They wait. If they could wait two thousand years to return and reinhabit Western civilization, they can wait a much shorter time. If we do not fill the house, the gods will return and with a vengeance. Then their temples will be reassembled, their altars, rebuilt, and the house, repossessed.

THE ANSWER

The fruit, the leaves, the branches, and the stems encompass every realm of culture. But the root is spiritual. One cannot solve a spiritual problem with a political, economic, societal, or cultural answer. One can only solve a spiritual problem with a spiritual answer. It began when America turned away from the God of its foundation and emptied itself of His presence. So it can only be undone and the answer only come if America returns to the God of its departing and receives back His presence into every void and hollow of His absence. It was a mass departure. So it must be answered by a mass return. It can only be answered by a societal, cultural, and civilizational return, awakening, and revival.

THE IF OF REVIVAL

As in the stone image of Jehu and the photographic image of Trump in Pennsylvania, each on his knees and bowed down to the ground, so we must humble ourselves before God, turn from our darkness, and seek His presence and mercy, as it is written,

> If My people who are called by My
> name will humble themselves, and
> pray and seek My face, and turn from
> their wicked ways, then I will hear
> from heaven, and will forgive their sin
> and heal their land.[1]

Revival is not optional; it is the only thing. Without revival, America as we have known it will have been lost. Without revival, America will, in the end, proceed to judgment or, worse, be consigned to an irreversible state of darkness and to the possession of the gods.

REDEMPTION

Without God, not only are nations lost and judged, but each of us is. And without God, we each become an empty house. We then spend our lives trying to fill the void but cannot. And as with nations, we all proceed to judgment. But nations are temporary; our souls are forever. And so the judgment or redemption of our souls is eternal.

It is written that there is only one name given under heaven by which we must be saved—Jesus. The name *Jesus* is a translation of His real name, Yeshua. *Yeshua* means *God is salvation*.[2] Yeshua, Jesus, is, has always been, and will always be our only way to salvation.

Jesus, Yeshua, said virtually nothing about religion. For salvation is not about being born Catholic, Protestant, Jewish, Muslim, Hindu, or any other label. It is about being *born again*. It was He who said that the only way one can be saved is that one be *born again*.[3]

What does that mean? It means turning away from the

Judgment, Redemption, and Eternity

old, from the darkness, from sin, and seeking for and receiving His forgiveness and cleansing. It means receiving His love and presence into one's heart, to fill every void and emptiness. And it means following Him every day of one's life. It can happen in any place and time—in the reading of these words.

FOR WHICH ONE THE TRUMPET WILL SOUND

As for America, it is now hanging in between God and the gods, between light and darkness, revival and judgment, and worse. Though its fall was, for a time, averted, its apostasy is in a deep state and an advanced stage. And so the line separating redemption from judgment is, for this nation, especially thin. And as, in ancient times, the trumpet of God sounded for both redemption on one hand and warning on the other, so the days of Trump may sound for the one or for the other. What happens to America with regard to its turning to or away from God will determine for which one it will sound.

WHAT MUST WE DO?

What then must we do? We must pray for revival as never before, fervently, wholeheartedly, and unceasingly. We must work as never before, act and minister, that revival may come. We must boldly spread the word of salvation, the good news of Messiah, to all who will hear it, that revival may come. And we must not only pray and work for revival, but we must *choose* revival, that revival will come. For it is not enough to seek revival to come to others, but to actually begin living in revival—with no reservations, no compromise, and no turning—all-out, total, and on fire for God. If we do that, then revival begins, then and there. Let us commit to doing so.

IN THE END

In the end the gods will fade away, but God will remain. And those who have stood for Him, who have upheld His ways, who have followed in His footsteps, who have trusted in His Word, and who have obeyed His will, they will, as it is written, shine as the stars of heaven. May that be said of the one who now reads these words.

Until that day stand strong for God and against the gods, steadfast, unfaltering, and immovable, and no matter what the future may bring, live your life in such a way that it will, in glory or reproach, in praise or persecution, in the light of day or the darkness of night, boldly declare that God alone is God.

ABOUT JONATHAN CAHN

Jonathan Cahn caused a worldwide stir with the release of the *New York Times* bestseller *The Harbinger* and his subsequent *New York Times* bestsellers. He was named, along with Billy Graham, as one of the top forty spiritual leaders of the last forty years "who radically changed our world." He has addressed members of Congress and spoken at the United Nations. He is known as a prophetic voice for our times and for the opening up of the deep mysteries of God. His teachings and prophetic messages on his YouTube channel have over one hundred million views.

Jonathan leads Hope of the World, a ministry of bringing the Word of God to the world and compassion to the world's most needy, and Beth Israel/the Jerusalem Center, his ministry base and worship center in Wayne, New Jersey, just outside New York City. He ministers and speaks throughout America and the world.

To get in touch, to receive prophetic updates, to receive free gifts from his ministry (special messages and much more), to find out about his over two thousand messages and mysteries, for more information, to contact, or to have a part in the Great Commission, use the following contacts. Go to: **HopeoftheWorld.org;** write directly to Hope of the World, Box 1111, Lodi, NJ 07644 USA; or email contact@hopeoftheworld.org.

To receive Jonathan's latest messages and prophetic updates, go to:

YouTube: Jonathan Cahn Official
Facebook: Jonathan Cahn (Official Site)
Instagram: jonathan.cahn
X: @Jonathan_Cahn

To find out how you can go with Jonathan on an Israel Super Tour, including his Book of Revelation and Footsteps of Paul tours, go to JonathanCahnSuperTours.com or email contact@hopeoftheworld.org.

*To see Jonathan's other books, go to: BooksByJonathanCahn. com or Amazon.com.

NOTES

CHAPTER 4

1. Paul Zacharia, "The Surprisingly Early History of Christianity in India," *Smithsonian,* February 19, 2016, https://www.smithsonianmag.com/travel/how-christianity-came-to-india-kerala-180958117/.

2. Zacharia, "The Surprisingly Early History."

3. Andrea Malji, "The Rise of Hindu Nationalism and Its Regional and Global Ramifications," *Education About Asia* 23, no. 1 (2018), https://www.asianstudies.org/publications/eaa/archives/the-rise-of-hindu-nationalism-and-its-regional-and-global-ramifications/.

4. "Anti-Christian Violence on the Rise in India," Human Rights Watch, September 30, 1999, https://www.hrw.org/news/1999/09/30/anti-christian-violence-rise-india.

5. "Politics by Other Means: Attacks Against Christians in India," Human Rights Watch, September 1, 1999, https://www.refworld.org/reference/countryrep/hrw/1999/en/22306.

CHAPTER 5

1. A. D. N., "Saint Thomas, the Apostle to Us Indians," *Times of India*, September 26, 2020, https://timesofindia.indiatimes.com/blogs/weltanschauung/saint-thomas-the-apostle-to-us-indians/.

2. Human Rights Watch, "Politics by Other Means."

3. Psalm 91:2–3, 5.

4. "V. Attacks Across the Country," Human Rights Watch, accessed April 25, 2025, https://www.hrw.org/reports/1999/indiachr/christians8-05.htm.

Notes

371

CHAPTER 6

1. "Taj Mahal," Digital India, accessed April 25, 2025, https://agra.nic.in/tourist-place/the-taj-mahal/.

2. "Krishna," University of North Carolina Wilmington, accessed April 25, 2025, https://people.uncw.edu/deagona/tricksters/Blank%20Page%2011.htm.

3. "The Sakatasura Demon," Hare Krsnas, accessed April 25, 2025, https://www.harekrsna.com/philosophy/associates/demons/vrindaban/sakatasura.htm.

CHAPTER 7

1. Numbers 10:9.

CHAPTER 8

1. Omar Rodriguez, "AfroCuban Religion and Syncretism with the Catholic Religion," Miami University, accessed April 25, 2025, https://scholar.library.miami.edu/emancipation/religion1.htm.

2. "'Santeria': La Regla de Ocha-Ifa and Lukumi," Pluralism, accessed April 25, 2025, https://pluralism.org/%E2%80%9Csanter%C3%ADa%E2%80%9D-the-lucumi-way.

3. "The Orishas," Indiana University, accessed April 28, 2025, https://legacy.cs.indiana.edu/~port/teach/205/santeria2.html.

4. Mercedes Cros Sandoval, *Worldview, the Orichas, and Santería: Africa to Cuba and Beyond* (University Press of Florida, 2006).

5. Rodriguez, "AfroCuban Religion."

6. Lily Gardner, "Cult of the Saints: An Introduction to Santeria," *Llewellyn*, September 29, 2009, https://www.llewellyn.com/journal/article/2048?srsltid=AfmBOoqNcS

rZ6WeJG7gvMDQFfNWM1uSpY0Hypmy9ZZxm8X0tST x0QdZ_.

7. Catherine Beyer, "The Orishas: Orunla, Osain, Oshun, Oya, and Yemaya," Learn Religions, January 23, 2018, https://www.learnreligions.com/orunla-osain-oshun-oya-and-yemaya-95923.

8. Gardner, "Cult."

9. "Priesthood," BBC, accessed April 25, 2025, https://www.bbc.com/religion/religions/santeria/structure/priesthood.shtml.

10. "Psalm 106:37," Bible Hub, accessed May 30, 2025, https://biblehub.com/text/psalms/106-37.htm.

11. Ikechukwu Anthony et al., "The Concept of Sacrifice in Yoruba Religion and Culture," in *Formation of the Human Person in the 21st Century*, eds. Gregory Ogbenika and Francis Ikhianosime (The Seminary of All Saints, Uhiele-Ekpoma, 2021), 383–90.

12. Andrew Walker, "Marketing 'Killing Nigerian Festival,'" BBC News, September 8, 2008, http://news.bbc.co.uk/2/hi/africa/7593852.stm.

13. Katherine Hagedorn, *Divine Utterances: The Performance of Afro-Cuban Santería* (Smithsonian Books, 2001), 126–27.

14. Margarite Fernández Olmos and Lizabeth Paravisini-Gebert, *Creole Religions of the Caribbean: An Introduction from Vodou and Santería to Obeah and Espiritismo* (New York University Press, 2003), 73.

15. Joseph Holbrook, "The Catholic Church in Cuba, 1959–62: The Clash of Ideologies," *International Journal of Cuban Studies* 2, no. 3/4 (2010): 264–75, https://www.scienceopen.com/hosted-document?doi=10.2307/41945906.

Notes 373

16. "Religion in Cuba," Global Security, accessed April 29, 2025, https://www.globalsecurity.org/military/world/cuba/religion.htm.

17. Holbrook, "The Catholic Church," 271.

18. Peter Lemass, "Fidel Castro's Cuba," *The Furrow* 36, no. 6 (1985): 365–75, https://www.jstor.org/stable/27678080.

19. Marilyn Stewart, "Imprisoned Under Castro, Cuban Pastor Obed Millan Shares Message of Hope," New Orleans Baptist Theological Seminary, September 17, 2018, https://www.nobts.edu/news/articles/2018/PrisonertoPrisonChaplain.html.

20. Kirsten Lavery, "The Santería Tradition in Cuba," fact sheet from United States Commission on International Religious Freedom, February 2021, https://www.uscirf.gov/sites/default/files/2021%20Factsheet%20-%20Santeria%20in%20Cuba.pdf.

21. Associated Press, "Cubans Seek Solutions and Solace in Santería Amid Crises," *El País,* April 10, 2023, https://english.elpais.com/international/2023-04-09/cubans-seek-solutions-and-solace-in-santeria-amid-crises.html.

22. Lavery, "The Santería Tradition."

23. Associated Press, "Cubans."

24. Christine Ayorinde, *Afro-Cuban Religiosity, Revolution, and National Identity* (University Press of Florida, 2004).

25. Angela N. Castañeda, "The African Diaspora in Mexico: Santería, Tourism, and Representations of the State," in *The African Diaspora and the Study of Religion*, ed. Theodore Louis Trost (Palgrave Macmillan, 2007), 131–50.

26. Lavery, "The Santería Tradition."

27. Bret Sigler, "Saving the Cuban Soul," UC Berkeley Graduate School of Journalism, updated April 5, 2002, https://projects.journalism.berkeley.edu/cubans2001/story-religion.html.

28. "Cuba: Year of the Firing Squad," *Time,* February 3, 1961, https://content.time.com/time/subscriber/article/0,33009,872043,00.html.

CHAPTER 9

1. "18. Despatch from the Consulate at Santiago de Cuba to the Department of State," Office of the Historian, US State Department, February 21, 1958, https://history.state.gov/historicaldocuments/frus1958-60v06/d18.

2. *Britannica,* "The Rise of Castro and the Outbreak of Revolution," in "Cuban Revolution," accessed May 30, 2025, https://www.britannica.com/event/Cuban-Revolution/The-rise-of-Castro-and-the-outbreak-of-revolution.

3. *Britannica,* "The Rise."

4. "El Cobre & San Lázaro," *World Pilgrimage Guide,* accessed April 25, 2025, https://sacredsites.com/americas/cuba/el_cobre_san_lazaro.html.

5. *World Pilgrimage Guide,* "El Cobre."

6. "El Cobre, Cuba," Sacred Destinations, accessed April 29, 2025, https://www.sacred-destinations.com/cuba/el-cobre.

7. "Cubans Speculate About Santeria Rites at Castro's Funeral," *Martinoticias,* November 29, 2016, https://www.martinoticias.com/a/fidel-castro-ritos-santeria-funerales-especulaciones/134467.html.

8. Fidel Castro, "Address on Arrival in Havana on 8 January 1959," Fidel Castro Internet Archive, accessed April 25, 2025, https://www.marxists.org/history/cuba/archive/castro/1959/04/14-apr-1959.htm.

9. Olmos and Paravisini-Gebert, *Creole Religions,* 44.

10. Suzanne Preston Blier, "Kings, Crowns, and Rights of Succession: Obalufon Arts at Ife and Other Yoruba Center,"

Notes

Art Bulletin 67, no. 3 (1985): 383–401, www.collegeart.org/
pdf/artbulletin/Art%20Bulletin%20Vol%2067%20No%20
3%20Blier.pdf.

11. "Obatala: The Orisha Who Created the Sky and Mankind,"
Original Botanica, June 8, 2023, https://originalbotanica.
com/blog/orisha-obatala-prayers-rituals.

12. "Fidel Castro Speech, Havana, Cuba," film recorded
January 8, 1959, *Getty Images*, accessed April 25, 2025, 13
sec., https://www.gettyimages.com/detail/video/havana-
cuba-january-8-1959-historic-footage-of-the-first-news-
footage/1218249436.

13. Ivor L. Miller, "Religious Symbolism in Cuban Political
Performance," *TDR* 44, no. 2 (2000): 38, https://www.jstor.
org/stable/1146846.

14. Yoe Suárez, "The Cuban Revolution as a Religious Faith,"
Evangelical Focus, April 10, 2024, https://evangelicalfocus.
com/features/26161/the-cuban-revolution-as-a-religious-
faith.

15. Lillian Guerra, *Visions of Power in Cuba: Revolution,
Redemption, and Resistance, 1959–1971*, ed. Louis A. Pérez
Jr. (University of North Carolina Press, 2012), 152.

CHAPTER 10

1. Olmos and Paravisini-Gebert, *Creole Religions*, 42.

2. Indiana University, "The Orishas."

3. Christopher Smith, "Indict Castro for Murder," *Wall
Street Journal*, February 26, 2001, https://www.wsj.com/
articles/SB983143798683748150.

4. "Chango, Lord of Fire and Lightning," About Santería,
accessed April 29, 2025, http://www.aboutsanteria.com/
changoacute.html.

5. Laura Betzig, "Fidel: An American Comandante," *Psychology Today*, December 4, 2016, https://www.psychologytoday.com/us/blog/the-political-animal/201612/fidel.

6. Juan Reinaldo Sanchez, "Hidden Wives, Mistresses and Kids: Fidel Castro's Secret Life," *New York Post*, March 20, 2016, https://nypost.com/2016/03/20/hidden-wives-mistresses-and-kids-fidel-castros-secret-life/.

7. Robert Smith, *Kingdoms of the Yoruba* (Methuen & Co., London, 1969), 33–34.

8. Imisioluwa Ogunsunlade, "Sàngó and His Wives," Oriire, January 7, 2023, https://www.oriire.com/article/sango-and-his-wives.

9. "Shango: Orisha of Justice and Protection," Trailblazer Travelz, accessed May 30, 2025, https://www.trailblazertravelz.com/shango-orisha-of-justice-and-protection/.

10. "Fidel Castro's Human Rights Legacy: A Tale of Two Worlds," Amnesty International, November 26, 2016, https://www.amnesty.org/en/latest/news/2016/11/fidel-castro-s-human-rights-legacy-a-tale-of-two-worlds/.

11. *Britannica*, "Fidel Castro," accessed April 25, 2025, https://www.britannica.com/biography/Fidel-Castro; Erika de la Garza, "Fidel Castro, Hero or Tyrant?," Baker Institute, November 28, 2016, https://www.bakerinstitute.org/research/fidel-castro-hero-or-tyrant.

12. "Shango: Orisha of Justice and Protection," Original Botanica, February 23, 2023, https://originalbotanica.com/blog/chango-shango-orisha-santeria.

13. Will Worley, "Fidel Castro Dies: From Exploding Cigars to Poison, Assassination Attempts the Cuban Leader Is Said to Have Survived," *Independent*, November 26, 2016, https://www.the-independent.com/news/

Notes 377

    people/fidel-castro-dies-dead-exploding-scigar-poison-assassination-cia-survived-cuba-a7440546.html.

14. "Shango: The Orisha King of Fire and Lightning," Oshaeifa, accessed April 28, 2025, https://en.oshaeifa.com/orisha/shango/.

15. Ogunsunlade, "Sàngó."

16. Catherine Beyer, "The Orishas: Aganyu, Babalu-Aye, Chango, and Eleggua," Learn Religions, February 3, 2019, https://www.learnreligions.com/orishas-gods-of-santeria-95915.

17. Beyer, "The Orishas: Aganyu."

18. "Orisha Shango: Yoruba God of Thunder and Justice," Wars and History, September 12, 2024, https://warsandhistory.com/orisha-shango/; R. E. Dennett, *Nigerian Studies: Or the Religious and Political System of the Yoruba* (MacMillan and Co., 1910), excerpted in "Shango," TOTA, accessed May 30, 2025, https://www.tota.world/article/3267/.

19. "The Cuban Missile Crisis, October 1962," Office of the Historian, US State Department, accessed April 25, 2025, https://history.state.gov/milestones/1961-1968/cuban-missile-crisis.

20. "Letter from Castro to Khrushchev, 10/26/62," PBS, accessed April 25, 2025, https://www.pbs.org/wgbh/americanexperience/features/jfk-attack/.

21. Alexander Martinez, "Cubans and Saint Barbara's Day: A Celebration Full of Tradition and Devotion," *Cuba en Miami*, December 4, 2023, https://www.cubaenmiami.com/en/los-cubanos-y-el-dia-de-santa-barbara-una-celebracion-llena-de-tradicion-y-devocion/; Claudia Rodriguez, "Santa Barbara Day, Venerating the Owner of the Ray," *Ashé*, accessed April 29, 2025, https://ashepamicuba.com/en/dia-de-santa-barbara-venerando--la-duena-del-rayo/.

378   **THE AVATAR**

22. Nathaniel Samuel Murrell, *Afro-Caribbean Religions: An Introduction to Their Historical, Cultural, and Sacred Traditions* (Temple University Press, 2010), 109, 133.

23. Yare Grau, "This Is How Famous Cubans Celebrated the Day of Santa Bárbara and Changó," CiberCuba, December 5, 2024, https://en.cibercuba.com/noticias/2024-12-05-u65722-e65722-s27065-nid293262-asi-celebraron-famosos-cubanos-dia-santa-barbara.

24. Fabiola Santiago, "A Threatening Trump Wants 'a Better Deal,' but Knee-Jerk Moves Won't Transform a Post-Fidel Cuba," *Miami Herald*, November 30, 2016, https://www.miamiherald.com/news/local/news-columns-blogs/fabiola-santiago/article117824148.html.

25. Daniela Reyes, "Religious Leaders Link Fidel's Death to the Yoruba Religion," *Cuba en Miami*, November 29, 2016, https://www.cubaenmiami.com/en/religiosos-vinculan-la-muerte-de-fidel-con-la-religion-yoruba/.

26. Alan Gomez, "Cubans Line Streets as Fidel Castro's Ashes Begin Journey Across Island," *USA Today*, November 30, 2016, https://www.usatoday.com/story/news/world/2016/11/30/cubans-fidel-castro-ashes/94668100/.

27. "Fidel Castro's Ashes Buried in Santiago de Cuba," BBC, December 14, 2016, https://www.bbc.com/news/world-latin-america-38201169.

CHAPTER 11

1. "Evangelicals Come Up for Air," *Christianity Today*, June 14, 1999, https://www.christianitytoday.com/1999/06/evangelicals-come-up-for-air/.

2. 1 Samuel 5:3–4, ESV.

Notes 379

CHAPTER 12

1. Rachel Beauvoir-Dominique, "Underground Realms of Being: Vodoun Magic," in *Sacred Arts of Haitian Vodou*, ed. Donald J. Cosentino (UCLA Fowler Museum of Cultural History, 1995), 153–77.

2. Paul Christopher Johnson, *Secrets, Gossip, and Gods: The Transformation of Brazilian Candomblé* (Oxford University Press, 2002), 14.

3. Elizabeth A. McAlister, "Vodou," *Britannica*, accessed April 25, 2025, https://www.britannica.com/topic/Vodou.

4. "Candomblé at a Glance," BBC, September 15, 2009, https://www.bbc.co.uk/religion/religions/candomble/ataglance/glance.shtml.

5. Rodriguez, "AfroCuban Religion"; "History of Candomblé," BBC, accessed April 25, 2025, https://www.bbc.co.uk/religion/religions/candomble/history/history.shtml.

6. Fernand Leroy et al., "Yoruba Customs and Beliefs Pertaining to Twins," *Twin Research* 5, no. 2 (2002): 132–36, https://www.scribd.com/document/36035892/Yoruba-Beliefs.

7. Stephen Goddard, "Ago That Became Oyo: An Essay in Yoruba Historical Geography," *The Geographical Journal* 137, no. 2 (1971): 207–11, https://www.jstor.org/stable/1796741.

8. Norma H. Wolff and D. Michael Warren, "The Agbeni Shango Shrine in Ibadan: A Century of Continuity," *African Arts* 31, no. 3 (1998): 36, https://www.proquest.com/docview/220957086?sourcetype=Scholarly%20Journals.

CHAPTER 13

1. "Ooni of Ife: Unraveling the Reign of Nigeria's Most Respected Monarch," FasterCapital, March 31, 2025, https://fastercapital.com/content/Ooni-of-Ife--Unraveling-the-Reign-of-Nigeria-s-Most-Respected-Monarch.html#Introduction-to-the-Ooni-of-Ife.

2. FasterCapital, "Ooni."

3. Murrell, *Afro-Caribbean Religions,* 15.

4. "Nigeria: Ooni and Globalisation, This Day," *All Africa,* November 9, 2001, https://allafrica.com/stories/200111090064.html.

5. Olufunke Adeboye, "The 'Born-Again' Oba: Pentecostalism and Traditional Chieftaincy in Yorubaland," *Lagos Historical Review* 7 (2007): 17–18, https://www.socialtheology.com/docs/THE_BORN_AGAIN_OBA_PENTECOSTALISM_AND_TR.pdf.

6. *All Africa,* "Nigeria: Ooni."

CHAPTER 14

1. Joshua J. Mark, "Oshun," *World History Encyclopedia,* October 1, 2021, https://www.worldhistory.org/Oshun/.

2. Mark, "Oshun."

3. Isaiah 9:2.

CHAPTER 15

1. "Millions Celebrate Opening of Hindu Temple Built on Mosque Ruins in India," PBS, January 22, 2024, https://www.pbs.org/newshour/world/millions-celebrate-opening-of-hindu-temple-built-on-mosque-ruins-in-india.

Notes 381

2. Maha Marouan, "Santería in Cuba: Contested Issues at a Time of Transition," *Transition* 125 (2018): 57–70, https://doi.org/10.2979/transition.125.1.09.

CHAPTER 16

1. Stefan Lovgren and Ted Chamberlain, "Ancient Olympics Had 'Spectacular' Opening Ceremony, Pagan Partying," *National Geographic*, July 27, 2012, https://www.nationalgeographic.com/travel/article/120727-2012-olympics-opening-ceremony-ancient-london-world-summer-games.

2. Lovgren and Chamberlain, "Ancient Olympics."

3. "Factsheet: The Olympic Games of Antiquity," Olympic Committee, September 26, 2022, https://stillmed.olympics.com/media/Documents/Olympic-Games/Factsheets/The-Olympic-Games-of-the-Antiquity.pdf.

4. "The Olympics and Ancient Greece: Religion and Ritual," Michael C. Carlos Museum at Emory University, accessed May 16, 2025, https://carlos.emory.edu/sites/default/files/2021-08/RA%20Religion%20and%20Ritual.pdf.

5. "Olympic Anthem," International Olympic Committee, accessed May 30, 2025, https://www.olympics.com/ioc/olympic-anthem.

6. "Olympic Flame Lighting Ceremony—Ancient Olympia," Why Athens, accessed May 30, 2025, https://whyathens.com/events/olympic-flame-ancient-olympia/.

7. Matthew 12:43–45, ESV.

8. Edward Togo Salmon and Ramsay MacMullen, "The Reign of Valentinian and Valens," *Britannica,* accessed May 16, 2025, https://www.britannica.com/place/ancient-Rome/The-reign-of-Valentinian-and-Valens.

382   THE AVATAR

CHAPTER 17

1. Jerome Pugmire, "Paris Olympics Organizers Say They Meant No Disrespect with 'Last Supper' Tableau," Associated Press, July 28, 2024, https://apnews.com/article/olympics-2024-opening-ceremony-last-supper-criticism-9dd5fc5f1849ce9b0720fa997f38ed27.

2. "Why Were the Early Christians Accused of Cannibalism?," Clarifying Catholicism, accessed May 16, 2025, https://clarifyingcatholicism.org/articles/why-were-the-early-christians-accused-of-cannibalism/#.

3. Anisia Iacob, "Paris Olympics Opening Ceremony: A New Twist on Old Traditions," The Collector, August 10, 2024, https://www.thecollector.com/paris-opening-ceremony-new-twist-traditions/.

4. "The Cult of Bacchus," Virtual Museum of Archaeological Science, accessed May 16, 2025, http://avirtualmuseum.org/exhibits/roman_wineii/bacchic/bacchus_4.html.

5. *World History Encyclopedia*, "Zagreus," last modified October 22, 2023, https://www.worldhistory.org/Zagreus/.

6. Virtual Museum of Archaeological Science, "The Cult of Bacchus."

CHAPTER 18

1. Walter Friedrich Otto, *Dionysus, Myth and Cult*, trans. Robert B. Palmer (Indiana University Press, 1965), 65, 76.

2. Friedrich Nietzsche, *The Gay Science*, ed. Bernard Williams, trans. Josefine Nauckhoff (Cambridge University Press, 2001), 120.

3. Max Whyte, "The Uses and Abuses of Nietzsche in the Third Reich: Alfred Baeumler's 'Heroic Realism,'"

Notes 383

Journal of Contemporary History 43, no. 2 (April 2008): 171–94, https://www.jstor.org/stable/30036502.

4. "Nietzsche's Letter 1 1889," The Nietzsche Channel, accessed May 31, 2025, http://www.thenietzschechannel.com/correspondence/eng/nlett-1889.htm.

CHAPTER 20

1. "Religion, England and Wales: Census 2021," Office for National Statistics, November 29, 2022, https://www.ons.gov.uk/peoplepopulationandcommunity/culturalidentity/religion/bulletins/religionenglandandwales/census2021#.

2. "Roll Call Vote 119th Congress—1st Session Vote Summary: Question: On Cloture on the Motion to Proceed (Motion to Invoke Cloture: Motion to Proceed to S.6 (A Bill to Amend Title 18, United States Code, to Prohibit a Health Care Practitioner from Failing to Exercise the Proper Degree of Care in the Case of a Child Who Survives an Abortion or Attempted Abortion.))," US Senate, accessed May 30, 2025, https://www.senate.gov/legislative/LIS/roll_call_votes/vote1191/vote_119_1_00011.htm.

3. Nadine Yousif, "Assisted Dying Now Accounts for One in Twenty Canada Deaths," BBC News, December 12, 2024, https://www.bbc.com/news/articles/c0j1z14p57po.

4. Wendy Wang, Brad Wilcox, and Lyman Stone, "New Census Data: Key Takeaways on Divorce, Marriage, and Fertility in the US," Institute for Family Studies, September 22, 2022, https://ifstudies.org/blog/new-census-data-key-takeaways-on-divorce-marriage-and-fertility-in-the-us.

5. "AMA Announced Policies Adopted on Final Day of Special Meeting," American Medical Association, June 16, 2021, https://www.ama-assn.org/press-center/

384   **THE AVATAR**

press-releases/ama-announced-policies-adopted-final-day-special-meeting.

6. Christopher Kane, "Biden Hosts Biggest-Ever Pride Month Event at the White House," *Washington Blade,* June 10, 2023, https://www.washingtonblade.com/2023/06/10/biden-hosts-biggest-ever-pride-month-event-at-the-white-house/.

7. Aamer Madhani and Associated Press, "Biden Hosts Pride Month Celebration at White House, Voices LGBTQ+ Support," PBS, June 11, 2023, https://www.pbs.org/newshour/politics/biden-hosts-pride-month-celebration-at-white-house-voices-lgbtq-support.

8. President Biden (@POTUS46Archive), "Today, the People's House—your house—sends a clear message to the country and to the world. America is a nation of pride," X, June 10, 2023, https://x.com/POTUS46Archive/status/1667715777145847808.

9. "White House Lit Up with Rainbow Colors in 2015," National Park Service, accessed April 30, 2015, https://www.nps.gov/places/white-house-lit-up-with-rainbow-colors.htm; Kristopher Fraser, "Inside the White House Respect for Marriage Act Signing: Rainbow Lights, Sparkling Drag Queens, Cyndi Lauper Singing and More," Women's Wear Daily, December 14, 2022, https://wwd.com/eye/scoops/respect-for-marriage-act-white-house-rainbow-colors-1235449747/.

CHAPTER 21

1. R. Albert Mohler Jr., "President Clinton's Spiritual Enablers," *SBC Life,* January 1, 1999, https://www.baptistpress.com/resource-library/sbc-life-articles/president-clintons-spiritual-enablers/.

Notes 385

2. Dan Carson, "How the 1992 RNC in Houston Started the 'Culture War' Politics We Know Now," *Chron,* December 25, 2022, https://www.chron.com/politics/article/1992-rnc-houston-culture-war-17487677.php.

3. Carson, "How the 1992 RNC."

4. Mark Hensch, "Clinton: 'Deep-Seated' Beliefs Block Abortion Access," *The Hill*, April 24, 2015, https://thehill.com/blogs/ballot-box/239974-clinton-deep-seated-beliefs-block-abortion-access/.

5. "Planned Parenthood Commemorates One Hundred Years of Care, Education, and Activism with the Celebration of a Century," Planned Parenthood, April 6, 2017, https://www.plannedparenthood.org/about-us/newsroom/press-releases/planned-parenthood-commemorates-100-years-of-care-education-and-activism-with-the-celebration-of-a-century.

6. Helen Kennedy, "President Clinton Admits He Lied Under Oath About His Affair with Monica Lewinsky in 2001," Daily News, updated January 11, 2019, http://www.nydailynews.com/news/politics/bill-feds-cut-dealsurrenders-law-license-escape-ind-article-1.904790; "A Chronology: Key Moments in the Clinton–Lewinsky Saga," CNN, accessed April 11, 2025, https://www.cnn.com/ALLPOLITICS/1998/resources/lewinsky/timeline/.

7. "President Bill Clinton: I Have Sinned," The History Place, accessed July 3, 2017, http://www.historyplace.com/speeches/clinton-sin.htm.

8. "1 Kings 21—the Murder of Naboth," Enduring Word, accessed April 30, 2025, https://enduringword.com/bible-commentary/1-kings-21/.

9. International Standard Bible Encyclopedia Online, "Jehoram; Joram," accessed April 30, 2025, https://www.internationalstandardbible.com/J/jehoram-joram.html.

10. "'Alter Egos' Dissects Hillary Clinton's Tenure as Obama's Secretary of State," *Fresh Air*, hosted by Terry Gross, NPR, April 25, 2016, https://www.npr.org/2016/04/25/475584003/alter-egos-dissects-hillary-clintons-tenure-as-obamas-secretary-of-state.

11. David Bernstein, "The Speech," *Chicago*, May 29, 2007, https://www.chicagomag.com/chicago-magazine/june-2007/the-speech/.

12. 2 Kings 3:1, LEB.

13. 2 Kings 9:14–24; 2 Kings 9:33.

14. 1 Kings 16:29.

CHAPTER 23

1. 2 Kings 9:5.

2. 2 Kings 9:12.

3. 2 Kings 9:13, author's translation.

4. 2 Kings 9:13.

5. 2 Kings 9:16.

6. "Watch Donald Trump's Grand Escalator Entrance to His Presidential Announcement," ABC News, June 16, 2015, https://abcnews.go.com/Politics/video/watch-donald-trumps-grand-escalator-entrance-presidential-announcement-31802261.

7. 2 Kings 10:15.

8. "Trump's VP Pick Mike Pence Introduces Himself to America as 'a Christian, a Conservative and a Republican,'" ABC News, July 20, 2016, https://abcnews.go.com/Politics/trumps-vp-pick-mike-pence-introduces-america-christian/story?id=40756471.

9. 2 Kings 9:24, NASB.

10. 2 Kings 9:33.

Notes 387

11. 2 Kings 9:6–7.

12. 2 Kings 9:7–8.

13. "2 Kings 10: International Standard Version," Bible Gateway, accessed April 11, 2025, https://www.biblegateway.com/passage/?search=2%20Kings%2010&version=ISV;ESV.

14. Anita Kumar, "The Clinton Dynasty Has Come to an End," McClatchy DC, November 10, 2016, https://www.mcclatchydc.com/news/politics-government/election/article113778808.html.

15. "2 Kings 10," Bible Project, accessed April 11, 2025, https://bibleproject.com/bible/nirv/2-kings/10/.

16. Paul Bois, "Donald Trump, Dynasty Killer: 2023 Will Mean No More Bush, Cheney, McCain, or Clinton in Office," Breitbart, August 17, 2022, https://www.breitbart.com/politics/2022/08/17/donald-trump-dynasty-killer-2023-will-mean-no-more-bush-cheney-mccain-or-clinton-in-office/.

CHAPTER 24

1. Ben Kamisar, "The Final Price Tag on 2024 Political Advertising: Almost $11 Billion," NBC News, November 8, 2024, https://www.nbcnews.com/politics/2024-election/final-price-tag-2024-political-advertising-almost-11-billion-rcna179341.

2. Paul Bedard, "TV News 'Most Lopsided' Ever: Trump 85 Percent Negative, Harris 78 Percent Positive," *Washington Examiner*, October 28, 2024, https://www.washingtonexaminer.com/news/washington-secrets/3205606/tv-news-lopsided-trump-85-negative-harris-78-positive/.

3. Lazaro Gamio et al., "Tracking Efforts to Remove Trump from the 2024 Ballot," *New York Times*, March 4, 2024, https://www.nytimes.com/interactive/2024/01/02/us/politics/trump-ballot-removal-map.html.

4. Freddy Gray, "The Lawfare Against Donald Trump Is Increasingly Farcical," *Spectator*, December 20, 2023, https://www.spectator.co.uk/article/the-lawfare-against-trump-may-end-up-backfiring/.

5. Helen Johnson, "Fact Check: How Many Criminal Charges Is Donald Trump Facing and Could He Go to Jail?," Channel 4 News, February 19, 2024, https://www.channel4.com/news/factcheck/factcheck-how-many-criminal-charges-is-donald-trump-facing-and-could-he-go-to-jail.

6. Michael R. Sisak et al., "Guilty: Trump Becomes First Former US President Convicted of Felony Crimes," Associated Press, May 31, 2024, https://apnews.com/article/trump-trial-deliberations-jury-testimony-verdict-85558c6d08efb434d05b694364470aa0.

7. Justin Sweitzer, "Three Key Findings on the Trump Assassination Attempt in Butler," *City and State*, December 12, 2024, https://www.cityandstatepa.com/politics/2024/12/3-key-findings-trump-assassination-attempt-butler/401632/.

8. Gustaf Kilander, "What Trump Said When He Saw His Raised-Fist Assassination Photo for the First Time," *Independent*, March 7, 2025, https://www.independent.co.uk/news/world/americas/us-politics/donald-trump-assassination-photo-butler-b2711010.html.

9. "Dana Perino: This Was Like Watching a 'Warrior President,'" video, Fox News, July 14, 2024, 4 min., 59 sec., https://www.centralcharts.com/en/news/4753202-dana-perino-this-was-like-watching-a-warrior-president.

10. Michael Goodwin, "Trump Just Proved That He's a Pure Warrior After His Heinous Assassination Attempt," *New York Post*, July 13, 2024, https://nypost.com/2024/07/13/opinion/

Notes

389

trump-just-proved-that-hes-a-pure-warrior-after-his-heinous-assassination-attempt/.

11. Robert Downen and William Melhado, "Trump Vows Retribution at Waco Rally: 'I Am Your Warrior, I Am Your Justice,'" Texas Tribune, March 25, 2023, https://www.texastribune.org/2023/03/25/donald-trump-waco-rally-retribution-justice/.

CHAPTER 25

1. 2 Kings 9:2, author's translation.

2. Brandon Showalter, "Witches Outnumber Presbyterians in the US; Wicca, Paganism Growing 'Astronomically,'" *Christian Post*, October 10, 2018, https://www.christianpost.com/news/witches-outnumber-presbyterians-in-the-us-wicca-paganism-growing-astronomically.html.

3. Rachel Elizabeth Jones, "A 'Witch-In' Targets Trump," Seven Days, October 26, 2016, https://www.sevendaysvt.com/arts-culture/a-witch-in-targets-trump-3774747.

4. Meera Raman, "Can Witches Defeat Donald Trump? They're Trying," *Toronto Star*, October 24, 2024, https://www.thestar.com/news/insight/these-witches-are-trying-to-use-their-power-to-defeat-donald-trump/article_aabeec6a-8b27-11ef-a73c-831e92a6fb58.html.

5. Raman, "Can Witches Defeat Donald Trump?"

6. Jonita Davis, "'Witches for Harris 2024' Activated Colorado Women Under the Harvest Supermoon," Black CAPE, September 20, 2024, https://theblackcapemag.com/witches-for-harris-2024-activated-colorado-women-under-the-harvest-supermoon-4fe02fbb42ea.

7. Jason Mankey, "Hillary Clinton as a Witch," Patheos, November 1, 2016, https://www.patheos.com/blogs/panmankey/2016/11/hillary-clinton-as-a-witch/.

8. Francis X. Clines, "White House Plays Down a New Age Visitor," *New York Times*, June 24, 1996, https://www.nytimes.com/1996/06/24/us/white-house-plays-down-a-new-age-visitor.html.

9. Hillary Clinton, "Witches Get Stuff Done. Happy Halloween!," Facebook, October 31, 2023, https://www.facebook.com/hillaryclinton/posts/witches-get-stuff-done-happy-halloween/872951727521412/.

10. Rebecca Schneid and Koh Ewe, "Here's Who Has Endorsed Kamala Harris for President So Far," *Time*, July 26, 2024, https://time.com/7001125/kamala-harris-endorsements-biden-bill-hillary-clinton/.

11. Hillary Rodham Clinton, "Hillary Clinton: How Kamala Harris Can Win and Make History," *New York Times*, July 23, 2024, https://www.nytimes.com/2024/07/23/opinion/kamala-harris-donald-trump.html.

12. Benjamin Gill, "Witches Report Their Spells Against Trump Aren't Working: 'He Has a Shield,'" CBN, October 28, 2024, https://cbn.com/news/us/witches-report-their-spells-against-trump-arent-working-he-has-shield.

13. Gill, "Witches Report Their Spells Against Trump Aren't Working."

14. Jessica Botelho, "Self-Proclaimed Witches Say Spells Won't Work Against Trump," ABC 33/40, October 24, 2024, https://abc3340.com/amp/news/beyond-the-podium/self-proclaimed-witches-say-spells-wont-work-on-trump-2024-presidential-election-politics-kamala-harris-tim-walz-jd-vance-magic-witchcraft-salem-halloween.

CHAPTER 26

1. 2 Kings 9:20–24.

Notes 391

2. "Trump vs. Biden Debate: Five Disastrous Moments," Times News, YouTube, June 28, 2024, 2 min., 39 sec., https://www.youtube.com/watch?v=Vq0G1TMCw4Y.

CHAPTER 27

1. "Women Presidential and Vice Presidential Candidates: A Selected List," Center for American Women and Politics, accessed April 12, 2025, https://cawp.rutgers.edu/facts/levels-office/federal-executive/women-presidential-and-vice-presidential-candidates-selected.

CHAPTER 28

1. 2 Kings 9:30–31.

2. 1 Kings 16:15.

3. Andrew Mercer et al., "Why 2016 Election Polls Missed Their Mark," Pew Research Center, November 19, 2016, https://www.pewresearch.org/short-reads/2016/11/09/why-2016-election-polls-missed-their-mark/; "US Election Polls: Who Is Ahead—Harris or Trump?," BBC News, November 5, 2024, https://www.bbc.com/news/articles/cj4x71znwxdo.

CHAPTER 29

1. 1 Kings 19:14–16.

2. Chris Cillizza, "Donald Trump's 'Chaos' Presidency Reaches Frightening New Levels," CNN, January 4, 2018, https://www.cnn.com/2018/01/04/politics/chaos-trump/index.html.

3. 2 Kings 10:23–27.

CHAPTER 30

1. 2 Chronicles 22:7–9.

2. 2 Kings 9:16.

CHAPTER 31

1. James B. Jordan, "Chronologies and Kings, Part Ten: Jehoram of Judah," Theopolis Institute, April 24, 1992, https://theopolisinstitute.com/chronologies-and-kings-part-10-jehoram-of-judah/.

2. "Jehosh'aphat," Bible Hub, accessed April 13, 2025, https://biblehub.com/topical/j/jehosh'aphat.htm.

3. 2 Chronicles 21:6.

4. Amy Wang and Blair Guild, "How Biden's Abortion Stance Has Shifted Over the Years," *Washington Post*, April 17, 2024, https://www.washingtonpost.com/politics/2024/04/17/biden-abortion-stances/.

5. Luisa Blanchfield, "Abortion and Family Planning-Related Provisions in US Foreign Assistance Law and Policy," Congressional Research Service, July 15, 2015, https://www.congress.gov/crs-product/R41360.

6. Jamie Joseph, "Biden DOJ Weaponized FACE Act to Imprison Pro-Life Activists, Attorney Tells House: 'Systematic Campaign,'" Fox News, February 26, 2025, https://www.foxnews.com/politics/biden-doj-weaponized-face-act-imprison-pro-life-activists-attorney-tells-house-systematic-campaign.

7. 2 Chronicles 21:6.

CHAPTER 32

1. 2 Samuel 8:13–14.

2. 2 Kings 8:20.

3. 2 Kings 8:21, NASB.

4. 2 Kings 8:21, NASB.

Notes

5. "The Long Shadow of Biden's Afghan Withdrawal Debacle," *Wall Street Journal*, September 9, 2024, https://www.wsj.com/opinion/afghanistan-withdrawal-report-house-foreign-affairs-michael-mccaul-joe-biden-kamala-harris-donald-trump-taliban-498a9b12.

6. *Wall Street Journal*, "The Long Shadow."

7. Imtiaz Tyab, "Taliban Holding On to $7 Billion of US Military Equipment Left Behind After Withdrawal," CBS News, February 4, 2025, https://www.cbsnews.com/news/us-military-weapons-left-in-afghanistan-taliban/; Madeleine May, "Thousands of Afghans Who Helped the US Military Blocked from Reaching American Soil," CBS News, March 12, 2025, https://www.cbsnews.com/news/afghans-helped-the-u-s-military-blocked-from-america/?intcid=CNI-00-10aaa3a.

8. Daniel Kochis, "Biden's Afghanistan Debacle Will Cast a Long Shadow Over Transatlantic Security," Heritage Foundation, November 9, 2021, https://www.heritage.org/middle-east/commentary/bidens-afghanistan-debacle-will-cast-long-shadow-over-transatlantic-security.

9. "2 Kings 8:21 Meaning," VideoBible, accessed April 13, 2025, https://www.videobible.com/meaning/2-kings-8-21.

10. Stephen Collinson, "Biden's Botched Afghan Exit Is a Disaster at Home and Abroad Long in the Making," CNN, August 16, 2021, https://www.cnn.com/2021/08/16/politics/afghanistan-joe-biden-donald-trump-kabul-politics/index.html. See also Paul LeBlanc, "Chaos Is Unfolding in Afghanistan. Here's What You Need to Know," CNN, August 15, 2021, https://www.cnn.com/2021/08/15/politics/taliban-kabul-afghanistan-explainer/index.html.

11. Albert Barnes, "2 Kings 8:21," in "Notes on the Bible," Bible Hub, accessed April 13, 2025, https://biblehub.com/2_kings/8-21.htm.

12. Marc A. Thiessen, "Biden's Disastrous Pullout from Afghanistan Could Cost Him Reelection," *Washington Post*, August 28, 2023, https://www.washingtonpost.com/opinions/2023/08/28/afghanistan-withdrawal-anniversary-biden-impact/.

13. Jim Inhofe, "Afghanistan Was a Predictable, Preventable Disaster," Foreign Policy, August 15, 2022, https://foreignpolicy.com/2022/08/15/afghanistan-withdrawal-pullout-military-taliban-chaos-evacuation-biden-inhofe/.

14. Nick Schifrin and Dan Sagalyn, "House GOP Blames Biden for Chaotic Afghan Exit While Ignoring Trump Administration's Role," PBS, September 9, 2024, https://www.pbs.org/newshour/show/house-gop-blames-biden-for-chaotic-afghan-exit-while-ignoring-trump-administrations-role.

15. VideoBible, "2 Kings."

16. Collinson, "Biden's Botched Afghan Exit."

17. 2 Chronicles 21:10.

18. *Wall Street Journal*, "The Long Shadow."

19. "Getting Answers on the Afghanistan Withdrawal," US House Foreign Affairs Committee, accessed April 13, 2025, https://foreignaffairs.house.gov/getting-answers-on-afghanistan-withdrawal/.

20. Haydon N. Parham, "It Started in Afghanistan: The Disastrous American Withdrawal from Kabul Triggered a Wave of Instability the World Over," *The National Interest*, February 3, 2024, accessed May 30, 2025, https://www.linkedin.com/in/haydon-n-parham-77a341165/.

21. Parham, "It Started in Afghanistan."

22. Con Coughlin, "Four Years of Biden Have Left the World in Flames," *Telegraph*, September 25, 2024, https://www.

Notes

telegraph.co.uk/news/2024/09/25/joe-biden-foreign-policy-
israel-ukraine-afghanistan/.

23. Charles John Ellicott, "2 Chronicles 21, Verse 9," in *Ellicott's
    Commentary for English Readers*, StudyLight, accessed
    April 13, 2025, https://www.studylight.org/commentaries/
    eng/ebc/2-chronicles-21.html.

24. "Afghanistan Withdrawal Has Taiwan Pondering Its
    Alliance with the US and China Is Upping the Pressure,"
    King's College London, accessed May 30, 2025, https://
    www.kcl.ac.uk/afghanistan-withdrawal-has-taiwan-
    pondering-its-alliance-with-the-us-and-china-is-upping-
    the-pressure.

CHAPTER 33

1. 2 Chronicles 21:16–20.

2. 2 Chronicles 21:16–17.

3. "Wrap Up: Biden Administration's Policies Have Fueled
   Worst Border Crisis in US History," US House Oversight
   Committee, January 17, 2024, https://oversight.house.gov/
   release/wrap-up-biden-administrations-policies-have-
   fueled-worst-border-crisis-in-u-s-history%EF%BF%BC/.

4. Selene Rodriguez, "How Porous Borders Fuel Human
   Trafficking in the United States," Texas Public Policy
   Foundation, January 11, 2022, https://www.texaspolicy.
   com/how-porous-borders-fuel-human-trafficking-in-the-
   united-states/.

CHAPTER 34

1. 2 Chronicles 21:17.

2. Richard Goldberg, "President Joe Biden's Got
   Blood on Hands After Appeasing Iran for Years,"
   Foundation for Defense of Democracies, January
   28, 2024, https://www.fdd.org/analysis/2024/01/28/

president-joe-bidens-got-blood-on-hands-after-appeasing-iran-for-years/; Jonathan S. Tobin, "Can Biden's Cognitive Dissonance Let Israel Win the War?," *Jewish News Syndicate*, December 15, 2023, https://www.jns.org/can-bidens-cognitive-dissonance-let-israel-win-the-war/.

3. 2 Chronicles 21:16.

4. "Who Are the Palestinians?," Palestine Children's Relief Fund, accessed April 16, 2025, https://www.pcrf.net/information-you-should-know/who-are-the-palestinians.html.

5. Douglas J. Feith, "The Forgotten History of the Term 'Palestine,'" Mosaic Magazine, December 13, 2021, https://mosaicmagazine.com/observation/israel-zionism/2021/12/the-forgotten-history-of-the-term-palestine/.

6. *Britannica*, "Israel-Hamas War," accessed April 16, 2025, https://www.britannica.com/event/Israel-Hamas-War.

CHAPTER 35

1. 2 Chronicles 21:11.

2. 2 Kings 11:18.

3. Wang and Guild, "How Biden's Abortion Stance Has Shifted Over the Years."

4. Jamie Joseph, "Biden DOJ Weaponized FACE Act to Imprison Pro-Life Activists, Attorney Tells House: 'Systematic Campaign,'" Fox News, February 26, 2025, https://www.foxnews.com/politics/biden-doj-weaponized-face-act-imprison-pro-life-activists-attorney-tells-house-systematic-campaign.

5. Michael Collins, "Joe Biden Helped a Movement When He Changed His Mind on LGBTQ Issues. Who Advises Him Now?," *USA Today*, August 19, 2023, https://www.

Notes 397

usatoday.com/story/news/politics/2023/08/19/joe-biden-gay-friendly-president-lgbtq-issues/70233287007/.

6. Andrew Chung, "US Supreme Court Upholds Tennessee Law Banning Youth Transgender Care," Reuters, June 19, 2025, https://www.reuters.com/world/us/us-supreme-court-rules-against-challenge-youth-transgender-care-ban-2025-06-18/.

7. 2 Chronicles 21:11, author's translation.

8. Albert Barnes, "2 Chronicles 21:11," in "Notes on the Bible," Bible Hub, accessed April 16, 2025, https://biblehub.com/commentaries/barnes/2_chronicles/21.htm.

9. Carlos Jamieson, "Biden Administration Releases Proposed Rules for Transgender Athlete Participation," Education Commission of the States, May 4, 2023, https://www.ecs.org/biden-administration-releases-proposed-rules-for-transgender-athlete-participation/.

10. "United States of America v. State of Idaho," Alliance Defending Freedom, December 9, 2024, https://adfmedia.org/case/united-states-america-v-state-idaho/; Caroline Downey, "Federal Court Blocks Biden Admin from Forcing Doctors to Perform Gender Transitions," *National Review*, August 26, 2022, https://www.nationalreview.com/news/federal-court-blocks-biden-admin-from-forcing-doctors-to-perform-gender-transitions/.

CHAPTER 36

1. "2006 Clip of Joe Biden's Opposition to Gay Marriage Surfaces," WIBC, July 22, 2020, https://wibc.com/90041/2006-clip-of-joe-bidens-opposition-to-gay-marriage-surfaces/.

2. Fraser, "Inside the White House."

3. Ben Johnson, "Senate Advances Bogus Religious Freedom 'Fix' to Radical Same-Sex Marriage Bill,"

The Washington Stand, November 28, 2022, https://washingtonstand.com/news/senate-passes-bogus-religious-freedom-fix-to-radical-samesex-marriage-bill-.

4. Ezra 10:9–10.

5. Fraser, "Inside the White House."

CHAPTER 37

1. 2 Chronicles 21:17.

2. "Joe Biden Loses First Wife and Daughter in Tragic Car Accident," History, accessed April 16, 2025, https://www.history.com/this-day-in-history/december-18/joe-biden-loses-first-wife-and-daughter-in-tragic-car-accident.

3. 2 Chronicles 21:17, NIV.

4. 2 Chronicles 21:17, NIV.

5. Kevin Liptak, "Beau Biden, Son of Vice President and Former Delaware AG, Dies at 46," CNN, May 31, 2015, https://www.cnn.com/2015/05/30/politics/obit-vice-president-son-beau-biden/index.html.

6. 2 Kings 8:27.

7. Sam Cabral, "Hunter Biden: The Struggles and Scandals of the US President's Son," BBC News, June 11, 2024, https://www.bbc.com/news/world-us-canada-55805698.

8. 2 Chronicles 22:4.

CHAPTER 38

1. 2 Chronicles 21:12–15, ESV.

2. Annie Linskey et al., "How the White House Functioned with a Diminished Biden in Charge," Wall Street Journal, December 19, 2024, https://www.wsj.com/politics/biden-white-house-age-function-diminished-3906a839.

3. Warren Wiersbe, Be Distinct (David C. Cook Publishing, 2002), 62.

Notes

4. Frederick Mabie, "1 and 2 Chronicles," in *The Expositor's Bible Commentary*, PreceptAustin, accessed April 16, 2025, https://www.preceptaustin.org/2-chronicles-21-commentary.

5. House Foreign Affairs Committee, "Willful Blindness: An Assessment of the Biden-Harris Administration's Withdrawal from Afghanistan and the Chaos That Followed," press release, September 9, 2024, https://foreignaffairs.house.gov/press-release/chairman-mccaul-releases-historic-comprehensive-report-on-biden-harris-administrations-afghanistan-withdrawal/.

6. Alfred Edersheim, "Chapter 15: Old Testament History by Alfred Edersheim, Volume 6," Bible Study Tools, accessed May 30, 2025, https://www.biblestudytools.com/history/edersheim-old-testament/volume-6/chapter-15.html.

7. *Oxford Dictionaries*, "feeble," accessed May 31, 2025, https://www.google.com/search?q=feeble&sca_esv=.

8. *Collins Dictionary*, "feeble," accessed May 31, 2025, https://www.collinsdictionary.com/us/dictionary/english/feeble.

9. *Merriam-Webster*, "feeble," accessed May 31, 2025, https://www.merriam-webster.com/dictionary/feeble.

10. Bret Stephens, "A Disgraceful Pardon," *New York Times*, December 2, 2024, https://www.nytimes.com/2024/12/02/opinion/biden-hunter-pardon-trump.html.

11. Zeke Miller et al., "Biden Drops Out of 2024 Race After Disastrous Debate Inflamed Age Concerns. VP Harris Gets His Nod," Associated Press, July 21, 2024, https://apnews.com/article/biden-drops-out-2024-election-ddffde72838370032bdcff946cfc2ce6; Michael D. Shear et al., "He Still Thought He Could Win: Inside Biden's Decision to Drop Out," *New York Times*, August 15, 2024, https://www.

400 THE AVATAR

nytimes.com/2024/08/15/us/politics/biden-2024-election-dropped-out.html.

12. 2 Chronicles 21:19–20.

13. 2 Chronicles 21:20.

CHAPTER 39

1. *Britannica*, "Athaliah," accessed April 13, 2025, https://www.britannica.com/biography/Athaliah.

2. Joel Ryan, "Was Queen Athaliah Really as Bad as Her Mother Jezebel and Father Ahab?," Bible Study Tools, June 12, 2024, https://www.biblestudytools.com/bible-study/topical-studies/queen-athaliah-bad-as-mother-jezebel-father-ahab.html.

3. Shawn McCreesh, "Clintons Endorse Kamala Harris to Be Democrats' Nominee for President," *New York Times*, July 21, 2024, https://www.nytimes.com/2024/07/21/us/politics/clintons-kamala-harris-endorsement.html.

4. "Hillary Clinton Passes the Torch to Kamala Harris at DNC, Fortune," WPTL, accessed April 26, 2025, https://wptlradio.net/dnc-crowd-roars-lock-him-up-as-hillary-clinton-slams-felon-trump-the-daily-beast/.

CHAPTER 40

1. Matt Tracy, "A Look at Vice President Kamala Harris' LGBTQ Record," *Gay City News*, July 22, 2024, https://gaycitynews.com/vice-president-kamala-harris-lgbtq-record/.

2. Tracy, "A Look at Vice President Kamala Harris' LGBTQ Record."

3. Paul Meara, "Political Siblings: Barack Obama and Kamala Harris Are More Alike Than Different," BET,

Notes 401

August 19, 2020, https://www.bet.com/article/sj6bvq/
obama-and-harris-cut-from-the-same-cloth.

4. Philip Sherwell and Laura Pullman, "Kamala Harris
   Has History to Rival Obama's," *Times*, January 20, 2021,
   https://www.thetimes.com/uk/politics/article/kamala-
   harris-mould-breaking-veep-hopeful-has-history-to-rival-
   obamas-v2lgmfr35.

5. Courtney Subramanian, "Key Moments When Harris
   and Obama's Political Paths Crossed," BBC News,
   August 20, 2024, https://www.bbc.com/news/articles/
   cj08mn24jplo; Katie Rogers, "Behind the Obama-Harris
   Friendship: A Key Endorsement and a Kindred Spirit,"
   New York Times, August 20, 2024, https://www.nytimes.
   com/2024/08/20/us/politics/harris-obama-friendship.
   html?smtyp=cur&smid=tw-nytimes.

6. Sherwell and Pullman, "Kamala Harris"; R.
   Champakalakshmi and Sanat Pai Raikar, "India,"
   Britannica, accessed April 26, 2025, https://www.
   britannica.com/place/India/The-Shunga-kingdom.

7. Kalyani Ganesan, "What Were Kamala Harris' Diwali
   Visits to India Like?," SheThePeople, July 23, 2024,
   https://www.shethepeople.tv/us/kamala-harris-vists-to-
   india.

8. Tanvi Misra, "What Does Caste Have to Do with Kamala
   Harris?," *Harpers Bazaar*, September 26, 2024, https://
   www.harpersbazaar.com/culture/features/a62372490/
   what-does-caste-have-to-do-with-kamala-harris/.

CHAPTER 41

1. 2 Chronicles 21:5–6.

2. 2 Chronicles 21:6.

3. Kim Parker and Amanda Barroso, "In Vice President
   Kamala Harris, We Can See How America Has

402 **THE AVATAR**

Changed," Pew Research Center, February 25, 2021, https://www.pewresearch.org/short-reads/2021/02/25/ in-vice-president-kamala-harris-we-can-see-how-america-has-changed/.

CHAPTER 42

1. Stephanie Armour et al., "Harris, Who Is Biden's Voice on Abortion Rights, Is Likely to Raise the Volume," NPR, July 22, 2024, https://www.npr.org/sections/shots-health-news/2024/07/22/nx-s1-5048045/harris-abortion-health-drug-prices-insulin-medicare.

2. A. S. Peake, "Elijah and Jezebel," reprinted from *Bulletin of the John Ryland Library* 11, no. 2 (1927), http://library.huc.edu/jer/39262.pdf.

3. Samantha Waldenberg et al., "Kamala Harris Becomes First VP to Visit Abortion Provider with Planned Parenthood Visit," CNN, March 14, 2024, https://www.cnn.com/2024/03/13/politics/kamala-harris-planned-parenthood-minnesota/index.html.

4. Kilian Melloy, "Kamala Harris Will Probably Be the Democratic Candidate—but Will She Defend LGBTQ+ Rights?," *Edge*, July 24, 2024, https://www.edgemedianetwork.com/story/334497#.

5. Kate Yandel, "Fact Check: Harris' Position on Health Care for Transgender Prisoners and Detainees," Factcheck.org and *Pittsburgh Post Gazette*, April 26, 2025, https://www.post-gazette.com/news/election-2024/2024/10/04/fact-check-harris-health-care-transgender-prisoners/stories/202410040110.

6. Glenn Garner, "Kamala Harris Becomes First Sitting Vice President to March in a Pride Event," *People*, June 12, 2021, https://people.com/politics/kamala-harris-first-sitting-vice-president-to-march-in-pride-parade/.

Notes 403

7. Cheryl Sullenger, "Planned Parenthood Donated $81,000 to Kamala Harris, Who Ransacked David Daleiden's Home," LifeNews, April 7, 2016, https://www.lifenews.com/2016/04/07/planned-parenthood-donated-81000-to-kamala-harris-who-ransacked-david-daleidens-home/.

8. Daniel Payne, "89-Year-Old Death Camp Survivor Convicted for Pro-Life Protest Faces Jail Time," Catholic News Agency, August 21, 2024, https://www.catholicnewsagency.com/news/258833/89-year-old-death-camp-survivor-convicted-for-pro-life-protest-faces-jail-time; Nancy Flanders, "Grandmother Pardoned After Pro-Life Activism: 'I Was Doing This in Obedience to His Word,'" Live Action, February 21, 2025, https://www.liveaction.org/news/grandmother-pardoned-pro-life-activism-obedience/.

9. Tyler Arnold, "Biden DOJ Sued for Allegedly Hiding Info on Attacks of Churches, Pro-Life Groups," Catholic News Agency, March 22, 2023, https://www.catholicnewsagency.com/news/253915/heritage-sues-doj-for-info-on-attacks-of-churches-pro-life-groups; Samantha Kamman, "Biden Admin Accused of Failure to Prosecute Church Attacks, 'One-Sided' FACE Act Enforcement," *Christian Post*, December 20, 2024, https://www.christianpost.com/news/biden-admin-failed-to-prosecute-church-attacks-under-face-act.html.

CHAPTER 43

1. 2 Kings 8:27.

2. 2 Chronicles 22:3.

3. 2 Chronicles 22:2–9.

4. 2 Kings 11:1; 2 Chronicles 22:10–12.

5. Gene Maddaus, "Kamala Harris Launches Presidential Bid: 'My Intention Is to Earn and Win This

Nomination,'" *Variety,* July 21, 2024, https://variety. com/2024/politics/news/kamala-harris-president- campaign-white-house-hollywood-favorite-1236079539/.

6. Jeffrey H. Tigay, "Ethbaal," University of Pennsylvania School of Arts and Sciences, accessed April 11, 2025, https://www.sas.upenn.edu/~jtigay/ethbaal.doc#; McClintock and Strong Biblical Cyclopedia, "Ethbaal," accessed April 26, 2025, https://www.biblicalcyclopedia. com/E/ethbaal.html.

7. McClintock and Strong Biblical Cyclopedia, "Jehoram, 5," accessed April 26, 2025, https://www.biblicalcyclopedia. com/J/jehoram.html.

8. 2 Kings 11:1; 2 Chronicles 22:10.

9. Sullenger, "Planned Parenthood."

10. Alan Blinder, "Harris and Usher Make Abortion Rights the Focus at Atlanta Rally," *New York Times,* October 19, 2024, https://www.nytimes.com/2024/10/19/us/politics/harris- atlanta-rally-abortion.html.

11. Chantelle Lee, "What a Kamala Harris Win Would Mean for Abortion," *Time,* November 5, 2024, https:// time.com/7096543/kamala-harris-abortion-plan-2024/; "2024 Democratic Party Platform," American Presidency Project, August 19, 2024, https://www.presidency.ucsb.edu/ documents/2024-democratic-party-platform.

12. Tyler Arnold, "Kamala Harris Rejects Religious Exemptions for Abortion Laws: 'That Cannot Be Negotiable,'" Catholic News Agency, October 23, 2024, https://www. catholicnewsagency.com/news/260035/kamala-harris- rejects-religious-exemptions-for-abortion-laws-that-cannot- be-negotiable.

13. Amanda Seitz, "In 60-Year-Old Tim Walz, Kamala Harris Found a Partner to Advocate for Reproductive Rights," Associated Press, August 23, 2024, https://apnews.com/

Notes 405

article/walz-harris-ivf-abortion-reproductive-rights-55cb772
464c99ba9c2b4c2043cb87560.

14. Steve Karnowski, "Minnesota Governor Signs Broad Abortion Rights Bill into Law," Associated Press, January 31, 2023, https://apnews.com/article/abortion-politics-minnesota-state-government-timothy-walz-11c3b1d5269c92 9e442b979ff1bac73b.

15. Alex Demas, "Claims About Children Born Alive After Abortion Attempts in Minnesota Are True," The Dispatch, August 13, 2024, https://thedispatch.com/article/claims-about-children-born-alive-after-abortion-attempts-in-minnesota-are-true/.

16. Mike DeBonis and Felicia Sonmez, "Senate Blocks Bill on Medical Care for Children Born Alive After Attempted Abortion," *Washington Post*, February 25, 2019, https://www.washingtonpost.com/politics/senate-blocks-bill-on-medical-care-for-children-born-alive-after-attempted-abortion/2019/02/25/e5d3d4d8-3924-11e9-a06c-3ec8ed509d15_story.html.

CHAPTER 44

1. Andi Ortiz and Ross A. Lincoln, "Planned Parenthood Mobile Clinic Provided 8 Medication Abortions, 9 Vasectomies Outside the DNC," The Wrap, August 21, 2024, https://www.thewrap.com/planned-parenthood-mobile-clinic-services-provided/.

2. 2 Chronicles 24:7.

3. Lauren Gambino, "Democrats Lose Senate Vote to Codify Abortion Rights into Federal Law," *The Guardian*, May 11, 2022, https://www.theguardian.com/us-news/2022/may/11/senate-abortion-rights-bill-vote.

4. American Presidency Project, "2024 Democratic Party Platform"; Kamala Harris (@VP46Archive), "Yesterday,

406 THE AVATAR

the Equality Act was reintroduced in Congress. The House and Senate must pass this long overdue legislation to guarantee every LGBTQI+ American the right to live freely and openly," X, June 22, 2023, https://x.com/VP46Archive/status/1671903371765137412.

5. Jonathan Turley, "A Harris-Walz Administration Would Be a Nightmare for Free Speech," *The Hill*, August 10, 2024, https://thehill.com/opinion/civil-rights/4820490-harris-walz-administration-free-speech/.

6. 2 Kings 11:1–3, author's translation.

7. 2 Chronicles 22:11.

8. 2 Kings 11:3.

9. Mattie Quinn, "California Abortion Ruling Puts Other States' Laws in Doubt," *Governing*, June 26, 2018, https://www.governing.com/archive/gov-supreme-court-abortion-california.html.

10. Tyler Arnold, "How Kamala Harris Targeted Pro-Life Pregnancy Centers in California," Catholic News Agency, August 28, 2024, https://www.catholicnewsagency.com/news/258969/how-kamala-harris-targeted-pro-life-pregnancy-centers-in-california.

CHAPTER 45

1. "Breaking: Planned Parenthood Sells Baby Parts for 'Valuable Consideration' of Owning University 'Intellectual Property,' New Documents Reveal," Center for Medical Progress, March 5, 2024, https://www.centerformedicalprogress.org/2024/03/breaking-planned-parenthood-sells-baby-parts-for-valuable-consideration-of-owning-university-intellectual-property-new-documents-reveal/.

2. Kate Quiñones, "California Settles with David Daleiden, Pro-Life Activist Who Exposed Planned Parenthood,"

Notes

Catholic News Agency, January 30, 2025, https://www.catholicnewsagency.com/news/261917/california-settles-with-david-daleiden-pro-life-activist-who-exposed-planned-parenthood.

3. Center for Medical Progress, "Breaking."

4. Quiñones, "California Settles."

5. Mary Margaret Olohan, "Exclusive: Kamala Harris Sent Agents to Raid Pro-Life Journalist's Home After She Met with Planned Parenthood, Emails Show," Daily Signal, August 7, 2024, https://www.dailysignal.com/2024/08/07/exclusive-kamala-harris-sent-agents-raid-pro-life-journalists-home-met-planned-parenthood-emails-show/.

6. Megan Cassella, "California Officials Seize Computers, Footage from Anti-Abortion Activist," Reuters, April 6, 2016, https://www.reuters.com/article/world/us/california-officials-seize-computers-footage-from-anti-abortion-activist-idUSKCN0X32GT/.

7. Cassella, "California Officials."

8. Barbara Grzincic, "Abortion Foe David Daleiden Seeks Right to Share Covert Recordings," Reuters, August 4, 2022, https://www.reuters.com/legal/litigation/abortion-foe-david-daleiden-seeks-right-share-covert-recordings-2022-08-04/.

9. Mark P. Meuser, "Brief of Amici Curiae, the Center for Medical Progress, and David Daleiden in Support of Petitioners," Supreme Court of the United States, May 22, 2025, https://www.dhillonlaw.com/wp-content/uploads/2025/05/20250522_Amicus-Brief.pdf.

10. Alexandra DeSanctis, "Big Abortion v. David Daleiden," Human Life Review, Ethics & Public Policy, May 21, 2021, https://eppc.org/publication/big-abortion-v-david-daleiden/.

CHAPTER 46

1. 2 Chronicles 23:9–11.

2. 2 Kings 11:13–14.

3. 2 Kings 9:23.

4. 2 Chronicles 23:14.

5. Amber Phillips, "'She Won't Stay Throwed!' Rep. Emanuel Cleaver Compares Hillary Clinton to Jesus, Brings the House Down," *Washington Post*, July 28, 2016, https://www.washingtonpost.com/news/the-fix/wp/2016/07/28/she-wont-stay-throwed-rep-emanuel-cleaver-compares-hillary-clinton-to-jesus-brings-the-house-down/.

6. Will Weissert et al., "Harris Introduces New Running Mate Minnesota Gov. Tim Walz as the 'Vice President America Deserves,'" Associated Press, August 6, 2024, https://apnews.com/article/harris-running-mate-philadelphia-rally-multistate-tour-02c7ebce765deef0161708b29fe0069e.

7. "Philadelphia Rally (First Rally with Gov. Tim Walz)—August 6, 2024," transcript, Iowa State University Archives of Women's Political Communication, August 6, 2024, https://awpc.cattcenter.iastate.edu/2024/08/08/philadelphia-rally-first-rally-with-gov-tim-walz-aug-6-2024/.

CHAPTER 47

1. Yaron Z. Eliav, "The Temple Mount in Jewish and Early Christian Traditions," in *Jerusalem, Idea and Reality*, ed. Tamar Mayer and Suleiman Ali Mourad (Routledge, 2008), 54.

2. 2 Chronicles 23:14–15.

Notes 409

3. *Encyclopedia of the Bible*, "Kidron," accessed April 17, 2025, https://www.biblegateway.com/resources/encyclopedia-of-the-bible/Kidron.

4. *Encyclopedia of the Bible*, "Kidron"; 2 Chronicles 29:16.

5. Sam Cabral et al., "Harris Revellers Leave Howard Campus Without Seeing Candidate Speak," BBC, November 5, 2024, https://www.bbc.com/news/articles/cx2n4g86dw9o.

6. Cabral et al., "Harris Revellers."

7. Anwar Ali (@hsafutureus and @horizoncolumbushs), "Howard University Campus Tour with HSA Columbus Class of 2024 Anwar Ali," Instagram reel, March 24, 2025, https://www.instagram.com/hsafutureus/reel/DHmYBsBPHqi/.

8. Ali, "Howard University Campus Tour."

CHAPTER 48

1. 2 Kings 9:20.

2. 2 Kings 9:20, The Voice.

3. Preacher's Homiletical, "Commentaries: 2 Kings 9," StudyLight, accessed April 17, 2025, https://www.studylight.org/commentaries/eng/phc/2-kings-9.html.

4. Preacher's Homiletical, "Commentaries: 2 Kings 9."

5. Nathaniel Rakich, "No, Trump Can't Cancel the 2028 Election. But He Could Still Weaken Democracy," ABC News, January 21, 2025, https://abcnews.go.com/538/trump-cancel-2028-election-weaken-democracy/story?id=117807079.

6. Laura Doan and Julia Ingram, "Trump Issues Record One-Hundredth Executive Order Within First One Hundred Days of Term. Here's a Breakdown," CBS News, March 26, 2025, https://www.cbsnews.com/news/

trump-issues-record-100-executive-order-of-second-term-breakdown/.

7. Damali Ramirez, "Here's All the Executive Orders Trump Signed During His First Week," WBALTV, February 3, 2025, https://www.wbaltv.com/article/donald-trump-record-executive-orders-week-one/63576990.

8. E. Judson, "The Good and Evil in Jehu," Bible Hub, accessed April 17, 2025, https://biblehub.com/sermons/auth/judson/the_good_and_evil_in_jehu.htm.

9. Matt Tullos, "Jehu: A Character Study," matttullos.com, January 5, 2016, https://matttullos.com/jehu-a-character-study/.

10. Front page of the November 7, 2024, *New York Times*, PDF accessed April 17, 2025, https://static01.nyt.com/images/2024/11/07/nytfrontpage/scan.pdf.

11. Peter Baker, "'The Return of the King': Trump Embraces Trappings of the Throne," *New York Times*, January 22, 2025, https://www.nytimes.com/2025/01/22/us/politics/trump-president-king.html.

CHAPTER 49

1. 2 Kings 9:7.

2. 2 Kings 10:27–28.

3. Peter J. Leithart, "Jehu on a Donkey," *First Things*, April 7, 2017, https://firstthings.com/jehu-on-a-donkey/.

4. Deena Zaru and Will Steakin, "Trump Set to Dismantle DEI Within Federal Government in First Day Executive Action," ABC News, January 20, 2025, https://abcnews.go.com/Politics/trump-set-dismantle-dei-federal-government-day-executive/story?id=117884488.

5. Associated Press, "Trump Has Said the Education Department Should Be Dismantled—What Would That

Notes

411

Mean?," *The Intelligencer*, November 21, 2024, https://www.theintelligencer.net/news/top-headlines/2024/11/trump-has-said-the-education-department-should-be-dismantled-what-would-that-mean/.

6. "Agenda47: President Trump's Plan to Dismantle the Deep State and Return Power to the American People," donaldjtrump.com, March 21, 2023, https://www.donaldjtrump.com/agenda47/agenda47-president-trumps-plan-to-dismantle-the-deep-state-and-return-power-to-the-american-people.

7. Jeannie Suk Gersen, "How Much of the Government Can Donald Trump Dismantle?," *The New Yorker*, January 16, 2025, https://www.newyorker.com/news/the-lede/how-much-of-the-government-can-donald-trump-dismantle.

CHAPTER 50

1. 2 Kings 10:11.

2. Sean Lyngaas et al., "Trump Administration Fires Director of National Security Agency," CNN, April 4, 2025, https://www.cnn.com/2025/04/03/politics/trump-administration-fires-director-national-security-agency/index.html; Michael Macagnone, "Appeals Court Allows Trump Removal of Hampton Dellinger," *Roll Call*, March 5, 2025, https://rollcall.com/2025/03/05/appeals-court-allows-trump-removal-of-hampton-dellinger/.

3. Eleanor Watson, "With Ousting of Admiral to NATO, Trump Administration Has Fired at Least Nine Senior Officers," CBS News, April 8, 2025, https://www.cbsnews.com/news/shoshana-chatfield-admiral-to-nato-fired-senior-military-officers-ousted/.

4. "2 Kings 9:1–10:36—Jehu Purges Israel," Enter the Bible, accessed April 17, 2025, https://enterthebible.org/passage/2-kings-91-1036-jehu-purges-israel.

5. Michael S. Moore, "Jehu's Coronation and Purge of Israel," *Vetus Testamentum* 53, no. 1 (2003): 97–114, http://www.jstor.org/stable/1518809.

6. "2 Kings 10, Lexham English Bible: Jehu Continues Purging the House of Ahab," Bible Gateway, accessed April 17, 2025, https://www.biblegateway.com/passage/?search=2%20Kings%2010&version=LEB.

7. Richard T. Ritenbaugh, "What the Bible Says About Jehu's Purge of Baal Worship in Israel," Forerunner Commentary, Bible Tools, accessed April 17, 2025, https://www.bibletools.org/index.cfm/fuseaction/Topical.show/RTD/cgg/ID/19728/Jehus-Purge-Baal-Worship-Israel.htm.

8. Caitlin Dewey, "Donald Trump Ramps Up His War on 'Woke' with Purge of Federal DEI Workers," *Vanity Fair*, January 22, 2025, https://www.vanityfair.com/news/story/with-purge-of-federal-dei-workers-trump-ramps-up-his-war-on-woke?srsltid=AfmBOormFilifoPKaeRKAoxxB5bHaGTjjJSaS_JHZpgSeAtGdqT1HFs5.

9. Andrew Curry, "Unprecedented Policy Purge: Trump's Single Order Attempts to Dismantle Biden's Legacy," *Los Angeles Magazine*, January 22, 2025, https://www.yahoo.com/news/unprecedented-policy-purge-trumps-single-030000278.html.

10. *USA Today*, "Trump Administration Purges Military Leadership," video, Facebook, February 22, 2025, https://www.facebook.com/share/v/1QKR2pc25p/.

11. Rebecca Beitsch, "Purges at FBI, DOJ Trigger 'Battle' for Career Staff," *The Hill*, February 4, 2025, https://thehill.com/homenews/administration/5124328-trump-administration-purge-fbi/.

12. "Trump's Unprecedented Purge at the Department of Justice Threatens Public Safety, National Security, and the

Notes 413

Rule of Law," House Committee on the Judiciary, accessed May 31, 2025, https://democrats-judiciary.house.gov/uploadedfiles/2025.01.29_fact_sheet_on_doj_changes.pdf.

13. Pauline Grosjean, "'A Sweeping Purge Is Taking Place Throughout American Administrations,'" *Le Monde*, February 13, 2025, https://www.lemonde.fr/en/opinion/article/2025/02/13/a-sweeping-purge-is-taking-place-throughout-american-administrations_6738128_23.html.

14. Emily Crane, "Trump Announces Purge of Over 1,000 Biden Appointees: 'You're Fired!,'" *New York Post*, January 21, 2025, https://nypost.com/2025/01/21/us-news/trump-to-remove-over-1000-biden-appointees-youre-fired/.

15. Michael Kruse, "The Executive Mr. Trump," *Politico Magazine*, August 2016, https://www.politico.com/magazine/story/2016/07/2016-donald-trump-boss-employer-company-hired-fired-employees-workers-management-business-214020/.

CHAPTER 51

1. 1 Kings 19:2–3.
2. 1 Kings 19:16–17.
3. 1 Kings 19:8, 16.
4. 2 Kings 9:6–7.
5. Susan B. Glasser et al., "A Spirit of Vengeance in Trump's First Week," The Political Scene Podcast, *The New Yorker*, January 25, 2025, 45 min., 6 sec., https://www.newyorker.com/podcast/political-scene/a-spirit-of-vengeance-in-trumps-first-week.
6. Freddy Gray, "Trump II: Back with a Vengeance," *Spectator*, March 9, 2024, https://www.spectator.co.uk/article/trump-ii-back-with-a-vengeance/.

7. Rev. C. J. Ball, "2 Chronicles 22:8," in *Ellicott's Commentary for English Readers*, Bible Hub, accessed June 2, 2025, https://biblehub.com/2_chronicles/22-8.htm.

8. "2 Kings 9:13 Meaning," The Bible Says, accessed June 2, 2025, https://thebiblesays.com/en/synopsis/2ki+9:13.

9. Alexandra Hutzler and Hannah Demissie, "Trump Has Moved Quickly to Exact 'Retribution.' More Revenge Could Come: Analysis," ABC News, January 29, 2025, https://abcnews.go.com/Politics/trump-moved-quickly-exact-retribution-revenge-analysis/story?id=118180327.

10. Michael Barbaro, host, featuring Maggie Haberman, Zolan Kanno-Youngs, and David E. Sanger, "Trump 2.0: Bans, Purges and Retribution," podcast, *New York Times*, January 24, 2025, https://www.nytimes.com/2025/01/24/podcasts/the-daily/trump-executive-orders-office.html.

11. "Former President Trump Speaks at CPAC," C-SPAN, March 4, 2023, https://www.c-span.org/program/campaign-2024/former-president-trump-speaks-at-cpac/624800.

12. "Donald Trump Dances with Sword After He and JD Vance Cut Cake at Commander in Chief Inaugural Ball," PalmBeachPost, YouTube, January 20, 2025, 4 min., 14 sec., https://www.youtube.com/watch?v=4i3mHK8ukM8.

CHAPTER 52

1. Abby Trivett, "President Trump Is 'On a Mission from God,'" Charisma News, May 30, 2025, https://charismanews.com/news/president-trump-is-on-a-mission-from-god/.

2. Trivett, "President Trump."

3. 1 Kings 12:25–33.

Notes 415

4. *Britannica*, "Engel v. Vitale," accessed April 18, 2025, https://www.britannica.com/event/Engel-v-Vitale.

CHAPTER 53

1. Brian Dunignan, "Donald Trump," *Britannica*, accessed April 18, 2025, https://www.britannica.com/biography/Donald-Trump#ref332843.

2. Donald J. Trump, "America Needs a President Like Me," *Wall Street Journal*, September 30, 1999, https://www.wsj.com/articles/SB938645589464803190.

3. Steve Kornacki, "When Trump Ran Against Trump-ism: The 1990s and the Birth of Political Tribalism in America," NBC News, October 2, 2018, https://www.nbcnews.com/think/opinion/when-trump-ran-against-trump-ism-story-2000-election-ncna915651.

4. Edward Helmore, "How Trump's Political Playbook Evolved Since He First Ran for President in 2000," *The Guardian*, February 5, 2017, https://www.theguardian.com/us-news/2017/feb/05/donald-trump-reform-party-2000-president.

5. Staff and Wire Reports, "Trump to Stay Out of the 2000 Presidential Race," CNN, February 14, 2000, https://www.cnn.com/2000/ALLPOLITICS/stories/02/13/trump.quits/.

6. "2000 Presidential Primary Election Results," Federal Elections Commission, accessed April 18, 2025, https://www.fec.gov/resources/cms-content/documents/FederalElections2000_PresidentialPrimaryElectionResultsbyState.pdf.

CHAPTER 55

1. Claus Westermann, "The Divine or Semidivine King," *Britannica*, accessed April 18, 2025, https://www.britannica.com/topic/sacred-kingship/

The-divine-or-semidivine-king; *Britannica*, "Hittite," accessed April 18, 2025, https://www.britannica.com/biography/Telipinus-Hittite-king.

2. Peter J. Brand, "A Family of God-Kings: Divine Kingship in the Early Nineteenth Dynasty," The Past, April 13, 2023, https://the-past.com/feature/a-family-of-god-kings-divine-kingship-in-the-early-nineteenth-dynasty/.

3. George Hart, *A Dictionary of Egyptian Gods and Goddesses* (Routledge, 1986), 170.

4. *Britannica*, "Horus," accessed April 25, 2025, https://www.britannica.com/topic/Horus.

5. Westermann, "The Divine."

6. "Tutankhamun (Tutankhaten)," Ancient Egypt Online, accessed April 18, 2025, https://ancientegyptonline.co.uk/tutankhamun/; "The Aten," Ancient Egypt Online, accessed April 18, 2025, https://ancientegyptonline.co.uk/amarnareligion/.

7. "Amun," Ancient Egypt Online, accessed April 18, 2025, https://ancientegyptonline.co.uk/amun/.

8. Westermann, "The Divine."

9. Beate Pongratz-Leisten, "Chapter 2—Sacred Marriage and the Transfer of Divine Knowledge: Alliances Between the Gods and the King in Ancient Mesopotamia," in *Sacred Marriages*, eds. Martti Nissinen and Risto Uro (Penn State University Press, 2008), 43–73.

CHAPTER 56

1. Matthew 12:43–45.

Notes 417

CHAPTER 57

1. Anuradha, "Vishnu Sustains the Universe," All About Hinduism, March 8, 2013, https://www.allabouthinduism.info/2013/03/08/vishnu-the-protector/.

2. Gaurav Balakrishnan, "Vamana Avatar of Vishnu: Tale of Lord Vishnu's Dwarf Incarnation," Svastika, July 3, 2023, https://svastika.in/blogs/blog/vamana-avatar-of-vishnu.

3. *Britannica*, "Parashurama," accessed April 18, 2025, https://www.britannica.com/topic/Parashurama.

4. Roshen Dalal, *Hinduism: An Alphabetical Guide* (Penguin, 2010), 188.

5. *Britannica*, "Brahman," accessed April 18, 2025, https://www.britannica.com/topic/Brahman-social-class.

6. Misra, "What Does Caste."

7. *Britannica*, "Lakshmi," accessed April 18, 2025, https://www.britannica.com/topic/Lakshmi.

CHAPTER 58

1. Sheikh Saaliq, "A Tiny Village in India Where Kamala Harris Has Ancestral Roots Is Praying for Her Victory," Associated Press, November 6, 2024, https://apnews.com/article/india-kamala-harris-village-us-election-a2c1bf50db407b8e9503d763bc9fd572.

2. Saaliq, "A Tiny Village in India."

3. Saradha Venkatasubramanian, "The Tiny Indian Village Claiming Kamala Harris as Its Own," BBC, July 23, 2024, https://www.bbc.com/news/articles/c9037j47pyzo.

4. "Following the Lotus Around the World," Storytrails, April 22, 2023, https://storytrails.in/religions/following-the-lotus-around-the-world/.

5. Wisdom Library, "Significance of Lotus," accessed May 2, 2025, https://www.wisdomlib.org/concept/lotus-flower.

418 THE AVATAR

6. Genesis 17:5.

7. Judges 8:1–21.

8. Ruth 1:16.

9. Prarthna Saran, "Brahma Kamal, the Divine Lotus," *Sunday Guardian*, May 25, 2019, https://sundayguardianlive.com/opinion/brahma-kamal-divine-lotus-4.

10. Tracy Grant and Gregory Lewis McNamee, "Kamala Harris," *Britannica*, accessed April 18, 2025, https://www.britannica.com/biography/Kamala-Harris.

CHAPTER 59

1. *Britannica*, "Lakshmi."

2. *Britannica*, "Lakshmi."

3. *Britannica*, "Lakshmi."

4. *Britannica*, "Lakshmi."

5. "Kamalatmika: Another Name for Goddess Lakshmi," Ramana Maharshi, accessed April 18, 2025, https://www.ramana-maharshi.org/kamalatmika-another-name-for-goddess-lakshmi/.

6. Jit Majumdar and Krishna Maheshwari (contributor), "Devī," Hindupedia, accessed April 19, 2025, https://hindupedia.com/en/Dev%C4%AB.

7. "Lakshmi Sahasranama Stotram," trans. P. R. Ramachander, Hindupedia, accessed April 19, 2025, https://hindupedia.com/en/Lakshmi_Sahasranama_Stotram.

CHAPTER 60

1. *Britannica*, "Krishna," accessed June 2, 2025, https://www.britannica.com/topic/Krishna-Hindu-deity.

Notes 419

2. Sophia Tareen, "'One of Us': South Asians Celebrate Harris as VP Choice," Associated Press, August 13, 2020, https://apnews.com/article/election-2020-ap-top-news-race-and-ethnicity-ca-state-wire-chicago-0dc9ab18344753 08435b7175bf0288d1.

3. *Britannica*, "Krishna."

4. Paul Steinberg, "Gopal," Jivamukti Yoga, August 2013, https://jivamuktiyoga.com/fotm/gopal/.

5. Venkatasubramanian, "The Tiny Indian."

CHAPTER 61

1. "Samudra Manthan: Churning the Ocean for the Elixir of Immortality," Glorious Hinduism, October 26, 2023, https://glorioushinduism.com/2023/10/26/samudra-manthan/.

2. Glorious Hinduism, "Samudra Manthan."

3. "Jaladhija Name Meaning," parenting.firstcry.com, accessed May 31, 2025, https://parenting.firstcry.com/baby-names/meaning-of-jaladhija/.

4. "Kamala Harris' Journey from Oakland to the White House," Visit Oakland, September 15, 2024, https://www.visitoakland.com/blog/post/kamala-harris-journey-from-oakland-to-the-white-house/.

5. Visit Oakland, "Kamala Harris' Journey."

6. Kitty Jackson, "Symbolism of the Sea Shell in Botticelli's 'The Birth of Venus,'" ArtDependence, September 30, 2021, https://www.artdependence.com/articles/symbolism-of-the-sea-shell-in-botticelli-s-the-birth-of-venus/.

7. "What Is Sea Foam?," National Ocean Service, accessed April 20, 2025, https://oceanservice.noaa.gov/facts/seafoam.html.

420   THE AVATAR

8. "Kamala D. Harris, 32nd Attorney General," California Attorney General Office, accessed April 20, 2025, https://oag.ca.gov/history/32harris.

9. "Harris, Kamala Devi," *Biographical Directory of the United States Congress,* accessed April 20, 2025, https://bioguide.congress.gov/search/bio/H001075.

CHAPTER 62

1. Jonathan Martin et al., "How Kamala Harris's Campaign Unraveled," *New York Times,* August 11, 2020, https://www.nytimes.com/2019/11/29/us/politics/kamala-harris-2020.html.

2. "Kamala Stotram," trans. P. R. Ramachander, Vedanta Shastras Library, accessed April 20, 2025, https://www.shastras.com/devi-stotras/kamala-stotram/.

3. Jayaram V., "Hindu God Vishnu, the Preserver," Hinduwebsite, accessed April 20, 2025, https://www.hinduwebsite.com/hinduism/vishnu.asp; James Lochtefeld, *The Illustrated Encyclopedia of Hinduism* (Rosen Publishing Group, 2002), 2:759.

4. Chutima Kuanamon, "Lord Vishnu Lady Lakshmi Lotus Flower Prosperity Hinduism Mythology Illustration," Alamy, accessed June 2, 2025, https://www.alamy.com/lord-vishnu-lady-lakshmi-lotus-flower-prosperity-hinduism-mythology-illustration-image345118671.html.

5. "Drew Barrymore Says America Needs 'Mamala' Harris Right Now," Breakfast Television, YouTube, May 1, 2024, 2 min., 46 sec., https://www.youtube.com/watch?v=Y3BwcOm13_E; Ariana Brockington, "Drew Barrymore Called Kamala Harris 'Momala.' The Internet Winced," Today, April 30, 2024, https://www.today.com/popculture/news/drew-barrymore-kamala-harris-momala-rcna150114.

Notes

6. Mark Cartwright, "Lakshmi," *World History Encyclopedia*, August 14, 2015, https://www.worldhistory.org/Lakshmi/.

7. "Lakshmi," Theosophy Trust, accessed April 20, 2025, https://theosophytrust.org/614-lakshmi.

8. Tom Porter, "Trump's Campaign Is Struggling to Find a More Damaging Nickname for Biden than 'Sleepy Joe,' Report Says," Business Insider, June 29, 2020, https://www.businessinsider.com/trump-struggles-to-find-better-biden-nickname-than-sleepy-axios-2020-6.

CHAPTER 63

1. David R. Kinsley, *Hindu Goddesses: Visions of the Divine Feminine in the Hindu Religious Tradition* (University of California Press, 1986), 18, 132.

2. Jae-Eun Shin, *Change, Continuity and Complexity: The Mahāvidyās in East Indian Śākta Traditions* (Routledge, 2018).

3. Ankita Chand et al., "Shaktism in Hindu Religion: Concepts and Chronology," *International Journal of Development Research* 13, no. 6 (2023): 62885–93, https://www.journalijdr.com/sites/default/files/issue-pdf/26713.pdf.

4. David R. Kinsley, *Tantric Visions of the Divine Feminine: The Ten Mahavidyas* (Motilal Banarsidass, 1998), 62, 229.

5. Kinsley, *Tantric Visions*, 229.

6. Kinsley, *Tantric Visions*, 229.

CHAPTER 64

1. Kinsley, *Tantric Visions*, 70.

2. Kinsley, *Tantric Visions*, 230.

3. Kinsley, *Tantric Visions*, 230.

THE AVATAR

4. Kinsley, *Tantric Visions*, 230.

5. Kinsley, *Hindu Goddesses*, 148.

6. Kinsley, *Tantric Visions*, 68.

7. "Sri Kamala Ashtottara Satanamavali," Manblunder, accessed May 31, 2025, https://manblunder.com/articlesview/sri-kamala-ashtottara-sata-namavali; David Kinsley, "Kamalā: The Lotus Goddess," in *Tantric Visions of the Divine Feminine: The Ten Mahavidyas* (University of California Press, 2023), 223–32.

CHAPTER 65

1. "'Is That Funny to You?': Kamala Harris Blasted Over Dismissive Laughing on Key Issues," Sky News Australia, YouTube, September 12, 2024, 5 min., 2 sec., https://www.youtube.com/watch?v=20JTKuOCfZ0; Victor Nava, "Kamala Harris' Dismissive Laugh on Full Display in First Presidential Debate with Trump," *New York Post*, September 10, 2024, https://nypost.com/2024/09/10/us-news/2024-presidential-debate-harris-dismissive-laugh-on-display-in-first-presidential-debate-with-trump/.

2. Amit Chaturvedi, "'Utterly Inappropriate': Kamala Harris Roasted for Laughing When Asked About Ukrainian Refugees," *NDTV World*, March 11, 2022, https://www.ndtv.com/world-news/utterly-inappropriate-kamala-harris-roasted-for-laughing-when-asked-about-ukrainian-refugees-2817262.

3. Charlie Spiering, "Why Kamala Harris' Laugh Has Sparked Concerns from Democrats as They Rush to Turn Around Dire Approval Ratings...as AOC Praises Her and 'the Authority that Comes with Having a Uterus,'" *Daily Mail*, April 22, 2024, https://www.dailymail.co.uk/news/article-13336543/kamala-harris-laugh-democrats-approval-ratings-aoc.html.

Notes 423

4. Phillip Hamilton, "Kamala Harris Laughing Hyena Comparisons," knowyourmeme.com, accessed April 21, 2025, https://knowyourmeme.com/memes/kamala-harris-laughing-hyena-comparisons.

5. Sakshi Venkatraman, "Trump's Campaign Works to Convince Voters that Harris Is 'Crazy' Because of Her Laugh," NBC News, July 30, 2024, https://www.nbcnews.com/news/asian-america/kamala-harris-laugh-criticism-trump-women-color-emotions-rcna164069.

6. "Mahishasura Rushes Towards the Spot from Where He Heard Devi's Laughter," Vedadhara, accessed June 11, 2025, https://www.vedadhara.com/mahishasura-rushes-towards-the-spot-from-where-he-heard-the-laughter-of-devi.

7. Wisdom Library, "Kamala, Kamalā, Kāmalā, Kāmāla, Kama-la, Kama-ala: 56 Definitions," accessed June 11, 2025, https://www.wisdomlib.org/definition/kamala.

8. Swami Jagdishwarnanda, "The Chandi," Critical Collective, accessed June 1, 2025, https://criticalcollective.in/ArtHistoryDetail.aspx?Eid=648.

9. The Art of Dialogue (@ArtOfDialogue_), "Jamal Trulove on Kamala Harris laughing at him when he was wrongfully convicted and sentenced to 50 years in prison for murder," X, August 12, 2024, https://x.com/ArtOfDialogue_/status/1823094968170283479.

CHAPTER 66

1. "Sharad Purnima 2024: Why Observing It This Way Is Important?," Astro Yogi, https://www.astroyogi.com/blog/sharad-purnima-vrat-date-time.aspx.

2. "Getting to Know All About Sharad Purnima 2020," Astro Yogi, March 5, 2025, https://www.astroyogi.com/blog/sharad-purnima.aspx.

3. Mahima Sharma, "Sharad Purnima 2024: Date, Time, Rituals and Significance of Ashwin Purnima," *Times of India*, October 17, 2024, https://timesofindia.indiatimes.com/religion/rituals-puja/sharad-purnima-2024-date-time-puja-rituals-and-significance-of-ashwina-purnima/articleshow/114222412.cms.

CHAPTER 67

1. "Kojagari Vrat Story: The Legend of the Auspicious Night," Acharya Ganesh, January 11, 2024, https://acharyaganesh.com/spirituality.

2. Ganesh, "Kojagari Vrat"; Aadrika Sominder, "Sharad Purnima 2024: How East and Northeast India Celebrate the Auspicious Occasion of Kojagari Lakshmi Puja," *Hindustan Times*, October 16, 2024, https://www.hindustantimes.com/htcity/sharad-purnima-2024-how-east-and-northeast-india-celebrate-the-auspicious-occasion-of-kojagari-lakshmi-puja-101729059307880.html.

3. Sominder, "Sharad Purnima."

4. Ganesh, "Kojagari Vrat."

5. Sominder, "Sharad Purnima."

6. "Lakshmi Puja in India in 2025," Office Holidays, accessed June 2, 2025, https://www.officeholidays.com/holidays/india/lakshmi-puja.

7. "Sharad Purnima 2025: True Reasons of Worshipping Goddess Lakshmi," mypandit.com, https://www.mypandit.com/festivals/purnima/sharad-purnima/.

8. Ganesh, "Kojagari Vrat."

9. Tiyasa Das, "Kojagari Lakshmi Puja: A Unique Festivity in Bengali Households on Sharad Purnima," LocalSamosa, October 16, 2024, https://www.

Notes

425

    localsamosa.com/people-culture/kojagari-lakshmi-puja-2024-7315754.

10. Priya, "Sharad Purnima 2025: Significance and Reason to Keep Kheer in Moonlight!," Sanatana Journey, December 17, 2024, https://sanatanajourney.com/blogs/sharad-purnima-2025-significance-and-why-kheer-is-kept-in-moonlight/.

11. Yogic Encyclopedia, "Avatar," https://www.ananda.org/yogapedia/avatar/.

CHAPTER 68

1. "Maha Lakshmi Mantra—Goddess Lakshmi Mantra," Drik Panchang, accessed May 31, 2025, https://www.drikpanchang.com/vedic-mantra/goddesses/lakshmi/mahalakshmi-mantra.html; translated via ChatGPT, response to a question from the author, OpenAI, May 31, 2025, https://chatgpt.com/c/683aff1a-7c30-8008-9a59-3571869c16db.

2. "Sri Kamala Stotram," Hindu Gallery, accessed April 22, 2025, https://hindugallery.com/sri-kamala-stotram/.

CHAPTER 69

1. "Ancient Egyptian Gods and Goddesses," British Museum, accessed April 23, 2025, https://www.britishmuseum.org/learn/schools/ages-7-11/ancient-egypt/ancient-egyptian-gods-and-goddesses#.

2. Frances Mulraney, "Kamala Harris' Niece Angers American Hindu Groups for Sharing an Image of the Democrat Photoshopped as Goddess Killing a Demon with Trump's Face," *Daily Mail*, October 21, 2020, https://www.dailymail.co.uk/news/article-8863665/Kamala-Harris-niece-angers-Hindu-groups-sharing-image-Democrat-photoshopped-goddess.html; Emily

426   THE AVATAR

Burack, "Meet Kamala Harris's Niece Meena Harris," *Town & Country*, November 4, 2024, https://www.townandcountrymag.com/society/politics/a61888915/who-is-meena-harris/.

3. Mulraney, "Kamala Harris' Niece"; Aditi Maheshwari, "Shankha: Conch of Power and Spirituality," *Times of India*, November 10, 2023, https://timesofindia.indiatimes.com/blogs/adi-bytes/shankha-conch-of-power-and-spirituality/.

4. Kinsley, *Tantric Visions*, 230; Wikipedia, "Kamalatmika," accessed June 9, 2025, https://en.wikipedia.org/wiki/Kamalatmika; "The Goddess of Royal Power and Grace—Kamala," Exotic India, accessed June 9, 2025, https://www.exoticindiaart.com/blog/the-goddess-of-royal-power-and-grace-kamala/; "Kamala Devi Jai Maaa!," Goddess Vidya, August 26, 2012, https://vedicgoddess.weebly.com/goddess-vidya-blog/kamala-devi-by-yogi-ananda-saraswathi-jai-maaa.

5. Mulraney, "Kamala Harris' Niece."

6. Mulraney, "Kamala Harris' Niece."

CHAPTER 70

1. *Britannica*, "Ishtar," accessed June 15, 2025, https://www.britannica.com/topic/Ishtar-Mesopotamian-goddess.

2. Mihindukalasūrya Ār. Pī. Susantā Pranāndu, *Rituals, Folk Beliefs, and Magical Arts of Sri Lanka* (S. Godage & Bros., 2000), 228.

3. "Mahalakshmi Riding Her Lion," Global Nepal Museum, accessed June 9, 2025, https://globalnepalimuseum.com/objects/mahalakshmi-riding-her-lion/; see also "Lakshmi: Everything You Need to Know," AstroVed, December 22, 2022, https://www.astroved.com/articles/lakshmi-everything-you-need-to-know.

Notes

4. "The Lion of Babylon," World Monuments Fund, accessed May 1, 2025, https://www.wmf.org/projects/lion-babylon.

5. "Anahita, Durga, Kali, Vajradakini, Ishtar," Okar Research, October 3, 2013, https://balkhandshambhala.blogspot.com/2013/10/anahita-durga-vajrayogini.html.

6. Jayesh Mathur and Supriya Lahoti, "Imagery of Goddess Lakshmi: From Primordial Depictions to Modern Calendar Art," *Sunday Guardian*, November 5, 2023, https://sundayguardianlive.com/news/imagery-of-goddess-lakshmi-from-primordial-depictions-to-modern-calendar-art.

7. Kashish Rai, "12 Auspicious Symbols of Goddess Lakshmi and Their Spiritual Meaning," English Jagran, May 23, 2024, https://english.jagran.com/spiritual/12-auspicious-symbols-of-goddess-lakshmi-and-their-spiritual-meaning-10162405.

8. Rivkah Harris, *Gender and Aging in Mesopotamia: The Gilgamesh Epic and Other Ancient Literature* (University of Oklahoma Press, 2000), 167.

9. Pandit Sri Rama Ramanuja Achari, *Hindu Iconology: The Study of the Symbolism and Meaning of Icons* (Simha Publications Australia, 2015), 34; Rai, "12 Auspicious Symbols"; Jackson, "Symbolism."

10. H. Rodrigues, "Kamala," Mahavidya, December 22, 2017, https://mahavidya.ca/2017/12/22/kamala/.

11. Miroslav Marcovich, "From Ishtar to Aphrodite," *Journal of Aesthetic Education* 30, no. 2, Special Issue: Distinguished Humanities Lectures II (Summer 1996): 45, https://www.jstor.org/stable/3333191?read-now=1&seq=3#page_scan_tab_contents.

12. "Aphrodite Estate," Theoi Project, accessed April 23, 2025, https://www.theoi.com/Olympios/AphroditeTreasures.html.

428 THE AVATAR

13. Krista Langlois, "The Symbolic Seashell," *Hakai*, October 22, 2019, https://hakaimagazine.com/features/the-symbolic-seashell/.

14. Steven W. Squyres, "Venus," *Britannica*, accessed April 23, 2025, https://www.britannica.com/place/Venus-planet.

15. P. James Clark, "Ishtar & Aphrodite—Part I," The Classical Astrologer, January 7, 2018, https://classicalastrologer.com/2018/01/07/ishtar-aphrodite-part-ib/.

16. Carl Rod Nave, "The Highlands of Venus," Hyperphysics, accessed April 23, 2025, http://hyperphysics.phy-astr.gsu.edu/hbase/Solar/venusland.html.

17. M. A. Ivanov and J. W. Head III, "Formation and Evolution of Lakshmi Planum, Venus: Assessment of Models Using Observations from Geological Mapping," *Planetary and Space Science* 56, no. 15 (December 2008): Introduction, https://www.sciencedirect.com/science/article/abs/pii/S0032063308002766.

CHAPTER 71

1. "Remarks by President Trump Announcing His Nominee for Associate Justice of the Supreme Court of the United States," Trump White House Archives, September 26, 2020, https://trumpwhitehouse.archives.gov/briefings-statements/remarks-president-trump-announcing-nominee-associate-justice-supreme-court-united-states/.

2. Jodi Kantor and Adam Liptak, "Behind the Scenes at the Dismantling of Roe v. Wade," *New York Times*, December 15, 2023, https://www.nytimes.com/2023/12/15/us/supreme-court-dobbs-roe-abortion.html.

3. "A Million Women Event—LIVE in D.C.," video streamed live October 12, 2024,

Notes

429

UpperRoom, YouTube, https://www.youtube.com/watch?v=FmTtIUcO4Bk&t=35278s.

4. Ryan Thoreson, "Trump Administration Moves to Reject Transgender Identity, Rights," Human Rights Watch, January 23, 2025, https://www.hrw.org/news/2025/01/23/trump-administration-moves-reject-transgender-identity-rights; "Defending Women from Gender Ideology Extremism and Restoring Biological Truth to the Federal Government," White House, January 20, 2025, https://www.whitehouse.gov/presidential-actions/2025/01/defending-women-from-gender-ideology-extremism-and-restoring-biological-truth-to-the-federal-government/.

5. Jo Yurcaba, "Government Agencies Scrub LGBTQ Web Pages and Remove Info About Trans and Intersex People," NBC News, February 3, 2025, https://www.nbcnews.com/nbc-out/out-politics-and-policy/government-agencies-scrub-lgbtq-web-pages-remove-info-trans-intersex-p-rcna190519.

6. Ashley Murray, "Trump Order Blocks Funds for Trans Care," Nevada Current, January 30, 2025, https://nevadacurrent.com/briefs/trump-order-blocks-funds-for-trans-care/.

7. White House, "Defending Women."

CHAPTER 72

1. "John Winthrop Dreams of a City on a Hill, 1630," *The American Yawp Reader*, accessed April 23, 2025, https://www.americanyawp.com/reader/colliding-cultures/john-winthrop-dreams-of-a-city-on-a-hill-1630/.

2. Laura Schulte, "'Oh, You Guys Are at the Wrong Rally': Kamala Harris Counters Hecklers at La Crosse Event," *Milwaukee Journal Sentinel*, updated October 18, 2024, https://www.jsonline.com/story/news/politics/2024/10/17/

430   **THE AVATAR**

kamala-harris-claps-back-at-rally-protesters-in-la-crosse-wisconsin/75724847007/; Emery Winter, "What We Can Verify About Exchange Between Kamala Harris and Protesters at Wisconsin Rally," WFAA, October 22, 2024, https://www.wfaa.com/article/news/verify/kamala-harris/harris-jesus-king-protesters-rally-fact-check/536-a189591f-1740-4a1d-9f69-9412840a6462.

CHAPTER 73

1. 2 Kings 9:13, author's translation.
2. 1 Corinthians 15:52, KJV.
3. 1 Thessalonians 4:16, KJV.
4. 2 Chronicles 23:12–13.

CHAPTER 74

1. "Parashat Beha'alotcha 5706 15 June 1946—16 Sivan 5706: Torah Portion: Numbers 8:1–12:16," Hebcal, https://www.hebcal.com/sedrot/behaalotcha-19460615?i=on; "Num 10:1–2," Sefaria, https://www.sefaria.org/Numbers.8.1-12.16?lang=bi&aliyot=1.
2. Sefaria, "Num 10:1–2."

CHAPTER 75

1. Numbers 10:10.
2. Leviticus 25:10.
3. Leviticus 25:9.
4. Micah Goodman, "The Jubilee Year of the Six-Day War," *Yale University Press*, December 16, 2019, https://yalebooks.yale.edu/2019/12/16/the-jubilee-year-of-the-six-day-war/.
5. Paolo Ondarza, "The Jobel at the Origins of the Jubilee," *Vatican News,* April 9, 2024, https://www.vaticannews.

Notes 431

va/en/vatican-city/news/2024-04/verso-il-giubileo-jobel-shofar-rabbino-di-segni.html.

6. Ondarza, "The Jobel at the Origins of the Jubilee."

7. Mark Landler, "Trump Recognizes Jerusalem as Israel's Capital and Orders U.S. Embassy to Move," *New York Times*, December 6, 2017, https://www.nytimes.com/2017/12/06/world/middleeast/trump-jerusalem-israel-capital.html.

CHAPTER 76

1. Babylonian Talmud, Chullin 105b:16, author's translation.

2. Babylonian Talmud, Rosh Hoshanah 16b, author's translation.

3. Jonah Rank, "Playing the Shofar in De-monic: Rashi on the Diabolus in Musica," *Journal of Synagogue Music* 41, no. 2 (2016): 54, https://www.academia.edu/27875796/Playing_the_Shofar_in_De_monic_Rashi_on_the_Diabolus_in_Musica.

4. Deuteronomy 32:17.

5. Numbers 10:9.

CHAPTER 77

1. 2 Kings 11:18.

2. 2 Kings 11:17.

CHAPTER 78

1. "The Beginning of the End for Judah," *Ligonier*, accessed April 24, 2025, https://learn.ligonier.org/devotionals/beginning-of-end-for-judah.

2. 2 Kings 10:30, NIV.

3. 2 Kings 10:28–29, NIV.

432 THE AVATAR

4. 2 Kings 10:31, NIV.

5. Joel Ryan, "4 Lessons We Can Learn from King Jehu's Violent Reign," Crosswalk, September 14, 2021, https://www.crosswalk.com/faith/bible-study/lessons-we-can-learn-from-king-jehus-violent-reign.html.

CHAPTER 79

1. 2 Kings 9:3.

2. Leviticus 8:12–30.

3. Lewis Kamb, "'Gunshots at the Trump Rally': First Audio of 911 Calls from Trump Assassination Attempt," NBC News, October 23, 2024, https://www.nbcnews.com/news/us-news/first-audio-911-calls-trump-assassination-attempt-rcna176757.

4. Ryan King, "Trump to Hold Rally at the Site of First Assassination Attempt in Butler, Pa. Next Week," *New York Post*, September 25, 2024, https://nypost.com/2024/09/25/us-news/trump-announces-return-to-butler-pa-site-of-first-assassination-attempt/.

5. Jack Jenkins, "At Inauguration, Trump Says He Was 'Saved by God to Make America Great Again,'" Religion News Service, January 20, 2025, https://religionnews.com/2025/01/20/at-trumps-inauguration-president-says-he-was-saved-by-god-to-make-america-great-again/.

6. Exodus 29:20.

7. Olivia Rinaldi et al., "Trump Shot at Rally in Failed Assassination Attempt. Here's What We Know So Far," CBS News, July 16, 2024, https://www.cbsnews.com/news/trump-shot-rally-assassination-attempt/.

8. Exodus 29:20.

9. Evan Vucci, untitled, July 14, 2024, photograph, WSBT, accessed April 24, 2025, https://wsbt.com/resources/

Notes 433

media2/original/full/1024/center/80/2093964e-2625-4d09-a07d-1ac55b569a09-AP24195806515160.jpg.

10. Exodus 29:20.

11. Jack Birle, "Trump Asked for Shoes After Secret Service Hit Him 'So Hard' They Went Flying," *Washington Examiner*, July 16, 2024, https://www.washingtonexaminer.com/news/campaigns/presidential/3084539/trump-ask-shoes-because-secret-service-hit-him-hard-flying/.

CHAPTER 80

1. Jonathan Homrighausen, "Forgetting the Forgetter: The Cupbearer in the Joseph Saga (Genesis 40–41)," *Journal for Interdisciplinary Biblical Studies*, accessed April 24, 2025, https://jibs.hcommons.org/2022/11/02/4-2-homrighausen-forgetting-the-forgetter/.

2. "Nehemiah: Cupbearer with Great Influence," *Church News*, September 29, 1990, https://www.thechurchnews.com/1990/9/29/23261340/nehemiah-cupbearer-with-great-influence/.

3. "2024 Republican National Convention: Day 4, Thursday, July 18," C-SPAN, accessed April 24, 2025, https://www.c-span.org/republican-national-convention-2024/.

4. Exodus 40:12.

5. C-SPAN, "2024 Republican."

6. C-SPAN, "2024 Republican."

7. Steven Shepard, "Trump's Garden Party: The Most Notable and Quotable Moments from the GOP Convention Finale," *Politico*, August 28, 2020, https://www.politico.com/news/2020/08/28/trump-rnc-thursday-superlatives-404184.

8. Shawn McCreesh, "Trump's Brush with Death as Political Theater, for One Night Only," *New York Times*,

July 19, 2024, accessed April 24, 2025, https://www.
nytimes.com/2024/07/19/us/politics/trump-rnc-shooting-
speech.html.

9. Evelina G., "The Second Temple in Jerusalem:
Everything You Wanted to Know," Judaica WebStore,
March 10, 2024, https://blog.judaicawebstore.com/what-
is-the-western-wall/.

10. Exodus 29:35, NET.

11. Leah Sarnoff, "Trump Assassination Attempt Timeline:
Witnesses Spotted Gunman 2 Minutes Before Shooting,"
ABC News, July 30, 2024, https://abcnews.go.com/US/
timeline-trump-assassination-attempt-unfolded-rally-
pennsylvania/story?id=111933309.

CHAPTER 81

1. J. Caleb Howard, "The Black Obelisk," Tyndale House
Cambridge, November 20, 2020, https://tyndalehouse.
com/explore/articles/the-black-obelisk/.

2. Howard, "The Black Obelisk."

CHAPTER 82

1. 2 Chronicles 7:14.

2. "Understanding the Names Yeshua and Yehoshua in the
Bible," Fellowship of Israel Related Ministries, August
19, 2024, https://firmisrael.org/learn/understanding-the-
names-yeshua-and-yehoshua-in-the-bible/.

3. John 3:3.